Principal 2.0

Technology and Educational Leadership

D1006384

edited by

Matthew Militello
North Carolina State University

Jennifer Friend
University of Missouri–Kansas City

INFORMATION AGE PUBLISHING, INC.
Charlotte, NC • www.infoagepub.com

Library of Congress Cataloging-in-Publication Data

A CIP record for this book is available from the Library of Congress
http://www.loc.gov

ISBN: 978-1-62396-301-9 (Paperback)
        978-1-62396-302-6 (Hardcover)
        978-1-62396-303-3 (ebook)

CONTENTS

Foreword: Ready Set Go! with Educational Technology ix
Governor Beverly Perdue

Acknowledgments xi

Introduction: Making the Case for Principal 2.0 xiii
Jennifer Friend and Matthew Militello

PART I

PERSPECTIVES ON TECHNOLOGY AND SCHOOLING

1 Augmenting Educational Realities 3
John Militello

2 The Role of For-Profit Firms in the Educational Ecosystem 13
Michael J. Schmedlen

3 Generation X Meets Generation Y: Reflections on Technology
and Schooling 25
Jennifer Friend and Alexander David Friend

4 Zen and the Art of Technology in Schools: Multigenerational
Perspectives 51
*Matthew Militello, Ronald Militello, Dominic Militello,
Luke Militello, and Gabriel Militello*

PART II

TECHNOLOGY EDUCATORS CAN USE TODAY

5 Digital Storytelling for Critical Reflection: An Educational Leadership Story... 67
Francisco Guajardo, Miguel A. Guajardo, John A. Oliver, Mónica M. Valadez, and Mark Cantu

6 Engaging Youth Voice: Collaborative Reflection to Inform School Relationships, Processes, and Practices................................... 81
Christopher Janson, Sejal Parikh, Jacqueline Jones, Terrinikka Ransome, and Levertice Moses

7 There's an App for That: 50 Ways To Use Your iPad 97
April Adams and Jennifer Friend

8 Student-Owned Mobile Technology Use in the Classroom: An Innovation Whose Time Has Come... 123
Tricia J. Stewart and Shawndra T. Johnson

9 Affective Learning Through Social Media Engagement 133
David Ta-Pryor and Jonathan T. Ta-Pryor

10 The Central Texas Community Learning Exchange Digi-Book: Fostering School and Community Engagement Through the Creation of a Digital Book.. 149
Lee Francis, IV, Mónica M. Valadez, John A. Oliver, and Miguel A. Guajardo

11 Leaders Online: Enhancing Communication with Facebook and Twitter.. 173
John B. Nash and Dan Cox

PART III

SOCIOPOLITICAL CONTEXT FOR TECHNOLOGY IN EDUCATION

12 Balancing Effective Technology Leadership with Legal Compliance: Legal Considerations for Principal 2.0...................... 185
Justin Bathon and Kevin P. Brady

13 Connected Principals: In Pursuit of Social Capital
via Social Media.. 211
Candice Barkley and Jonathan D. Becker

14 School Leaders' Perceptions of the Technology Standards........... 233
Matthew Militello and Alpay Ersozlu

15 Supporting Effective Technology Integration and
Implementation.. 249
Scott McLeod and Jayson W. Richardson

About the Contributors... 273

FOREWORD

READY SET GO! WITH EDUCATIONAL TECHNOLOGY

Governor Beverly Perdue

Educating our youth is an important and demanding enterprise that takes place in our homes, our communities, and our schools. It is this education that is the foundation of our democratic society—providing opportunities for career advancement, self-efficacy, and participatory citizenship in order to fuel our economy and to create socially just communities.

I have always put education front and center. My own education includes a BA in history, a MEd in community college administration, and a PhD in educational leadership. I also worked as a kindergarten and secondary school teacher. My most important role as an educator was as a mother to my two sons. Finally, as a public servant, I have been able to influence education by expanding the pre-K program, raising teacher salaries, increasing technology funding in schools, and beginning the *Ready Set Go!* initiative to prepare all students to graduate ready for a career, college, or technical training; in 2011 our state was awarded $400 million in federal Race to the Top funds and a spot on the list of states to watch in education.

I was delighted to hear about this book. Every child has unique gifts, talents, and challenges. To educate each and every child it will certainly take a village of families, community members, and school educators. But it will

Principal 2.0: Technology and Educational Leadership, pages ix–x
Copyright © 2013 by Information Age Publishing
All rights of reproduction in any form reserved.

also take the purposeful, creative, and thoughtful implementation of technological innovations. School principals are well-positioned to influence how educational technologies are used in our schools. This book provides today's school leaders with practical steps to advance their own use of educational technology as well as applications for their teachers and students.

Each article in this volume is powerful for a number of reasons. To begin, the content is focused on technologies that a school leader *can use right now!* Each chapter not only provides a description of the technology, but also a *step-by-step guide* to advance the use of the technology for the reader. Additionally, the chapters provide vivid examples of the technologies in action. That is, there are a number of examples including external links to videos that demonstrate what these technologies look like in schools. Finally, and perhaps the most intriguing facet of these chapters, there are multiple voices in this book. Specifically, the editors have included authors that represent a wide and wise array of ages and occupations:

- Professors with expertise in educational technology;
- Undergraduate and graduate students;
- Technology industry personnel from Lenovo and Google;
- Current and former school principals, superintendents, and technology specialists;
- And, most importantly, current students in elementary, middle, and high schools.

Principal 2.0 provides the *just-in-time* learning school leaders need. This book will advance work in the field and provide school leaders the motivation to advance their own technology dispositions, in addition to the knowledge and skills needed to enact these innovations.

This is an important contribution with a noteworthy set of contributors.

ACKNOWLEDGMENTS

This book could have been dedicated to our kids. Not only because they sacrificed time with us while we engaged in this project, but also as thanks for the ways they challenge us to explore new technologies in our lives and our work. We want our children, as well as our students, to live technology in their learning—in and out of formal schooling. We could have dedicated this book to our elders and our mentors—individuals who have impacted our thinking, teaching, and learning. We could have dedicated this book to the authors of each chapter in this volume. Without their thoughtful contributions this book would not have been possible. We could also have dedicated this book to Governor Perdue, a leader whose actions demonstrate her dedication to educational issues on the state and national levels. Lastly, we could have dedicated this book to Information Age Publishing, to our graduate research assistants, and our administrative assistants for their support preparing this publication.

However, we want to dedicate this book to a "mind shift" related to technology and schooling. That is, *if* the future generation of students, leaders, and teachers are to support learning effectively, *then* we must align teaching, learning, and leading with the tools of today and tomorrow. This will take more than idiosyncratic practices by teachers and leaders. It will take more than one policy or budget line item. It will take a revolutionary mind shift where learning with educational technologies are demanded as normative practices in schools by policymakers, educators, parents, and students themselves.

This great technological revolution begins with those brave enough to read and implement lessons from this book. So we dedicate this book to the leaders of this mind shift revolution!

Principal 2.0: Technology and Educational Leadership, page xi
Copyright © 2013 by Information Age Publishing
All rights of reproduction in any form reserved.

INTRODUCTION

Making the Case for Principal 2.0

Jennifer Friend and Matthew Militello

Fiction has historically provided vivid insights into future realities. From Bradbury's *Fahrenheit 451* that envisioned a world without books to Vonnegut's *Player Piano*, Huxley's *Brave New World*, and Asimov's *I, Robot* that describe technology-based, dehumanized worlds, in many ways yesterday's fantasies have become today's realities. A recent novel by Ernest Cline, *Ready Player One*, depicts virtual schools where students simply put on a visor and gloves in order to travel to places in a synchronous fashion. Cline's novel is set in a future world; however, augmented reality and virtual schools are already here and accessible to anyone with an Internet connection.

Technology and education are synonymous terms. That is, one cannot think about schools without thinking about the technologies that are used. Parents scouting new schools have added the presence of technology in the classrooms to their checklist for "good schools." This has not always been the case. As recently as 20 years ago, technology in schools was found only in isolated classrooms. Then technology was viewed as a tool for remediation, acceleration, and efficiency. Today there are clear focus areas regarding the potential of educational technology to enhance teaching and improve student learning, and a present press to implement these technologies.

Principal 2.0: Technology and Educational Leadership, pages xiii–xviii
Copyright © 2013 by Information Age Publishing
All rights of reproduction in any form reserved.

We know technology has a pivotal role in the education of youth today and in their future careers. We also know principals matter in schools. As a result, the focus of advanced technologies for current and future school leaders is a matter of great importance. This book is aimed at teaching, learning, and leading with technology. While some books have been written about one or the other, this volume seeks to bind the triumvirate of teaching, learning, and leading together. Only when these three aspects of schooling are considered simultaneously will educational technology impact the pedagogy (teaching), achievement (learning), and policy (leading) in schools.

Research in educational technology has been relegated to the study of economics (supply and demand) and pedagogy (teacher use). Besides the number of studies that summarize the technologies that are, and are not, in schools, investigations of teachers and technology have increased. The development of TPACK: Technological Pedagogical Content Knowledge captures the essential qualities of teaching with technology (Mishra & Koehler, 2006). The advanced research today focuses on the technology tools themselves. Current educational interactive technology platforms exist that merge tools and pedagogy (see Dede & Richards, 2012). Universal design provides access to previously ignored populations (see Rose, Meyer, & Hitchcock, 2005). In the midst of all the advancements and research, there is still a dearth of conceptualization and empirical evidence around educational technology looking at the school leader as the unit of analysis.

There are examples of new technologies used to enhance education. Surely technology can be a simple tool of efficiency, but there are also examples of technology assisting teachers in advancing learning though higher-order thinking, not just simply the regurgitation of facts. For instance, it has been reported that close to 40% of students do not have access to requisite college courses—technology can have a role in ameliorating this issue. Or take an example from Europe where Danish upper schools have allowed the use of the Internet during written exams. We also know that this type of analytical thinking is a highly sought-after trait for employers (see Rothstein, 2004). In fact, employers are seeking socially adapted and thoughtful workers that are team players. These characteristics often go untested in school, yet they are proven attributes of future success. While the past decade's drive for standardization and testing created a narrative based in prescription and multiple choice assessments, technology, in concert with leadership and teaching, has the ability to render this type of teaching and learning obsolete.

Learning is about discovery and inquiry. So why has it been so difficult to provide the resources, support, and implementation of technologies in schools? King (1996) stated that, "the shift from steam to electric power was gradual and costly, not just because of the required investments in technology, but because the technology both enabled and required fundamentally new ways of organizing and conducting work" (p. 248). Mechanisms of all sorts have been introduced to assist the teacher in teaching children. From the New England Primer to Guttenberg's printing press and the McGuffey Reader to the chalkboard to the electronic media of the 20th century, innovations have focused on making teaching more efficient and learning more fruitful. The innovations that had staying power in schools were simple to manipulate, easy to access, and efficient for teachers (Cuban, 2001). Chalkboards, textbooks, and the duplicating machine captured these important characteristics. Additionally, cognitive science tells us, "People who use tools actively rather than just acquire them, by contrast, build an increasingly rich implicit understanding of the world in which they use the tools and of the tools themselves" (Brown, Collins, & Duguid, 1989, p. 33).

As a result, it can be deduced that the electronic innovations that failed to take hold in schools lacked the essential characteristics of accessibility, versatility, compatibility, and adaptability for teacher use (see Rogers, 2003). In the 1930s, educational radio promised to transform the classroom. When radio technology failed to innovate teaching, John Thomas (1932), a district principal in Clippert Schools in Detroit, stated that radio technology was "retarded by many factors: Lack of adequate funds for equipment and research, mechanical developments too rapid to keep pace with, [and] stable teaching practice" (p. 980).

New technologies are challenging what we understand as teachers, leaders, and learners in school today. Advanced technologies flip the script where learners become the teacher and teachers become the learners (see Collins & Halverson, 2009). Rittel and Webber's work on social policy led to coining the term "wicked problems." They found that social policy creation and implementation was stymied by complexity, contradiction, incomplete information, fluid requirements, and a lack of risk-taking. Sounds familiar! Education is all of the above. Moreover, because most everyone in our society has attended school, there are millions of "experts" who *know* the tonic to cure problems in education. Yet we know there are no simple answers to such complex problems as social or educational policy. Rittel and Webber (1973) stated that "science has developed to deal with 'tame' problems, but 'wicked' problems have no scientific answer" (p. 155). So the solutions to "wicked" problems need a new science to derive solutions. We believe that educational technology is a classic case of a wicked problem that needs a new kind of inquiry to generate solutions.

Technology today looks very different than technology used in earlier decades. The form of technology has changed to smaller, mobile, and cloud-based. The function has also transitioned from mere efficiency to the potential to add to inquiry, reflection, and discovery. Moreover, technology has become more accessible, not only to rural populations but for individuals with unique needs. Mobility, instant communication, and interactivity have become nomenclature for technology today. Soon small, handheld devices will outnumber computers. How will schools react? Will these new mobile technologies be the latest in a long line of technologies marginalized and buffered? Demonized or banned from schools with the claim they distract rather than inform?

The philosophical "why technology" debate is over. Schools are now replete with electronic technologies. However, public schools have inundated themselves with hardware (computers and networks) without much thought to software (to compliment the curriculum) and "peopleware" (supportive technical maintenance and professional development for curricular integration). The ubiquitous nature of technology and the demassification and democratization of information from physical to digital states have revolutionized the way we live and work. But has it changed the way we teach and learn? Has educational leadership changed the philosophy and the structure of the organization to mediate pedagogy, learning, and educational technology? Such questions motivated us to put this book together.

OVERVIEW OF THE BOOK

This volume of essays provides insights into educational technology from a diverse set of vantage points. Each chapter provides school leaders with both conceptual insights and practical guides. Moreover, the authors of these insights and guides are an eclectic group, including current K–12 school educators and students, professors and graduate students of educational technology and educational leadership, and technology industry leaders. Our goal was to provide a thoughtful and thought-provoking set of essays that propels your own work in the world of educational technology forward.

The audience for this book includes teachers, school and district leaders, educational technologists, educational policymakers, and higher education faculty. Chapters demonstrate a number of specific uses of advanced technologies in schools, in educational leadership, and in leadership preparatory programs. Chapters are accompanied by screen-captured images and links to multimedia examples that are accessible to readers via the Internet, including digital artifacts of leadership and learning that will guide readers to implementation in diverse educational settings.

We chose to organize the chapters into three sections. The four essays that anchor Part I, *Perspectives on Technology and Schooling*, provide highlights from the technology industry as well as insights from adolescents and young adults. The chapters by Schmedlen (Lenovo) and Militello (Google) offer highlights from technology-based industries and illustrate how schools can learn from how these organizations think about technology. Next, two essays elucidate how current K–16 students and their families think about and use technologies. In Friend and Friend, changes in technology available in schools between 1970 and 2010 are explored through the experiences of the mother/son co-authors, along with recommendations for today's educators to keep up with the rapid changes associated with Generation Z and advancements in technology. Finally, Militello and family invite the reader into a fireside chat about technology from three generations of learners and educators.

Part II is titled *Technology Educators Can Use Today*. Here we shift the conversation from the philosophical dialogue to practical examples. Guajardo, Guajardo, and colleagues illustrate the power of digital storytelling for school community leaders while Janson and colleagues demonstrate the power of digital discourse among educators and students. Adams and Friend provide school educators with 50 ways to use an iPad, including recommendations for professional development and principal preparation programs, methods for technology acquisition and software updates, and policy development for schools and districts. Stewart and Johnson focus on the use of student owned mobile devices in schools. Ta-Pryor and Ta-Pryor provide information about social media and affective learning, while Francis and colleagues offer an example of how a digital book can be useful for school leaders. Finally, Nash and Cox explore the world of online synchronous and asynchronous discussions with Facebook and Twitter.

In Part III, *Sociopolitical Context for Technology in Education*, we highlight important elements of educational technology including law, standards, and social media. Bathon and Brady begin with an up-to-date accounting of the law and technology in schools today. Barkley and Becker author a chapter filled with links that demonstrate how social capital can be strengthened through social media. Then, Militello and Ersozlu offer original research about how school leaders perceive the current school technology standards. We conclude with a powerful chapter by McLeod and Richardson, who provide a message of hope and a call for technology integration by our school leaders.

*   *   *   *   *

We believe this collection of essays does indeed make the case for the need for a *Principal 2.0*. Moreover, this book provides specific strategies for current and future educational leaders to embody the Principal 2.0 vision for innovative and effective use of technologies in schools.

REFERENCES

Brown, J., Collins, A., & Duguid, P. (1989). Situated cognition and the culture of learning. *Educational Researcher, 18*(1), 32–42.

Cline, E. (2011). *Ready player one.* New York, NY: Broadway.

Collins, A., & Halverson, R. (2009). *Rethinking education in the age of technology: The digital revolution and the schools.* New York, NY: Teachers College Press.

Cuban, L. (2001). *Oversold and underused: Computers in the classroom.* Cambridge, MA: Harvard University Press.

Dede, C., & Richards, J. (Eds.). (2012). *Digital teaching platforms: Customizing classroom learning for each student.* New York, NY: Teachers College Press.

King, J. (1996). Where are the payoffs from computerization? Technology, learning, and organizational change. In R. Kling (Ed.), *Computerization and controversy: Value, conflict and social choices* (2nd ed., pp. 239–260). New York, NY: Academic Press.

Mishra, P., & Koehler, M. (2006). Technological pedagogical content knowledge: A new framework for teacher knowledge. *Teachers College Record, 108*(6), 1017–1054.

Rittel, H., & Webber, M. (1973). Dilemmas in a general theory of planning. *Policy Sciences, 4,* 155–169.

Rogers, E. (2003). *Diffusion of innovation* (5th ed.). New York, NY: Free Press.

Rose, D., Meyer, A., & Hitchcock, C. (Eds.). (2005). *The universally designed classroom: Accessible, curriculum and digital technologies.* Cambridge, MA: Harvard Education Press.

Rothstein, R. (2004). *Class and schools: Using social, economic, and educational reforms to close the black-white achievement gap.* New York, NY: Teachers College Press.

Thomas, J. (1932). Radio as teacher. *Michigan Educational Journal, 9*(7), 980.

PART I

PERSPECTIVES ON TECHNOLOGY AND SCHOOLING

CHAPTER 1

AUGMENTING EDUCATIONAL REALITIES

John Militello

INTRODUCTION

I had no idea why I was invited to share my perspectives on technology and education. I am a father, husband, brother, son, artist, technologist—not someone who should be writing about education. I graduated high school with an abysmal grade point average. Yet somehow I made it *through* and ultimately *to* a prestigious college. I built a solid career, landing a leadership role working at Google, one of the best companies in the world. And, get this, now I teach an advertising class one day a week at the School of Visual Arts in New York City! I don't think making it through should be the goal of education. So maybe my story of technology and education can make a contribution. My journey may in fact speak to teachers and leaders of disenfranchised students. You never know which student that frustrates you most may become the next Bill Gates, Steve Jobs, Mark Zuckerberg, or even John Militello.

A BRIEF HISTORY OF A SLACKER

My scholastic journey didn't start out so bad. I tested very well and was identified as "gifted and talented"; however, there were no specialized programs

Principal 2.0: Technology and Educational Leadership, pages 3–11
Copyright © 2013 by Information Age Publishing

in rural Michigan. There was nothing wrong with my education. It was perfectly mediocre and probably indicative of most schools in the country in the 70s and 80s. My academic downward spiral started in the fifth grade. I got bored quickly and enjoyed making friends with the slackers sitting in the back of the classroom. It surely looked like they were having fun in school. By the time I hit middle school I was woefully behind.

By the seventh grade, I had pretty much given up on school. I was a totally obnoxious middle school hellion. They didn't know what to do with me. After an altercation with the gym teacher, I was given a project to paint a mural for two hours each day. I was given a budget, a purchase order number, and a pass to walk off campus to buy paint and supplies. In the end I hated the mural, but I learned so much about myself through the individualized work and responsibility. By my junior year of high school I had exhausted all of the drafting offerings in our curriculum. A special advanced course was created for me, but that did not last long as I managed to get kicked out of that! It should not come as a surprise to anyone that I ended up graduating in the bottom 5% of my high school class.

Within all this failure there were a number of lessons. In middle school I realized that there was an attempt to recognize and tap the artist in me. It certainly would have been easier to suspend me. In high school I came to understand that I was given many chances and breaks because my dad was the principal. That's right—he had to intervene numerous times to keep me in school. I do consider myself lucky to have been given so many chances—so many chances to fail! I do not remember much from my history classes, but I do recall a quote that stuck with me: "Only those who dare to fail greatly can ever achieve greatly" (Robert F. Kennedy).

So when and how did my destructive behavior and academic failures pay off? When I enrolled in community college. This gave me the opportunity to restart, rethink schooling. In college I was able to learn at my own pace. In some classes, such as English, I had to start at a remedial level. Meanwhile I quickly excelled in my art classes. The most important motivator was the day I had to go ask the school for a loan to buy books heading into my second semester. They pulled up my GPA, an amazing 3.5, and asked me, "How much do you need?" I was floored. Those three years in community college were a second chance to clean up the past. That experience afforded me the opportunity to attend the College for Creative Studies in Detroit. Four years later I had a Bachelor of Fine Arts degree.

THE ADVERTISEMENT

My life changed when I saw Apple's 1984 Macintosh advertisement on television. This commercial, directed by Ridley Scott of *Alien* and *Blade Runner* fame, premiered during the Super Bowl. At the time I had experience with Apple II and IIe because my younger brother had a computer. (I had a mechanical drafting table.) After seeing this ad, I knew the Macintosh was coming. A few years later I got my hands on a Macintosh and I immediately understood the future. The computer could and would augment me—my talents and my future.

A TECHNOLOGY ROMANCE

During high school I studied some computer programming in the business lab, and it was there I saw my first Apple Macintosh. I had heard about a computer mouse, but I had never seen one let alone used one. I was drawn to it, and I sat down and started moving the mouse and clicking. It was more than just a device to replace keystrokes, there was an aesthetic beauty in the design principles of the mouse—it was both elegant and useful. I began to use it immediately. I stumbled onto a drawing program and within minutes I was drawing cartoons. I was turned on. Computers were finally for artists! At that point I truly discovered how computers would change the world forever. It was then I realized these devices augment anything you want to do, and they would just get better and better.

So that is how I fell in love with the computer. It was a high school romance. It was a tough romance, because back then technology was moving slowly, at least by today's standards. I could see the future but there were still so many barriers to overcome. To make computers and technology integral in day-to-day academic studies would take time. When it comes to technology, schools are both advanced and behind. My school adopted computers in the early 1980s and I thought that was very progressive, but access to computers was limited to students taking vocational classes. I had wonderful advanced printing classes, but the technology remained well behind the industry standards. I felt back then that schools would have to change the way they think about technology resources.

That's the rub. I am an advocate for advanced technologies in schools. If our schools are to remain among the best in the world, then how we resource, think about, and use technologies in schools is of paramount importance. Now I am experiencing the public school system as a parent. I see tremendous variations in thinking and quality and the integration of technologies. Yesterday we debated the use of calculators in the classroom; today we debate mobile devices and social media in our schools. If we are to learn from the past, we must harness and embrace technology in our schools. Educators must forge ahead and bring the best of the past with the promise of the future.

AN AUGMENTED EDUCATION

For me, the computer first augmented my education with writing. I paid little to no attention to English classes in my primary and secondary education. In college I had no choice but to face my lack of writing skills head on. Living away from home, I had no history or connections at my university. I knew I could not get more "chances" or special classes just for me. My grammar and spelling were atrocious; some say it still is. I went on to discover that I could use Microsoft Word to write, rewrite, and layout my papers. The program had spell check, which augmented my grammatical skills just enough to get me from grades of C's and D's, to grades of B and even a few A's. If it were not for the computer and access to word processing, I honestly don't think I would have made it through college.

As I dove deeper into my art education, I quickly discovered how the computer allowed me to design a logo, create an illustration, retouch a photo, and layout a page. I was an early adopter, a habit that continues to this day. In college I learned the craft of graphic design, art direction, and graphic communications. Desktop publishing hit the scene and was revolutionizing the industry. I quickly realized desktop publishing was just as important a learning tool for me as the word processor—maybe more so.

Even though technology was on the horizon, I still had to start my art education and professional life using traditional methods. Rulers, pens, knives, rubber cement, and paint thinner gave me an understanding of exactly what technology delivered over those traditional methods. Sometimes my attempts to learn how to complete my art projects with technology took longer than just doing the work traditionally. I had to write more lines of code than I'd like to remember just to generate a block image of something I had already drawn by hand. The beauty was that now my work was forever in cyberspace, it was now scalable, and I could share it with a worldwide online audience.

AN AUGMENTED REALITY

In addition to education applications, technology intended to augment reality has been around for a long time. As happened with many technological advancements, the military led the way. Remember the heads-up display? In the 1950s and 1960s pilots were using HUD devices for weapons sighting and flying military aircraft. Today there is a commercial use for the technology: the line of scrimmage and first down mark on TV during football broadcasts. Today augmented reality is also being used in smartphones in applications like Yelp's Monocle, which uses the camera in the phone to share virtual information (see Figures 1.1 and 1.2). We are now moving

Figure 1.1 This is a standard YELP search for restaurants in an area I'm in. Using the GPS in my phone, it shows restaurants nearby.

Figure 1.2 My camera is turned on using Monical. Using the GPS, compass, and the gyroscope in my phone, the application overlaid the locations of the restaurant that I may like to go to.

from an augmented reality to an augmented humanity. That is, these devices are able to mimic human behaviors and decisions in a common and organic fashion.

I think the technology that can change the world is already here today: for example, the mobile smartphone. Having a device that can access the world's information shared through multisensory displays, all in a tiny form that fits in your pocket, is simply amazing! Advances in mobile technology are moving at a breakneck speed. Why? Because mobile devices are small and inexpensive. In some parts of the world, people may never own a PC or have access to an Internet connection, but many own mobile devices that can be used to augment learning.

With augmented reality, a person could take an individualized course based upon anything seen in the "real world." Walking in a city with your mobile device becomes similar to taking an audio tour at an art museum. You can learn about any location throughout that city simply by watching a video or image on your device. History, culture, geography, music, literature, architecture—the possibilities are endless. This technology knows exactly where you are, yet allows for individual choice of information available for that location. A group of students could be touring different moments in time of a city's history, maybe even seeing neighborhoods as they once were. One person could see New York's Greenwich Village in 1960 while someone else could see it in 1850.

Imagine walking through a city where you don't speak the language, but with a smartphone you can now translate and people can speak to each other in their own native language. Voice translation technology is absolutely amazing. In fact, I'm writing parts of this chapter using voice-to-text technology. I'm speaking this sentence right now and it's being translated to text! I think all technology is a form of augmentation of humankind's abilities by its very nature. We have created technological tools to make this happen. That is what separates humans from most other animals. We use tools to further our abilities. These new sets of tools are beyond our wildest dreams and moving at an ever-increasing pace.

AUGMENTING EDUCATION TODAY

So the question becomes, will this render education useless? If I can simply download an app to my phone and augment my skills and ability with little or no effort, why would I still need a formal education? What role do teachers have? Why would we need physical structures called classrooms? Well, an app isn't going to be able to provide us with the fundamentals both academic and social. We still have to know certain things and learn how to behave within our society. We need to know what norms and standards are acceptable. *Augment* doesn't mean to deconstruct or replace, it means *to add on to*. So by augmenting my reality I can expand learning opportunities and acquire new information faster. A person can download a skill set, but it is not a "plug and play" skill set. We still need teachers, mentors, and leaders to support and enhance the learning process through practice.

Many new inventions and innovations have immediately sparked criticism by the establishment. Some people might not support augmented reality, arguing that it could take the organic moments or serendipity out of learning. I disagree. I travel regularly for work, as do many of my colleagues, friends, and family members. If I'm traveling and I check in on Foursquare Facebook or Google+, everybody in my social network knows where I am, and I know where they are. As we all travel the country, we may discover that we are in the same city and be able to meet up for a coffee or dinner while on a layover, or share a ride somewhere, finding more moments of serendipity. For those with privacy concerns, these mobile device features are not trackable unless individuals "opt-in."

Societies, by their very definition, are built on relationships. I speak to brand advertisers all the time about how brands are like people and people are brands. I tell them that today it is important to be a brand rather than "just" a company; organizations stand for ideas. We now live in a world that commodifies many relationships, and technology allows this to occur on a much larger scale. Technology allows us to break down all sorts of barriers, such as language and distance. It allows advertisers to say the right thing to the right person at the right time, delivering exact product information that is relevant to the end user. This can get very sophisticated, but I think it would be beneficial to learners and to schools if we could apply these types of algorithms to education.

I recently gave a presentation at the South by Southwest Interactive Festival that was titled, "Your five-year-old is more digitally savvy than the average Chief Marketing Officer." Part of my research consisted of interviewing my daughter's preschool friends and their parents. Most parents were delighted to participate, but some were apprehensive about allowing me to ask preschoolers about technology and advertising. I learned that some parents exhibited a technophobia related to their youngsters' activities, stating that they are waiting as long as possible before allowing their children to watch television or play with an iPad or any other kind of computer device.

Other parents embraced this new technology, sometimes out of necessity. Many of the parents relied on handing over their smartphones to keep their kids quiet, if only for two or three minutes in line at the grocery store. Some parents, as in past generations, pacified children with television, believing that programming was available to enable their kids to learn something. In my own family, we limit our daughters' time using the tablet or smartphone, and television time is spent watching PBS KIDS videos and playing games. They are learning valuable new things, and best of all they are not watching any commercials.

I submit to you that advanced technologies are about strengthening relationships and making societies greater. By augmenting relationships and skills, technology is a democratizing force—the walls created by language differences or geographic distances that keep us apart are knocked down. Today I see my children, ages 4 and 2, using tablets and smartphones intuitively, as if access to these technologies has always existed in this way. I am astounded to see children who have autism using technology to reveal new sides of their personalities that their parents and educators never saw before. That is what technology is all about.

RANDOM ACTS OF LEARNING

So what can you all glean from my story? I overcame my early school failures. I used technology and I found my way. I had many great teachers, although at the time I didn't realize it. I was my own worst enemy but also my own champion. I don't think my story is unique, as evidenced by our nation's appalling high school graduation rates hovering around 70%. I feel that I survived the system and it survived me, but my interest in education today is much more vested. I have kids and I want them to experience better methods of education than I did. I believe that today's technology needs to be available at a 1:1 ratio in schools. Curriculum and instruction need to adapt in ways that would enable students to use technology to learn at their own pace, to explore unique interests, and to augment their diverse skills. With more power in our hands than at any moment in history, there is no reason any child should be left behind.

Ultimately I think it is all about scale. Can educational systems deliver the promise of every student having access to cutting-edge technologies? It's a promise that empowers people and society by democratizing information and access to education. When you think of Sal Khan and the Khan Academy born on YouTube, it really makes you wonder if our educational system is nimble enough to take advantage of discoveries such as the "flipped classroom" today. Creating policies and selecting technologies are not enough. If I gave you an example here, by the time you read this chapter it would be outdated. Educators must have a mindset that: (a) learning never stops—you as an adult must keep pace with emerging technologies, and (b) technologies are tools that can speak to a diverse set of learners. Technology is not the sole answer to problems in schools, but our inability to embrace it will have detrimental effects on kids today who will become the teachers and leaders of tomorrow.

ARE YOU READY?

Are educators ready to launch early and iterate *? Take risks and then stay nimble enough to fix issues that arise.* Are you willing to be open and share knowledge throughout the system? *Learn in public and create technology-enhanced and -supported relationships.* Do you believe that good ideas can come from anywhere? *Turn consequences, intended or not, into opportunities.* Are you willing to make the leap and believe technology does more good than harm? *Learn, lead, and teach with technology in mind.* If your answer to these few basic questions is yes, then the future of augmenting education using technology is in your hands. Our students deserve nothing less. Our school leaders and teachers can change the trajectory of education in the United States and augment our current educational reality.

CHAPTER 2

THE ROLE OF FOR-PROFIT FIRMS IN THE EDUCATIONAL ECOSYSTEM

Michael J. Schmedlen

INTRODUCTION

Education is a long-term investment for governments and societies. If each student who graduated with a bachelor's degree were viewed as a separate research and development (R&D) project, the return on investment horizon would be more than 17 years. According to Yale professor Richard Foster, this is longer than the average lifespan of companies listed in the S&P 500 index (Gittleson, 2012). Students who earn a high school diploma spend 13 years in development. Students who have finished 8th grade—middle school—spend 9 years in development. Conversely, many commercial technology R&D projects that are estimated to take more than *nine weeks* are shelved. For each student, society makes very significant investments in time and money.

Education is also a big business. Education is the single largest vertical market in the world for personal computers (International Data Corporation, 2012). Each year, over 30 million laptops, desktops, and tablets are purchased by schools, colleges, and universities. Education PC and mobile

Principal 2.0: Technology and Educational Leadership, pages 13–24
Copyright © 2013 by Information Age Publishing
All rights of reproduction in any form reserved.

device revenue is estimated at over $15 billion annually, and this is in addition to the billions of dollars in content, assessment, learning management, services, and infrastructure businesses (IDC, 2012). Economic rent, or a significant return on investment, is available immediately to profit-seeking firms. There is no 17-year waiting period for investments to mature for technology businesses. Corporate actors are incented to compete, to deliver value to education clients, and to deliver value to governments and society.

By identifying both free cash flows and incentives to compete, it becomes clear why investing in education makes sense for technology firms. There are two important short-term motives for companies: revenue and profit. There are two equally important long-term motives: developing healthy economies in which to compete and building firms' future workforces. Firms must, in the words of Justin van Fleet, "realize how a better-educated society benefits both the global community and the business community" (van Fleet, 2011, p. 3). Firms must also compete and increase value for shareholders.

RETHINKING FIRMS' SOCIETAL ENGAGEMENT

The traditional rationalization for spending corporate profits on philanthropic endeavors has been simple: The allocation of resources toward something other than the firm's immediate profit and loss statement will improve the firm's reputation, increase brand awareness, and, therefore, increase the long-term value of the firm. For example, a local insurance agency will sponsor a food bank, or a corporation will sponsor the national Olympic team in the country were their firm is based. While such actions do benefit these organizations directly, they have little impact on society as whole and, arguably, little impact on the long-term sustainability of the firm.

There is a better way. Instead of traditional "ivory tower" philanthropy, firms should break down internal corporate barriers and start solving critical societal issues within their core businesses (see Figure 2.1). Much has been written recently on this subject, including Michael Porter and Mark Kramer's excellent article "Creating Shared Value" in *Harvard Business Review* (2011) and the paper *Shaping the Future: Solving Social Problems Through Business Strategy* (2010) offered by the Committee Encouraging Corporate Philanthropy (CECP) based on McKinsey & Company's research. My own brief (and much more pedestrian!) treatise, "Africa: Sharing Value through Society-Centric Design" (Schmedlen, 2012), attempts to demonstrate how applying these theories actually worked, citing my firm, Lenovo, as a specific example. The general idea: investing in education allows firms to simultaneously differentiate their brands and products while materially improving students' learning outcomes and schools' operational efficiency.

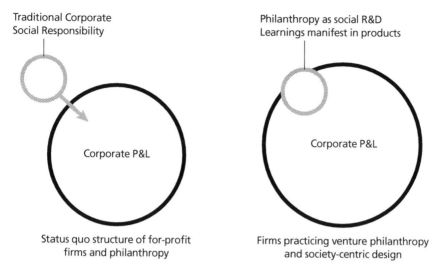

Figure 2.1 Migrating from traditional CSR by infusing philanthropy into the firm's core business.

In this chapter, I will attempt to illustrate what, exactly, I mean by "venture philanthropy in educational technology," citing three world-leading projects that were funded fully, or in part, by my firm. I'll also attempt to show how these research activities simultaneously benefitted society and Lenovo in significant ways. My hope is that more companies will invest to fuel innovation, share ideas, and conduct good, empirical science. Hopefully, the next time Matt Dunleavy needs a partner for virtual reality, project-based learning research or Shelly Blake-Plock needs funding for the fantastic Digital Harbor Foundation, corporations will respond.

THE EXHIBITS: CREATING THE STATE OF THE ART

Lenovo is a personal technology company and the world's second-largest PC vendor. We have more than 26,000 employees in more than 60 countries serving customers in more than 160 countries. While Lenovo has been extremely fortunate to be involved in many education technology research projects, I've selected three for *Principal 2.0* that I believe will have substantial lasting impact and relevance:

- *Developing mobile apps: A next-generation interdisciplinary curriculum* with the National Academy Foundation and the Massachusetts Institute of Technology

- *Center for Faculty Excellence* at the University of North Carolina, Chapel Hill
- *Student Global Leadership Institute* founded at Punahou School in Hawai'i

As education—indeed, the entire process and industry of learning—is transformed by technology, these projects may be seen as harbingers of mass innovation.

CREATING AN APP DEVELOPMENT CURRICULUM: CONTEXT AND RELEVANCE IN THE TIME OF MOBILITY

In late 2011, the National Academy Foundation (NAF) expressed interest in partnering with Lenovo to help integrate technology into its Academies of Information Technology (AOITs). NAF is a network of over 500 schools serving 60,000 students in the United States, which include "industry-focused curricula, work-based learning experiences, and business partner expertise" (NAF, 2012, p. 1).

The conversations first focused on the traditional role of corporate actors: Lenovo should donate PCs and laptops for computer labs at the schools. However, through a thoughtful dialog between the organizations, a more innovative idea presented itself: Lenovo and NAF could create—ex nihilo—a new curriculum for Mobile Application Development and test its efficacy and participation at a geographically diverse selection of academies. This idea leveraged key strengths of both partners: educational innovation and technology development.

After several months of collaboration, it became clear that a third partner would be needed to complete visioning and the assessment of the project. We chose to approach the Massachusetts Institute of Technology (MIT) because of its strength in education technology, computer science, and management education, as well as its free educational content activism best illustrated by MIT OpenCourseWare. Lenovo was fortunate to have OpenCourseWare Director Cecilia d'Oliveira keynote our ThinkTank conference held at Babson College in 2008.

Now that the partners were established, work was finalized on the rubrics, lesson plans, and other guidelines for the academies. Sam Morris of Lenovo led the federation of content from open source content providers. He used this content to create a syllabus and lesson plans for application development with the help of Andy Rothstein of NAF. In order to make the course even more relevant, several project-based aspects were added. Students would work in teams and would be expected to deliver a strategy and marketing plan in addition to the app itself. Lucky for us, MIT also has a world-class

Grover Cleveland High School New York, NY	*Find Your Way:* an app assisting people with disabilities using public transportation.
Apex High School Apex, NC	*Shop Local Raleigh:* an app helping users find and shop at locally owned and operated businesses.
Pathways to Technology Magnet High School Windsor, CT	*Social Onion:* a professional networking app.
Downtown Magnets High School Los Angeles, CA	*Recycle It:* a game-based social app encouraging recycling.
A.J. Moore Academy Waco, TX	*KiwiPad:* an assistive text to sound app.

Figure 2.2 A sample of student-created mobile applications from National Academy Foundation schools in the United States.

management school, and we asked for the Sloan School's support in advising on the marketing and strategy assessment, which they provided.

In total, five Academies of Information Technology were selected to participate in piloting the new course: New York, NY; Hartford, CT; Los Angeles, CA; Waco, TX; and Apex, NC. Teams of two to three students began work learning how to code and deciding what market opportunities existed in the current ecosystem. For this pilot year, Android technology was chosen based on the large proliferation of devices and the availability of development tools (http://developer.android.com).

There was some initial doubt about the ability of high-school students to plan, develop, and publish a mobile app in one semester. Fortunately, this anxiety was unnecessary. By the end of the course, over 50 functioning apps had been created. Over 25 were uploaded, approved by Google, and made available on the Android Market, now known as Google Play (see Figure 2.2).

What drove these students to action? Why was this experiment so successful? Three ingredients combined to create the result:

1. *Curricular relevance and contemporary context.* While the principles of project management, product strategy, and computer science are, essentially, timeless, mobile applications are an emerging industry. By contextualizing these principles and presenting them in the captivating and ultramodern world of mobile technology, the students were engaged and highly motivated.
2. *Project-based learning.* The course deliverables were a culmination of strategy, marketing, and computer science created by a team of

students. Because students had to dynamically construct content and knowledge gleaned from diverse disciplines, they did not have to merely retain and regurgitate information; they had to synthesize information and create something new.

3. *Organizational capabilities or the partner organizations.* Drawing on the strengths of education experts, the host schools, a research university, and the private sector, the course was authentic. Combining domain expertise, curricular expertise, and real-world technology expertise produced great results.

CENTER FOR FACULTY EXCELLENCE: INNOVATION IN UNDERGRADUATE AND GRADUATE INSTRUCTION THROUGH THE INNOVATIVE USE OF TECHNOLOGY

In 2008, the University of North Carolina at Chapel Hill's new chancellor, Holden Thorp, invited Lenovo to campus to discuss potential areas of collaboration. We had a lot in common: Chancellor Thorp was one of the youngest leaders in higher education (Ferreri & Stancil, 2008), and Lenovo was the youngest multibillion dollar companies in personal technology, having just acquired the IBM Personal Computing Division a few years prior (Lohr, 2004).

The university had a crazy idea: use their campus, including their faculty and students, as an incubator for instructional technology innovation. They also wanted to create an environment where faculty would compete for support based on the merits of their instructional hypotheses. The timing was good: UNC Chapel Hill had just formed its Center for Faculty Excellence (CFE). CFE is the successor to UNC's Center for Teaching and Learning, the storied professional development organization.

Over the next few months, ideas from this meeting materialized into a proposal for instructional innovation grants that would "promote innovation in the areas of collaborative learning, global education, and engaging large class sections" (CFE, 2012, p. 1). We were sold. Within four months, the Center for Faculty Excellence became one of the four founding sites for Lenovo's Education Research Initiative (E School News, 2009).

Since the program's inception, the grants have enabled a variety of faculty from diverse fields to test and hone innovative uses of technology in instruction. Instead of focusing on science and technology fields alone, the grant seekers came from across disciplines. Diverse topics such as "Students' Writing beyond the Classroom" from an English faculty member, "Lumbee Indian History: Using Technology to Tell Our Own Stories" from the history department, "Using Virtual Worlds to Make Poster Presentation an Iterative Process" from the school of pharmacy, and "Re-thinking

Communities of Practice for Teacher Education" from the school of education, all contribute to a rich body of research. Regardless of the discipline,
the program "emphasiz[es] innovative strategies for addressing the diverse
learning needs of both students and faculty members in higher education"
(CFE, 2011, p. 1).

The instructional innovation grants scale beyond Chapel Hill. Under the
leadership of Todd Zakrajsek and Bob Henshaw in 2010, the Center began
publishing the qualitative and quantitative outcomes of the research and
publishing them online (Zakrajsek & Henshaw, 2011). These annual reports document the winning grants, their hypotheses, and the results. They
are a treasure trove of insights on the effective use of technology. Accessible
by domain experts and generalists alike, these experiments serve as a guide
to faculty around the world.

What makes the Lenovo Instructional Innovation Grants valuable?

1. *The grants are specifically tied to innovation in teaching.* By earmarking
   funding specifically for technology interventions in teaching, the
   program narrowly focuses faculty efforts on technology, providing a
   comparable, tightly linked set of experiments.
2. *Success and failures are well documented.* By creating annual reports
   and hosting annual faculty meetings where results are presented,
   the Center for Faculty Excellence practices high-quality knowledge
   management. The experiments both add to existing instructional
   research and inspire new experiments.
3. *Diversity of participating departments.* By convening faculty from such
   a diverse set of disciplines, traditional biases—such as technology
   being only for hard sciences—evaporate. By including economics,
   literature (and the sciences!), UNC is extending technology's relevance to all departments at universities.

"LEGACY-FREE" INTERNATIONAL RELATIONS: HOW THE STUDENT GLOBAL LEADERSHIP INSTITUTE IS ENABLING INTERNATIONAL PROJECT-BASED LEARNING

In 2007, I was approached by a group of Hawai'ians from Punahou School
while attending a National Association of Independent Schools conference.
In addition to having a high degree of confidence in one of their graduates
to win the U.S. Presidential election later that year, the group also had a
vision of how technology could enable new approaches to international understanding and collaboration among students. Jim Scott, Wendi Kamiya,
Hope Staab, and Colleen Sotomura, among others, made their case for

Lenovo to help establish one of the most innovative education technology programs ever created, the Student Global Leadership Institute.

Soon after our meeting in Chicago, the first U.S. partner schools were announced: Cary Academy in North Carolina, Phillips Exeter Academy in New Hampshire, and Sidwell Friends School in Washington, DC. Delegations led by Hope Staab of Punahou then identified partner schools in China. Each of the schools from the U.S. and China then selected three to five student delegates. In late summer, these students began an "intensive two-week summit that had challenged them to develop the collaborative style of leadership needed to solve worldwide problems in the 21st century" (Donnelly, 2010, p. 1). In less than three years, SGLI would expand to include over 20 institutions from 8 countries (see Figure 2.3).

Each year, a theme is selected based on international relevance and curriculum capabilities. Themes such as water, energy, and healthcare are chosen to ensure global relevance and to engage students in globally significant subjects. After the two-week residency at Punahou, the students are then asked to apply these themes to local context, producing projects in their local communities.

China	Beijing Huiwen Middle School High School Affiliated to Fudan University (Shanghai) High School Affiliated to Renmin University of China (Beijing) Shanghai #3 Girls School
Japan	Gakushin Boys Senior High School (Tokyo) Gakushuin Girls Junior and Senior High School (Tokyo) International Christian University High School (Tokyo)
Jordan	King's Academy (Madaba–Manja)
Singapore	Raffles Institution
Sweden	Viktor Rydberg School (Djmsholm)
United Kingdom	Hitchin Girls School (Hertfordshire)
United States	Cary Academy (Raleigh, NC) Castilleja School (Palo Alto, CA) The Chapin School (New York, NY) Lakeside School (Seattle, WA) Noble and Greenough School (Dedham, MA) Phillips Exeter Academy (Exeter, NH) Punahou School (Honolulu, HI) Sidwell Friends School (Washington, D.C.) St. Paul's School (Baltimore County, MD)

Figure 2.3 Student Global Leadership Institute (SGLI) participating institutions.

During the residency, students are exposed to live presentations and conversations with domain experts ranging from Michael Horn and Chris Dede on distance education; U.S. Secretary of Energy Steven Chu on energy; and Punahou alumnus Steve Case on how healthcare can be transformed by technology (Donnelly, 2012). By engaging in a direct dialog with the thought leaders in each discipline, the students are inspired, but, more importantly, are given practical advice on how to proceed with their projects in their home countries.

Once the students return from Hawai'i, they begin work in their communities. Despite being separated by several continents, cultures, and various forms of government, they stay in constant contact with their peers and program administrators using social media tools. These tools enable collaboration, while maintaining an intellectual and emotional link among the students. From the first posts about missing Honolulu's weather to the celebration of a completed project and college acceptances, these students create a permanent transnational cohort.

Why is SGLI so successful?

1. *The hybrid program structure.* The combination of an on-premise introductory program and massively distributed distance learning has proven very effective. Using this approach, SGLI enables profound relationships—personal and intellectual—among students.
2. *Partner selection and management.* Punahou is uniquely positioned (geographically and historically) to bring east and west together. In addition to the schools recruited to participate, Punahou also recruited both foundation and corporate partners, as well as top domain experts, to increase the relevance and production value of the program.
3. *Global relevance.* By selecting annual themes relevant to all cultures and nations, SGLI engages emerging student leaders and encourages rigorous study and substantial actions. Because of this diversity of participating institutions, each theme is seen through the lens of multiple cultures, providing a more complete, global view of the issues.

CONCLUSION: ASSESSING THE VALUE FOR THE FOR-PROFIT ACTORS

As described in the introduction to this chapter, the traditional goal of corporate social responsibility is to improve the firm's reputation. In addition to these reputational benefits, the three programs described here yield much greater value for the firm. As a direct result of these interventions at a research intensive university, an education foundation, and a collective of globally significant independent schools, the sponsoring for-profit firm was able to create new value for itself and its customers.

First, through the deep engagement with these institutions and the creation of technical and organizational assets, the firm gained a profound understanding of the market. Combined with other knowledge management activities within the firm, these programs generate primary-source information. From this information, the firm can create valuable, rare, inimitable, or nonsubstitutable capabilities within its products and corporate organization. Further, visceral, on-the-ground understanding of the technical and financial requirements of the customer environment allows for solutions that specifically address vertical markets (see Figure 2.4).

In the longer term, producing evidence based on findings—qualitative and quantitative—from investments like these can accelerate the adoption of technology to increase access to education and improve learning outcomes. Educational improvement is highly correlated to economic growth (Hanushek & Woessmann, 2010). Investing in education makes sense in the short-term and for the long-term (see Figure 2.5).

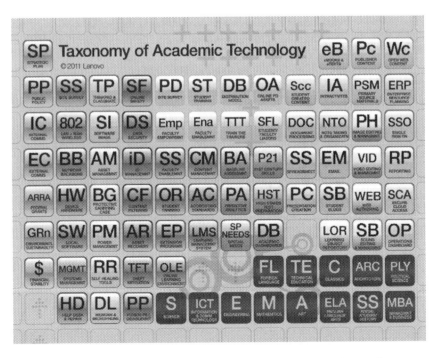

Figure 2.4 Applied research helps firms develop a profound understanding of the market environment: The diverse landscape of academic technology (Schmedlen & Welles, 2011).

Value to for-profit firms as a result of investing in education research	
Short Term [revenue and profit]	**Long Term** [sustainability]
Profound market knowledge	Economic development
Differentiated products	Political stability
Differentiated organizational structures	Infrastructure development
Solutions-based approach	Skilled employee pipeline
Increased brand equity (immediate)	Increased brand equity (generational)

Figure 2.5   Value to for-profit firms as a result of investing in education research.

Therefore, by supporting educational innovation, firms can support economic development. While especially useful in growing developing economies, education is also useful in sustaining and supporting mature economies. Improving education, particularly in the areas of access, outcomes, and efficiency, ensures a robust future marketplace for firms.

REFERENCES

Committee Encouraging Corporate Philanthropy. (2010). *Shaping the future: Solving social problems through business strategy.* Retrieved August 1, 2012 from http://www.corporatephilanthropy.org/research/thought-leadership/research-reports/shaping-the-future.html

Donnelly, C. (2010). *Facing the future together: The 2010 Student Global Leadership Institute.* Punahou School Bulletin. Retrieved August 1, 2012 from http://www.punahou.edu/page.cfm?p=2975

Donnelly, C. (2012). *Students rise to global challenge.* Punahou School Bulletin. Retrieved August 1, 2012 from http://www.punahou.edu/page.cfm?p=3816

E School News Staff. (2009). Lenovo to research tech's effect on learning. *ESchoolNews.* Retrieved August 1, 2012 from http://www.eschoolnews.com/2009/06/05/lenovo-to-research-techs-effect-on-learning/

Ferreri, E., & Stancil, J. (2008). Holden Thorp named UNC Chancellor. *The News and Observer*, May 8, 2008, B1.

Gittleson, K. (2012). Can a company live forever? *British Broadcasting Company News.* Retrieved September 12, 2012 from http://www.bbc.co.uk/news/business-16611040

Hanushek, E. A., & Woessmann, L. (2010). *The high cost of low educational performance: The long-run economic impact of improving PISA outcomes.* OECD Publishing. Retrieved September 12, 2012 from http://hanushek.stanford.edu/sites/default/files/publications/Hanushek%2BWoessmann%202010%20OECD_0.pdf

International Data Corporation. (2012). *Worldwide quarterly personal computer tracker.*

Lohr, S. (2004). Sale of I.B.M. PC unit is a bridge between cultures. *The New York Times.* Retrieved December, 2, 2012 from http://www.nytimes.com/2004/12/08/technology/08computer.html?_r=0

National Academy Foundation (2012). *About NAF.* Retrieved August 23, 2012 from www.naf.or/about-naf

Porter, M., & Kramer, M. (2011). Creating shared value. *Harvard Business Review, 89*(1/2), 62–77.

Schmedlen, M. (2012). Sharing value through society-centric design. *This is Africa.* Retrieved August 23, 2012 from http://allafrica.com/stories/201208270709.html

Schmedlen, M., & Welles, R. (2011). *Taxonomy of academic technology.* Lenovo Group Limited. Retrieved November 20, 2012 from http://blog.lenovo.com/education/taxonomy-of-academic-technology

University of North Carolina at Chapel Hill Center for Faculty Excellence (CFE). (2012). *Lenovo instructional innovation grants.* Retrieved August 23, 2012 from http://cfe.unc.edu/lenovo/index.html

van Fleet, J. (2011). *A global education challenge: Harnessing corporate philanthropy to educate the world's poor.* Washington, DC: Brookings Institution Center for Universal Education. Retrieved August 23, 2012 from http://www.brookings.edu/research/reports/2011/03/04-corporate-philanthropy-fleet

Zakrajsek, T., & Henshaw, R. (2011). *Lenovo Global Education Research Initiative: 2011 Annual Report—University of North Carolina at Chapel Hill.* Retrieved August 23, 2012 from http://cfe.unc.edu/pdfs/LenovoERI_UNC-CH_Report_2011.pdf

CHAPTER 3

GENERATION X MEETS GENERATION Y

Reflections on Technology and Schooling

Jennifer Friend and Alexander David Friend

INTRODUCTION

Analysts have defined generational groupings in the U.S. in different ways depending on the source of information used. Gordinier (2008) asked, "Is it worth asking whether or not a generation even exists? Can any one thread be said to unify a group of people who were born at the same time, or is that merely a convenient and romantic fiction?" (p. xxii). Every generation has its own unique characteristics, but too often these are reflective only of the dominant culture. A person who grew up in the 1950s may or may not have experienced family values seen on the television program "Leave it to Beaver" that included a stay-at-home mom, buzz-cut hair for boys, and poodle skirts for girls. A Generation X teenager in the 1980s may or may not have spent hours watching music videos on MTV or VH1 and playing Asteroids on their Atari game system. And a Generation Y child may or may not have been a fan of Pokemon, had access to a home Internet connection, and carried a personal cell phone.

Principal 2.0: Technology and Educational Leadership, pages 25–49
Copyright © 2013 by Information Age Publishing

When examining different generations, it is important to realize that the individuals who are part of a particular generation have their own unique experiences. As Werth and Werth (2011) have noted, "Although labeling a person as belonging to one generation or another based solely on the year they were born is stereotypical, it can be a useful tool for making general statements about the likely characteristics that exist in a group of individuals" (p. 12). For the purposes of this chapter, we will define generations using Tapscott's (2009) time periods: Baby Boomers (born between 1946 and 1964), Generation X (born between 1965 and 1976), Generation Y or Millennials (born between 1977 and 1997), and Generation Z (born between 1998 and present).

Changes in society such as rapid technological advancements are experienced according to the unique perspectives of the members of each generation. In terms of technology and schooling, the Baby Boomers in the 1950s had chalkboards, slide rules, and typewriters. By the late 20th century, Generation X students had dry erase boards, scientific calculators, and desktop computers. And the Millennials, also known as Generation Y, had SMART Boards, smartphones, and a variety of desktop, laptop, and tablet computers to choose from in schools.

Teachers and educational leaders, in addition to the faculty members in the programs that prepare these professionals, must act as lifelong learners themselves in order to provide every student with a first-class education and to bridge the gaps between generations and cultural contexts. According to Werth and Werth (2011):

> In addition to blurring the generational boundaries, the size of these categories has educational ramifications. Someone who is 50 and returning to school will likely have different educational needs and expectations than someone who is 29, even though they both could be called Gen Xers. In this situation, the 29 year old is more likely to align educationally with a Millennial than a fellow Gen X student. (p. 12)

A university professor from the Baby Boomer generation may have made monthly payments to purchase an expensive four-function calculator when it first became available. A practicing principal from GenX may have owned a Casio calculator watch and a TI-30 calculator for more advanced mathematics while in school. And a GenY early career teacher may have experienced a calculator as one of many functions in a cell phone or computer. Yet they all need to understand the technological experiences and learning needs of the current students in their learning organizations.

It is difficult for many people to understand new technologies, let alone incorporate them into their lifestyles as fast as they are being created. Computer power and memory storage are expanding exponentially. For instance, libraries used card catalogues to store information for many generations. In the 1980s a floppy disk stored 1.5 megabytes (MB) or the equivalent of 1.5 million characters. Floppies were widely used for over a decade, until zip drives capable of storing up to 75 MB became available in the mid-1990s. By 2003, zip drives were outpaced by flash memory sticks that could hold 4 gigabytes (GB). And these were rapidly replaced by secure digital (SD) cards that were smaller in size yet capable of storing between 32 GB and 2 terabytes (TB) of information. In the current educational context, by the time a cohort of students graduates from high school, their experiences with technologies in school already are obsolete.

This chapter will explore some of the characteristics and experiences of Generation X and Y, who will comprise the majority of educators in the workforce through the early 21st century, relative to technology and schooling. The first part of the chapter will examine the changes in U.S. society and technology that occurred for members of Generation X and Y. The second part of the chapter will share reflective narrative from the mother/son co-authors, one a member of GenX and one from GenY. The chapter will conclude with information related to Generation Z and recommendations for teachers, educational leaders, and preparatory program faculty to help them remain connected to technological advancements throughout changing generations.

DIGITAL IMMIGRANTS AND DIGITAL NATIVES: MEETING GEN-X AND GEN-Y

When the first Generation X babies were born in 1965, Lyndon B. Johnson was beginning his elected term as the 36th President of the United States. The Vietnam War was escalating overseas and the Social Security Act introduced Medicare and Medicaid as part of the War on Poverty at home. *The Sound of Music* played at the cinema and The Beatles played the first rock music stadium concert in New York. The August 1965 Watts Riots in Los Angeles resulted in 34 deaths, over 1,000 persons injured, and nearly 4,000 arrests, demonstrating "much about the underlying realities of race and class relations in America" (Rustin, 1966, p. 1). In terms of technology, a person could purchase a 12-bit PDP-8 "minicomputer" from the Digital Equipment corporation for around $18,000 (Smithsonian National Museum of American History, 2012).

By the time the last of the GenXers were born in 1976, the nation had seen President Richard Nixon's tenure and resignation, Gerald Ford's term in office, and Jimmy Carter's election as the 39th President of the U.S. The Apollo 11 mission had successfully enabled humans to walk on the moon and the video game *Pong* was released by Atari. In 1976, Apple Computer Company was founded by Steve Jobs and Steve Wozniak to sell their hand-made Apple 1 personal computer (PC) model with an amazing 4 KB of memory for $666.66 (oldcomputers.net, 2012). This was definitely a good investment, as Christie's (2012) recently sold an Apple 1 for $212,267 and Sotheby's auctioned the motherboard from an Apple 1 for $374,500 (CBS News, 2012).

For all of the advancements in technology during these years, GenX members had few opportunities to interact with computers at home or at school. A GenXer born in the 1970s may have experienced a first encounter with technology through playing video games at a friend's house or through a special lesson utilizing the PC stationed on a cart in the classroom at school. As such, GenX members are "digital immigrants"—they approach technology from the perspective of a generation whose childhoods occurred at a time when there was no Internet, there were no cell phones, and most kids did not have a PC or video game system in their homes. Prensky (2001) stated that, "As Digital Immigrants learn—like all immigrants, some better than others—to adapt to their environment, they always retain, to some degree, their 'accent,' that is, their foot in the past" (p. 1).

For members of the Baby Boomer generation, that accent is more pronounced. Faculty members who request a hard copy of their students' assignments or dissertation drafts in lieu of reading and providing feedback digitally are one example of the "digital immigrant accent" described by Prensky (2001). GenXers have the advantage of immigrating into the world of technology earlier in life than the Baby Boomers. As such, GenX members may be called upon by their generational predecessors to translate technology, similar to the manner in which English-language-learner students translate for their non-English-speaking parents during school conferences.

In contrast, the members of Generation Y were the first "digital natives," described by Prensky (2001) as those for whom "[c]omputer games, email, the Internet, cell phones and instant messaging are integral parts of their lives" (p. 1). The earliest members of Generation Y, or Millennials, started kindergarten in 1982, which coincided with the time that computers started to appear in schools. Ronald Reagan was President and Michael Jackson released his record-breaking *Thriller* album. The Cold War between the Western and Communist worlds was in its final years, *Time* magazine's "Man of the Year" was "The Computer," and video gamers had their own anthem with Buckner and Garcia's *Pac-Man Fever*. Black (2010) described the members of this new generation:

> Digital natives, fluent in acquiring and using technological tools and learning this technology quickly with an intuitive understanding of digital language, seem to use these tools as an extension of their brains. As members of the first generation to grow up with digital technology, they can speak its language. (p. 95)

However, it is important to consider that the "digital native" term does not apply to every member of Generation Y. There are those who were raised in environments that may not have been technologically saturated due to time, location, and available resources. The experiences with technology at home and at school for a GenY member born in the late 1970s were significantly different than those of a GenY person born in the mid-1990s. The access to technology was different for a GenY teenager in a middle-income family who attended a wealthy suburban district compared to a teenager attending impoverished urban or rural schools and living in a family with income below the poverty level.

Many GenY childhoods were spent with their primary forms of entertainment and information derived from a technological source. Whereas GenX youth were raised in a world where computers were seen as too complex and expensive for children to use, GenY children had access to rapidly expanding technological power. According to Emeagwali (2011):

> The Millennials, also known as the Net Generation and Generation Y, are a generation like no other. With their love of technology, social networking, collaboration, innovation, and a "Yes We Can!" attitude, Millennials are forcing established systems, be it education, the workplace, or corporate America, to take them seriously; to reevaluate how they do business in order to accommodate what is the first digital generation in recorded history. (p. 23)

While educational institutions are being transformed by acquisitions of new technologies, teachers and leaders struggle to keep pace and to communicate with the digital natives who inhabit their classrooms. According to Werth and Werth (2011), "While a great deal has been written describing the characteristics of Millennials as well as what they value, much has yet to be discovered regarding best practices for the education and training of this group" (p. 12). One response to the frustrations associated with demands for continuous adaptation and new understanding on the part of digital immigrants is to devalue or marginalize the members of the digital native generation.

Emeagwali (2011) reviewed literature associated with Generation Y from a variety of sources and found that "many have called them lazy, dumber than they should be, too entitled, lacking in social skills, and unable to handle the real world" (p. 26). The changes in communication and relationships among members of the digital native generation make up a common theme that emerges in the literature. Black (2010) stated, "Ironically, Gen Y may be simultaneously the most-socialized generation in the digital world and the most-isolated generation in the physical world" (p. 96).

While schools struggled to adapt quickly enough for the first generation of digital natives, most of these students passed through their classrooms without picking up any new technological knowledge and skills before moving on to the next phase of their lives. The last cohort of Generation Y students will graduate from high school in 2015. A new generation of students, commonly referred to as Generation Z or the Net Generation, already have taken over as the majority and they possess even more advanced levels of technology fluency and proficiency. Generation X and most of GenY are now relegated to the roles of teacher, principal, and higher education faculty member instead of being the ones served by our schools. Their stories related to technology and education can inform the ways in which schools adapt for Generation Z, as evidenced by the following reflections from one GenX and one GenY product of U.S. schools.

GENERATION X: A FUTURE SO BRIGHT, THEY HAD TO WEAR SHADES (JENNIFER)

As a teenager in the 1980s, I remember the popularity of sunglasses. Tom Cruise wore Ray-Bans in the films *Top Gun* and *Risky Business,* Corey Hart's song and video "Sunglasses at Night" reinforced the coolness of shades at any hour, and "shutter shades" were introduced to the world. With Generation X, clothing and accessories were all about being totally cool. I recall being the first female student at Ashland Junior High School in Ohio to wear black parachute pants (purchased at the mall with money saved from my paper route). And I remember when a classroom lab of brand-new Commodore 64 computers appeared in the summer between my seventh- and eighth-grade school years.

At the time I was an adolescent super-nerd who played the flute in band and orchestra with braces on my teeth, had permed hair like Barbara Streisand in *The Main Event,* and wore oversized Holly Hobby glasses. My neighbor, Mr. Kowalka, worked for the school district and he invited me to teach a summer enrichment class in the new computer lab for the Incredible Saturdays program. Mr. K. knew that my father was a technology fanatic and that I had been living with home computers since Dad acquired his first Heathkit in the late 1970s. My dad was compelled to have the first new technology available, even though it cost more and was not as sophisticated as later models. Instead of Atari, we had the Interact as our video game system, which featured knock-offs like "Packrat" and "Alien Invaders" running software off a cassette tape deck.

Teaching at Incredible Saturdays was the beginning of a lifelong association between technology, schools, and my role in the vanguard. At school, word got around that I could work the computers, and some of the teachers asked me questions or gave me the role of assistant on the occasions that we went to the lab. It was a great feeling to be valued—I had something to contribute to our school community and to learning and was not treated as a "kid." At home I experimented with BASIC programming using type-in programs found in the computer magazines of the time. We had a Wang 2200, a computer so powerful it took up half the space in the room. A typical program looked like this:

```
10 PRINT "WHAT IS YOUR NAME?"
20 INPUT A$
30 PRINT "HELLO"; A$
40 END
```

The novelty of seeing the computer using my name to say hello cannot be oversold. I remember this computer had a text-based game called "Hammurabi" that required careful strategy and allocation of resources (which I am sure developed skills that later served me as a principal).

I also had access to my dad's "laptop," an Osborne, to record observations about people as practice for my future career as an international secret agent. While digging through old copies of *Byte* magazine and the technology through the ages stored in my parents' basement, I actually found a floppy disk from high school labeled "Jenny Personal Profiles I" that somehow survived the last few decades intact.

What is interesting about these experiences is that the new learning that I acquired related to technology did not occur at school but at home, where I had access to more advanced technology and resources like computer programming magazines. At school my lessons involving computers were highly scripted, but at home I could play games on the computer or adapt the available technology to my own purpose and interests. The fact that my teachers valued my experience and expertise with computers was extremely positive in terms of my own self-efficacy and motivation to learn.

Generation Xer Goes to College

My freshman year of college in 1988 coincided with the advent of computer labs on campus. As a member of the Honors Club, I was among 40 students who were provided with an email address to pilot student user accounts provided by the university. Instead of using our real names, everyone created nicknames—my roommate was "Home Slice" and I was "Stan the Man" for no particular reason. People would just throw out a name and it stuck. We spent hours in the computer lab sending each other emails instead of talking to one another while sitting in the same room. We even made up new words when necessary, such as the term "daddamizing" to describe one student's attempt to stand behind another student to read what was on the monitor.

Email wasn't just for fun and games, as we discovered in the summer of 1989 during the Tiananmen Square student protests in China. My three roommates and I were clustered around our PC in our basement apartment emailing with a Beijing university student who shared stories as events were occurring. For the first time in my life, instead of relying on a television news program or a newspaper article to tell me about a global event, I had the opportunity through technology to speak with people of my generation who were in the middle of an event while it was happening. It was a powerful realization, and the significance of what we were doing became a moment that we remembered.

Reflecting on these experiences, it is interesting that our early-adopter group—like later, more digital generations—explored and played with digital identities, as expressed through our choices to use nicknames to present ourselves to one another in the digital context. We also were the first generation to sit in a room among friends and choose to communicate via technology instead of using our vocal chords. My dad said we were "people separated by mass communication." However, the use of a dial-up modem or networked computer also made our email communication with the university student in China possible, just as in the Arab Spring of 2011 when technology facilitated on-the-ground communication in the midst of social upheaval. Technology made it possible to form and strengthen social relationships and to circumvent the typical methods of accessing information and communicating with people in a global context.

Generation Xer Enters the Workforce

When I became a middle school language arts teacher in 1992, I once again had the opportunity to pilot a technology initiative. My school district had over 35,000 students attending nearly 50 schools. The technology at the time consisted of random computer stations in classrooms or on a cart featuring the Apple IIe or newer versions of the Commodore 64. Teachers did not have computer stations in the classrooms for their own use. Most communication relied on printed letters or flyers, and conversations happened face-to-face or via one of the shared telephones located throughout the building. At my school there was a phone in the custodian's closet at the end of each hallway, a phone in the faculty lounge, and a phone in the front office for teacher or student use.

The district began a technology plan by offering a desktop computer and printer to 20 teachers through a district-wide application process. I was excited to be selected for the program, and I set up my computer in the family room at home along with a box of "tractor feed" paper for the dot matrix printer. Each sheet of paper was connected at the top and bottom of each page, and there were holes on the left and right side of each page to enable it to feed into the printer. After printing, one had to tear off the sides and separate each sheet of paper using the perforated edges. I used the computer to prepare lesson plans and to create student handouts with interesting visual graphics.

In my third year as a teacher, my colleagues across the district returned to school to find computers on their desks. The district technology department had been hard at work over the summer wiring the building for networked computers, and every teacher and administrator now had an email account and the Microsoft Office software suite with Word, Excel, and PowerPoint. Teachers still could choose to maintain their grades in a paper gradebook, but new gradebook software was provided, along with training for any teacher who wanted to learn. There was a 30-station computer lab with IBM PCs to use with our students

I became a technology trainer to help other teachers learn how to use the computers sitting on their desks and to explore how we might integrate technology into instructional plans. I taught technology classes offered by the district professional development department, and the principal in my building asked me to mentor individual teachers as needed. This was my first exposure to "technophobia," as some teachers were beyond reluctant to interface with their new desktop stations. I explained data storage using a filing cabinet to show how virtual folders could be created in which to save and retrieve documents. For one extreme case of technophobia, I even brought a hat and scarf from home to dress up the computer monitor to make it appear more human to alleviate one senior teacher's anxiety. It seemed to work, because she laughed and was willing to put her hands on the keyboard.

In my language arts classes, students worked in the computer lab to create historical diaries and short story collections using word processing software (see Figure 3.1). We also used the new computers to create a school-wide literary magazine. Students used PowerPoint to enhance classroom presentations, and my classes used the school's video camera during a science fiction unit to create their own short films based on scripts they collaborated to write (see Figure 3.2).

During my first four years of teaching, every teacher and administrator in my district transitioned into the digital world through email communication and individual desktop computers. I recall my cooperating teacher telling me that, when she started out, students knew how to operate a record player but that by the 1990s most students did not even know what a record album was or how to play one using the box covered in dust that sat on a shelf in the classroom. Teachers were expected to use new technology in ways that improved instruction, communication, and record-keeping, and most administrators were learning at the same time as the teachers, although administrators had the opportunity to learn while not in view of the students.

Figure 3.1 Jennifer Friend working with students in the computer lab in the early 1990s.

Figure 3.2 Students sharing classroom computers in Jennifer's English class in the early 1990s.

Generation Xer Becomes a Middle School Administrator

By the time I became an assistant principal, my stellar technological expertise could not keep up with the times. I could utilize the technology that was available through work, but I no longer spent time playing with new technologies as a hobby. I continued to facilitate professional development sessions related to technology in my district because I was more adept than my colleagues (see Figure 3.3). But we were all falling behind in terms of what our students were doing with technology outside of school.

At home I found myself getting technology tips on things like advanced PowerPoint functions from my first-grade son, Alex. And the video games that Alex played were so much more sophisticated than the ones I had enjoyed as a teenager. I could get high score on Ms. Pacman, but I couldn't figure out all the buttons on the remote for his Nintendo games. My encounters with new technology occurred only when necessary, such as when the district purchased cell phones and PDAs for all administrators (see Figure 3.4 and Figure 3.5).

Figure 3.3 Jennifer Friend using a computer cart to facilitate a professional development session in the mid-1990s.

Figure 3.4   Jennifer Friend's cutting-edge cell phone in the mid-1990s.

Figure 3.5   Jennifer Friend's cutting-edge palm pilot in the mid-1990s.

As a school leader I knew it was important to advance teachers' technology proficiencies related to organizational functions and instructional enhancements. One year our district adopted "Parent Connect" so that families could access students' grades and upcoming assignments, but only a few teachers maintained current records and posted the week's activities. The same occurred when each teacher was provided with a webpage on the school's website to post classroom information. We used capital outlay funds to purchase mobile wireless laptop carts and SmartBoards for classroom use, but there were many days that this equipment sat unused.

One successful practice at my school for teacher technology growth was to have "open lab" times before school two days each month. These optional sessions in the computer lab involved demonstration of available technology, one-on-one and small group instruction when requested, and time to share successful practices with other teachers. Another activity in the middle school involved scheduling each advisory class in the computer lab on a monthly basis for a 45-minute technology lesson. Since every teacher was assigned an advisory group, our faculty was present for these lessons in addition to the students. With so many priorities in our school, we had to be creative to find ways to make time for technology.

Generation Xer as Faculty in Principal Preparation

After nine years as a middle school administrator I decided to seek a position as a faculty member in higher education. I wanted to be involved in the preparation of new school leaders and to influence educational policies and practices through research and writing activities. As the only Gen X member in my department, I quickly became the unofficial technology support person for my new colleagues. Our official technology department offered telephone and email help desk support and frequent technology training sessions, but it seemed to me that faculty preferred sitting down with a peer in a one-on-one setting. Each year there were new advancements in available technology for our campus.

My first "blended" course was School Finance, where we met on-campus eight times using an every-other-week schedule, alternating with asynchronous online sessions. In order to facilitate direct instruction during the online classes, I volunteered to pilot Tegrity podcasting for the university (which coincidentally was the same institution where I had participated in the student email project as an undergraduate). The next year I utilized Wimba Classroom to facilitate synchronous online classes as part of a doctoral program, enjoying the freedom of teaching from any location with Internet access.

Soon, the use of Blackboard became a requirement for every faculty member when the university automatically generated an online component for every course. The students who enrolled in these classes had new expectations for faculty members to provide access to information and to communicate with faster response times than the previous norms for voicemail or email. As more blended and online courses emerged across campus, a newly hired "instructional technologist" created opportunities for faculty development.

I enrolled in an online teaching certification course that was facilitated through Blackboard by our instructional technologist. This was an extremely valuable opportunity to see what distance education was like from a student's perspective and to learn new ways in which Blackboard could facilitate learning. After completing this course, I applied for and received a technology grant for our division faculty to collaborate and redesign many of our classroom-based courses in the superintendent preparation program. This effort led to the creation of an online degree in district-level administration that was recently accredited by our state department of education and by the National Council for Accreditation of Teacher Education (NCATE).

As a member of Generation X, my first learning experiences involved being physically present in the classroom, looking up unfamiliar words in a dictionary, and using a pen or pencil to complete assignments on notebook paper. My dissertation research involved pushing a cart with a squeaky wheel through the library to collect back issues of journals that I wanted to photocopy. Now when I review research literature, I can access sources through the Internet, and it amazes me that with one click my computer will read a journal article aloud to me or translate it into Spanish.

Sometimes I drag my feet when it comes to acquiring new technology because I am comfortable with my own status quo, and sometimes there are gaps in my technological understanding. For instance, my son had to explain the difference between an .mp3 and an .mp4 file when I first encountered these options for my students to download my podcasts. I tried a Twitter account, but I soon abandoned the effort because of the difficulty in regularly generating clever and informative tweets of 140 or fewer characters. I finally joined the ranks of e-readers by purchasing a Kindle this summer. I have a Facebook page and I recently used some of my research account funds to order an iPad. The future of technology seems blindingly bright at times, which brings me back to wearing those sunglasses to cut down on the glare.

GENERATION Y: A FUTURE DISCONNECTED
FROM SCHOOLING (ALEXANDER)

I hear a complex array of chirps as a phone line is disabled. Someone is signing on to the Internet in 1997. My grandparents' house hummed with

Figure 3.6 Alexander Friend learning about electronics with his grandfather, David Baker.

electricity and technology (see Figure 3.6). Outfitted with two phone numbers, a person could connect to the Internet and talk to someone on the telephone at the same time! When I visited their house there were few things I wasn't allowed to do. Playing outside, having fun with music, toys, or candy, and so on were all great options. Mostly, though, I wanted to gaze into glowing screens for hours at a time. Television, video games, and websites were a hypnotizing possibility that was always sure to offer a sense of awe and exploration. My parents and their parents hold an attitude of eagerness to obtain and incorporate novel technology into their lives. By the time I came around, they had already amassed a great amount of information on how to use instruments of media, and they provided the tools required for me to do so (see Figure 3.7).

Generation Y in Middle School

After completing my seventh-grade year in a traditional school setting in Kansas, any possible alternative to middle school was appealing. At the beginning of eighth grade, I was offered the chance to escape from the physical confines of that institution to become an official student of E-School in a strange set of imaginary confines. "Alex...Alexander...Alexander Friend?" said our answering machine one afternoon upon returning to our house. It was one of the teachers from Texas calling to discuss something to do with this E-School business. I don't really remember what they wanted then, or any other time for that matter. In theory, with enough effort I could have pieced together the strange set of clues on their poorly de-

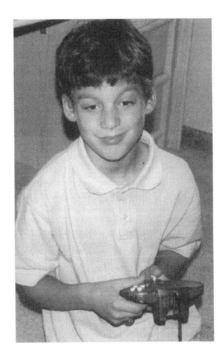

Figure 3.7 Alexander Friend playing videogames in the late 1990s.

signed, confusing webpage as to what my assignments were and how to turn them in. That didn't sound like a fun idea, so instead I talked to friends over Instant Messenger or debated with folks from around the world who appeared more than willing to argue about any topic at all with a twelve-year-old in Kansas through various forums and blogs.

Not that anyone knew I was twelve. Countless public service announcements and in-school movies on stranger danger warned us all to never tell anyone on the Internet anything about your real life, or else a lunatic or bogeyman might discover your whereabouts and steal you away. In part, this was sound advice. Being freed from the limits of any superficiality was wonderful. All those hours I spent with groups of strangers cursing at each other taught me that people can always find ways to be angry, even if they have no idea who you are or what you look like. You couldn't take anything personally. It was a place where all communication had almost zero consequence. There also was almost zero consequence to the E-School experiment as well. Sometime before returning to high school for ninth grade, I took a multiple choice Scantron test, and the nonvirtual school system welcomed me back as though nothing had ever happened.

Generation Y in High School

During my third and final year of high school I enrolled in an off-site vocational program focused on technology that was offered by my district. This "Technical Center" was a great way to spend more time on a bus. A camera monitored our every move but perceived nothing but a silent group of passengers holding glowing devices. In the noiseless, motionless world of the wired and wireless, though, we were roughhousing in pixelated arenas and chatting about whatever we wanted without being overheard by a gruff driver. We would be ferried to and from a separate building outfitted with computer labs, projectors, interactive whiteboards, and every other gadget that could be crammed into our classrooms.

Most of the students at the Tech Center, it seemed, knew quite a bit more about how to operate computers than their teachers. While the teachers probably went through training to prepare themselves for the ocean of gizmos they were tasked not only to learn but to teach, most of my classmates were skilled enough to have been using these "new" technologies and programs for years before attending. With impunity they would run servers off of the school networks to host video game tournaments. Excuses for any oddities on the computers could be explained away with enough technical jargon to confuse the teachers.

I was warned early in the school year by a returning student not to mess with the computers in the graphics design lab. The lab director, it was rumored, actually knew about technology. It was apparent in watching him work that this was true. He spoke with his students in a vocabulary that they understood, and his on-screen lessons demonstrated a proficiency not seen in most other instructors. He fluently used hotkeys instead of dropdown menus. When scripted lesson plans weren't enough to explain a concept, he could improvise in ways unexplained by the school manuals.

▪ This was proof enough for me to know that any computerized hijinks would not go unnoticed, but playing games in his class wasn't something we wanted to do anyway. Those distractions were just something we students defaulted to when there wasn't anything to be learned from paying attention. This lab director was a person who just liked technology so much that he wanted to show others how to use it too. I looked forward to college as a place where all educators used this strategy of sincerity to further the enrichment of themselves and others.

Generation Y in College

In college, my learning experiences did not go as expected. Professors at college showed wildly different attitudes towards technology. Some insisted that we never contact them through e-mail and devised assignments that required hard copies of newspapers as sources. Students who brought in copies of the same articles printed from the newspaper's website received a lower grade on that factor alone. Another professor insisted that we all check our e-mail addresses multiple times a day in order to be up to date on class plans and that we should use electronic sources so as not to waste paper. The technological fluency of my instructors and their willingness to bridge the technology literacy gap between them and their students played a huge role in whether I succeeded or failed at an assignment.

I received my first smartphone as a way of keeping up with the more complex responsibilities of being a college student. Being able to access the Internet anywhere was like something out of science fiction. I gleefully gazed into that touch-activated rectangle for hours. This was no telephone; it was a computer that fit in your pocket! It wasn't as powerful as a desktop computer, but it had a certain charm that made getting online feel like a whole new activity again, much like a book read by flashlight is somehow more fun despite being more dimly lit.

Despite the freedom that seemingly unlimited information and communication gave me, I felt trapped on campus. I wasn't being kept against my will in a windowless building under penalty of law any more, but it still had too many similarities to the strange and unjust power dynamics of past school years. Somehow, what I was doing just didn't seem correct. Earth is an amazing place, but I spent almost all of my time thinking about whatever was on the Internet or whatever was going on at school instead of exploring the rest of this glorious reality. After three semesters, it just wasn't worth sticking around, so I left.

Generation Y Signs Off

Leaving the educational system was the most educational thing I have ever done. I was no longer taught, I learned! I found an organization that provided a link between organic farms searching for volunteers and those who were interested in the field. After moving to a nearby farm further west in Kansas, the first step in my 180-degree turn from virtual reality to old-fashioned reality was complete. As the sprawl of the suburbs gave way to passing fields, I was filled with excitement like the first day of school. This is where I would live and work, at least for a time, while I figured out what this planet was all about outside of homework and checking e-mail. The owner of the farm was a kind, grey-haired woman who was quite knowledgeable about agriculture. She took my relative youth as a sign of technological proficiency and asked if I would transcribe things about the farm onto the

Internet. Not wanting to lose sight of my intentions, I replied: "Sorry, I am not very good at computers." It wasn't true then, but it would be very soon.

So the rules went: answer only every other phone call, respond to text messages only after at least twenty-four hours have passed, no social media, no instant messaging, no posting anything of any kind on the Internet. I was able to break the addiction just fine, but everyone I knew seemed to have serious problems with it. Friends thought that I had some sort of personal vendetta against them, for they assumed that they had been blocked. I can only imagine how many times I heard "Well, if you were still on Facebook..." in response to being oblivious to some social current event. In middle school, being on a computer all the time felt like being a part of some geeky subculture, but now choosing to be offline was a transgression of expected behavior for which one was scolded.

After a spring and summer at the farm, I decided to move to Florida to check out a different sort of ecosystem. I had never actually lived outside of the Midwestern United States. This was going to be great! Or so I thought. When I arrived it was a strange new place. Smart phones were now no longer something only a few people had. They were absolutely everywhere. Billboards and newspapers had strange symbols of dots that had to be explained to me. "Well, you use your phone to take a picture of this square, and you see your sites!" an elderly man on an iPhone told me on a bus. My twenty dollar handset from a general store had no such function. Bus rides through Orlando had an interesting slice of the populous on board. There were retired folks enjoying the warm weather, New Yorkers in exile, and always people yelling profanities into a Bluetooth headset as though they were in a private argument instead of a cramped vehicle.

That last bit really bugged me. Would they have been so bold as to scream at another person if they were right there in front of them, or was this a false courage gained from being far apart in distance? I observed during one bus ride when everyone's calls were dropped that amazing things happened in this technological dead-zone. People looked out the window at the world outside. Two people who had been in angry phone calls discussed how it was odd that both of their handsets stopped working at once. I overheard the dialogue shift from topic to topic until their stop came up. They left amicably with pockets full of best wishes.

My time was up, though. Remaining outside of the educational complex any longer would mean falling too far behind to easily catch up. Immersion into the world without technology for two years was like speaking a foreign language in a foreign land. I learned a lot from the experience but my contact with those still absorbed in the wired and wireless suffered from my lack of practice speaking in our common tongue. Things in the real world change slowly and steadily. Things in the world of technology changed so much that now I was the one who could be tricked with enough jargon and modern parlance. Difficulties were certainly caused by choosing to become disconnected, but I do not regret it. These might be the final days where maintaining an online presence is a choice and not a requirement. It may actually be too late already....

Generation Y Returns to College

Returning to a university setting after this time away was a future shock. All of my classes have much greater levels of online interaction, which was a difficult adjustment. A course scheduled to meet weekly actually has only one physical meet-up during the first six weeks. All class material in this time is done independently on an automated teaching and evaluation website. I am surprised to find that all of my textbooks now come with myriad codes on the inside of the front pages. If you enter some of their arcane phrases incomprehensible to humanity, such as PK7X3V29, you can gain access to a duplicate of the book in a virtual format that then can be put onto an electronic reader of some sort. Although it takes no resources or effort to create these electronic copies, they are valued and purchased as though they were real. This is definitely a different place than when I left.

I fumble with a tablet computer, awkwardly trying to coordinate my touchscreen gestures. We have many new technologies at our university's writing center where I work, but none of this was incorporated when I last worked there some years ago. I just don't get these apps, but if my younger cousin were here she would probably be able to show me a thing or two. She has been using a tablet computer since she was three years old and has navigated through the sliding colorful icons for longer than she could tie her shoes. It is a scene I have witnessed more than once: a plasma screen drones in the background as a toddler sits next to a box of juice and an iPad. Maybe if I ever get on a chat client again I can message her for technology support.

Trying to jump back on the bandwagon has been tough; the freedom and beauty of living only in the "real" world is not fun to give up. Everyone in my peer group is living less and less in the realm of here. There are fewer face-to-face conversations and social activities that take place in the same physical space. "Your worst flaw right now," said a very close relative in all seriousness, "is that you do not answer your cell phone." One thing seems to be universal: Students and professors from all walks of life demonstrate an experience of sheer wonder towards technology. There is a buzz of distrust and amusement towards our university's new advanced library robot. New Internet connection technology being pioneered by Google in Kansas City will increase the availability of data tenfold at less cost by this year's end. All the while, a bewildered teacher stands at the front of a classroom trying to placate an uncooperative machine asking, "Is anyone here any good with computers?" Hardly a day goes by without hearing someone or another sing praises or curses at what they saw on a glowing screen.

GENERATION Z, TECHNOLOGY, AND SCHOOLS

For individuals born after 1998, their childhoods may include spending significant amounts of time interacting with various computing devices on a mutually communicative level before they are even able to speak with other human beings fluently. This was not the case for individuals from Generations X and Y, whose first contact with less-advanced technology was at a later age with less user-friendly interfaces and fewer opportunities available. There are Generation Z infants who have e-mail accounts and social networking profiles before they have even been born.

Through better understanding of students' unique perspectives related to technology, educators and other adults who work in schools have the opportunity to engage in reflection and to expand their own mental models regarding academic and behavioral applications of technology to support learning for diverse students. Our mental models are the foundation from which we make meaning of the world, created from prior knowledge and experiences that form our core beliefs. These mental models have the power to influence professional practices such as teaching. The images, assumptions, and stories in our minds about other people, institutions, and technology shape how we act (Senge, 1990). Our mental models often exist without examination or analysis, because the process of reflection and change associated with mental models and core beliefs can be an uncomfortable exercise.

Educators' mental models may include their beliefs about cultural differences, their levels of expectations for diverse learners, and their understanding of ways in which technology can be used in schools. Just as thought precedes action, these mental models become manifested in educators' practices within schools. We can observe the practices within classrooms that hint at teachers' underlying mental models, some of which are detrimental to high levels of achievement for all students. If such mental models are transformed, educators may improve outcomes for student learning and for their schools. Listening to students' experiences with technology within classrooms and outside of school provides insight into how current instructional practices that involve technology are being received and interpreted. We can change the practices of educators when we change mental models.

Educators may carry out-of-date understandings about how technology can be used to support learning. They may view technology as a hindrance. Examples might be when they see cell phones, laptops, or iPads that Generation Z students try to bring into the classroom as problems that need to be confiscated or banned from school grounds. This is a very different mental model than seeing students arrive at school with technology that supports their unique strengths and talents, and seeing technological innovations that need to be incorporated into the learning process. These mental models can be observed in the classroom, where one teacher may provide instruction using technology to reinforce basic skills while another teacher may provide a challenging unit of instruction that incorporates students' interests and prior knowledge utilizing advanced technologies.

The rate of change within fields such as technology, social networking, media, and popular culture is now so rapid that the experience of children growing up four years apart in the same family can be as qualitatively different as children growing up in the 1950s versus the 1960s. Even with the best intentions to stay current and informed, it requires a sustained effort to be aware of new trends in technology that impact the lives of students within our classrooms. According to Black (2010):

> The nature of human interaction with the digital world is evolving in both speed and sophistication. Most digital immigrants view each technological device as a new challenge to learn, while digital natives see each device as a continuously evolving and improving facet of their lives to use, not just figure out. (pp. 98–99)

Today's vocational education can provide "students a learning environment that is aligned with their seemingly preferred learning style—a more hands-on approach" (Emeagwali, 2011, p. 24). However, this is no longer a track designed solely to prepare students to enter the workforce upon graduation from high school. Students in career and technical education programs need to be engaged in a rigorous curriculum in order to be prepared for success in college.

CONCLUSION AND RECOMMENDATIONS

The generation gap and mental models formed by experiences associated with technology are excellent examples of rapid change within our society. And the gap between advances in technology and educators' own technological expertise only gets wider with each passing year. There have been, there are, and there will be things that children and teens of all ages and cultural backgrounds know and can do with technology that their teachers and other adults in schools can only understand through listening to the students. Students' and educators' lived experiences are different, not just in terms of trends in technology, fashion, or music, but also in ways related to elements of cultural diversity such as race, socioeconomic status, gender, religion, language, ability/disability, sexual orientation, and more. There is much that we can learn from our students.

Many educators struggle with today's digital technologies because they are fairly technologically illiterate. The adults in schools are trying to prepare this current generation for their entry into higher education and the workforce. However, if the teachers and principals don't have an accurate idea of what the world will look like ten years from now, there is no hope of achieving this essential learning outcome. As Black (2010) noted, "In a sense, little has changed: good teaching has always focused on students' needs. The combination of the new generation and new digital tools, however, is forcing a rethinking of the very nature of education in both content and delivery" (p. 100).

After reflection on our own experiences with technology in schools, and an examination of the current context for education, we offer the following recommendations for principals and for programs that prepare educational leaders:

1. *Bring back the AV Club.* Back in the days of filmstrips and 16mm film projectors, many schools had audiovisual clubs where students assisted teachers by sharing their knowledge of the technology that was available to enhance instruction. With the introduction of computers in schools, AV Club students were replaced with information technology support staff hired by the district. Every educational organization needs a formal structure, such as a technology advisory committee or an "AV Club 2.0," to provide current students with a regular forum to share their knowledge and skills related to technology with their teachers and administrators in pre-K–12 settings, and with their faculty instructors in higher education programs.

2. *Provide ongoing professional development related to technological advancements for teachers, principals, and faculty members in educational preparatory programs.* Educators and educational leaders are expected to model lifelong learning for their students and colleagues, and the field of technology provides an ideal area for professional growth. Tapscott (2009) encouraged educators to "reinvent yourself as a teacher, professor, or educator," stating, "You too can say, 'Now, I can hardly wait to get up in the morning to go to work!'" (p. 148). Demonstration of new technologies is a good start, but there need to be opportunities for educators to collaborate regarding ways that digital technologies may support learning and active engagement for all students.

3. *Allocate resources to provide access to new technologies for teachers, principals, and faculty members in higher education.* In addition to the desktop or laptop computer that is typically provided for each educator within a school or university system, there needs to be access to

funds for cutting-edge technologies that educators can experiment with in the context of both work and play. Within institutions that do have funding for technology, there must be encouragement for the digital immigrant faculty to apply and utilize available resources. Manafy and Gautschi (2011) suggested, "Digital immigrants need to increase their interest and skill in modeling the use of digital tools and helping students become confident users of computer technology in their future work and leisure activities" (p. 359). Before this goal can be realized, however, educators must develop higher levels of efficacy with regard to their own understandings and proficiencies related to advanced technologies.

4. *Require at least one course in technology leadership for principals.* As instructional leaders for schools, the role of the principal must include fluency in the language of digital natives if they are to help teachers to improve technological literacies. It is important that this class be focused on creation and facilitation of cognitively complex, technology rich learning environments, not just on new tools. Educational leaders also need advocacy skills to acquire technological resources for their students and programs. Principals are also in a position to encourage partnerships with students, parents, local community organizations, and businesses in order to expand the opportunities that exist for learning with technology.

Technology is a native language for this new generation of students, while the adults in schools are second-language-learners trying to teach students their own language with minimal successes. "Many educators, as digital immigrants, are still teaching in ways that worked for them ten years ago or more" (Black, 2010, p. 97). Principals and other educators must strive to maintain an understanding of the technology that is being utilized by the current students who are part of each school's unique context. Educators also must understand new technologies as they become available, since these have an impact on the proficiencies that will be needed by all graduates in a globally competitive economy. Factors related to equity of educational outcomes, such as access to technology outside of school, are important considerations when engaging in strategic planning around technology and education.

REFERENCES

Black, A. (2010). Gen Y: Who they are and how they learn. *Educational Horizons*, 88(2), 92–101.

CBS News. (2012, June 15). Original Apple 1 computer motherboard sells for $374,500 at Sotheby's. *Techtalk*. Retrieved August 15, 2012 from http://www.

cbsnews.com/8301-501465_162-57453990-501465/original-apple-1-computer-motherboard-sells-for-$374500-at-sothebys/

Christie's. (2012). *Sale 7882 / Lot 65: Apple-1 Personal Computer.* Retrieved August 12, 2012 from http://www.christies.com/LotFinder/lot_details.aspx?from=searchresults&intObjectID=5370965&sid=1d221fae-dbba-4746-9922-8ca3e066b4bf

Emeagwali, N. S. (2011). Millennials: Leading the charge for change. *Techniques: Connecting Education and Careers, 86*(5), 22–26.

Gordinier, J. (2008). *X saves the world: How Generation X got the shaft but can still keep everything from sucking.* New York, NY: Viking.

Manafy, M., & Gautschi, H. (2011). *Dancing with digital natives: Staying in step with the generation that's transforming the way business is done.* Medford, NJ: Information Today, Inc.

oldcomputers.net (2012). *Apple 1.* Retrieved August 15, 2012 from http://oldcomputers.net/applei.html

Prensky, M. (2001). Digital natives, digital immigrants: Part 1. *On the Horizon, 9*(5), 1–6.

Rustin, B. (1966, March). The Watts. *Commentary Magazine.* Retrieved August 22, 2012 from http://www.commentarymagazine.com/article/the-watts/

Senge, P. (1990). *The fifth discipline: The art and practice of the learning organization.* New York, NY: Doubleday Currency.

Smithsonian National Museum of American History. (2012). *Computer history collection: The Digital Equipment Corporation PDP-8, 1965.* Retrieved August 7, 2012 from http://americanhistory.si.edu/collections/comphist/objects/pdp8.htm

Tapscott, D. (2009). *Grown up digital: How the Net Generation is changing your world.* New York, NY: McGraw-Hill.

Werth, E. P., & Werth, L. (2011). Effective training for Millennial students. *Adult Learning, 22*(3), 12–19.

CHAPTER 4

ZEN AND THE ART OF TECHNOLOGY IN SCHOOLS

Multigenerational Perspectives

Matthew Militello, Ronald Militello, Dominic Militello, Luke Militello, and Gabriel Militello

INTRODUCTION

When you consider an object, it is what you see that makes the object beautiful and what you don't see that makes it useful.

—Zen saying

Over the centuries, Zen Buddhists have developed koans, or "knotty problems" upon which to meditate in order to spark insights into the nature of things. If we apply this practice to reflections on technology in education, we could sit for hours pondering questions such as: What is the nature of technology in schools today? How does technology differ today from yesterday? And, what might technology look like in schools tomorrow?

Educational researchers and practitioners try to answers these questions on a regular basis. But, there are voices from other generations that are conspicuously missing: youth and elders. To begin, those who are impacted

Principal 2.0: Technology and Educational Leadership, pages 51–63
Copyright © 2013 by Information Age Publishing
All rights of reproduction in any form reserved.

most by policy and practice, the students, are rarely asked about their beliefs, knowledge, and skills as they relate to emerging technologies that surround their daily lives. Additionally, we often overlook our elders as keepers of lessons from the past related to common factors that have inhibited or fostered the implementation of technology innovations.

The purpose of this chapter is to seek three generational perspectives on technology and schooling in order to include student and elder voices. To approach this puzzle, I enlisted a panel of experts! Actually, I asked my family to sit around the dining room table to discuss technology and education. The "we" are (see Figure 4.1):

- Matt Militello (Age 42): former public school teacher, administrator, and current professor
- My dad, Ron Militello (Age 78): former public school teacher, principal, and superintendent
- My sons:
  - Dominic (Age 15): current 10th grader
  - Luke (Age 12): current 7th grader
  - Gabriel (Age 9): current 4th grader

This chapter features a dialogue among three generations of family members that was purposefully structured to include student and elder voices. This heuristic approach supported each participant in the dialogue

Figure 4.1 Photo of the Militello family taken by Elizabeth Militello in 2012.

to make meaning of the phenomenon of technology and schools. Patton (2002) stated that heuristics are "concerned with meanings, not measurements; with essence, not appearance; with quality not quantity; with experience not behavior" (p. 7). As we engaged in self-reflection on experiences with technology and education, we also realized that the experiences from different generations were equally important in that "the other can be understood only as part of a relationship with the self" (Vidich & Lyman, 1994, p. 24). Listening to each other's voices was essential to this inquiry. What follows is the transcript of our conversation.

WHO WE ARE AND HOW WE USE TECHNOLOGY

Matt

You all know me! I am 42 years old and a father of four amazing boys. I went to college to become a teacher. I followed in the footsteps of my dad who was my high school principal, and my mom, who never finished high school, yet she has always been the most influential teacher in my life. I was a middle and high school teacher and principal. I then went back to school and started teaching in the university setting.

I have always been an early technology adopter. In the mid 1980s, the home gaming industry was just burgeoning. My brother and I had a Colecovision and played many hours of Donkey Kong against each other.

I became hooked, if not addicted, to everything Apple from the first time I used a Macintosh II. Since then I have always been at the forefront of technology. From being a frequent user of the very first computer lab at the University of Michigan to incorporating technologies into my teaching and leadership, I have found ways to use technology in my work. Now as a university teacher, I press my students to use movie-making and Podcast technologies. Technology has been and continues to be integral in all aspects of my work.

Luke

I am Luke Militello and I am 12 years old and in 7th grade. I use Mac products such as iPads, the Mac Book Air, and I just got an iPhone. I mainly use apps—mostly games. I also look up stuff online. All my class grades and assignments are online so I look that up a lot. I also Skype with my friends. Most of the time just for fun like sharing music, but sometimes we will do our homework together.

Dominic

I am 15 years old and in 10th grade. I use a lot of technology, including digital cameras, video cameras, Mac computers, iPad, and I have an iPhone. I search the Web, use Facebook, and Skype with my friends. I also use Google Docs with the new STEM program I am in at school. This is where our teachers post all of our homework and our projects and our due dates and we do things through Google Docs and Gmail. For the iPad I just mainly play games, surf—same with my iPhone, just text, play games and that kind of stuff.

I am also involved in a project that my dad has at the university. I am the youth evaluator so I travel with him and conduct interviews and then cut videos with iMovie. I am trying to learn Final Cut Pro.

Gabe

My name is Gabe, I am 9 years old and in 4th grade. I usually use Apple products: iPod, iPad, iPhone, and Macs. I usually play games and use the calculator on the iPad to check my work. I also have a computer with me while I watch football on Sundays. My dad and I have a Fantasy Football team so I am able to keep track of the scores during the games.

Ron

I am Ron Militello, and I am 78 years old. I am a retired educator. I use my iMac quite often. I use it to look up information that I am not familiar with, especially when I am helping my grandsons with their homework. I use Facebook to keep up with old friends. I use it to do all of my reading of newspapers and magazines. I usually go on the Drudge Report because it has every major newspaper and magazine and I try to read a little bit of all of it just to see where they are coming from. I also use the iChat to visit with my older son and grandchildren in New York City.

HOW DO YOU DEFINE TECHNOLOGY?

Gabe

I define it as a learning tool. You can go and search things to learn and you can check if your answers are right or wrong.

Matt

I would define technology as something that makes life more efficient—like getting things done and having access to information faster. For example, when Guttenberg invented the printing press, spreading the news this way became more efficient. Instead of having people walking around the countryside yelling out the news, people could actually read it. The steam engine was another big technology breakthrough. In World War II, it was barbed wire and tanks.

Technology also offers affordances of efficacy. Efficacy is a basic human need. Innovations and the implementation of innovations are often tethered to emotions. The aesthetics of a technology prompts (or not) emotive responses. People become endeared to certain technologies surely for the ease of use (efficiency), but also for the comfort or absence of anxiety (efficacy). So the consumer's end-uses—type of computer one uses, the software and applications they employ, and the dimensions of interactivity—help us define technology.

Luke

I define technology as helpful, but sometimes it just slows us down. Like playing games, they distract us—they are pretty fun, I can admit that, but as my dad said, technology is very efficient so maybe we should take advantage of that more.

Dominic

I define technology as a tool. There are a lot of tools that help people. I see some of these tools as making things safer. For example, technology has helped our military keep us safer. But these technology tools can also be used as a weapon too like cyber hackers and bullies.

Ron

I agree with all of the above definitions. Another good example of technology that is helping with health and wellness—my insurance company called yesterday and wants to give me a new modem to hook up to my computer that will electronically send all of my vital statistics, my blood pressure, my glucose count, directly to my doctor's office and then also to the health nurse they are supplying so that if they notice any sudden variations they will contact me. So technology is helping with health and wellness.

WHAT DOES TECHNOLOGY LOOK LIKE
IN YOUR SCHOOL TODAY?

Dominic

Before this year, I used very little in my classes. We would occasionally use laptops and computers, but that was about it. This year I am in the STEM academy. We use a lot more with Google Docs—this is where I get assignments and read announcements. In our classrooms we have laptops and our teachers have iPads. We all have Gmail accounts and that is how we communicate with one another.

Gabe

This year I have to bring an iTouch to school. We usually search stuff and we sometimes play educational games. We pretty much use it to learn at our school.

Luke

In elementary school we used iTouches. I have not done much with technology in middle school. I have created some brochures with information I got online, but this was mostly done at home.

Matt

Just yesterday I taught a class and during the class I realized I needed some help with talking about technology for future school principals in my class. So I went on Google+ and I looked up my brother. He works at Google and was online. With a simple Internet connection, camera on my laptop and portable speakers, I was able to bring him into the classroom. We had a really interesting discussion with my 21 students.

As a professor, I see a lot of rooms now that are refurbished—they have a lot of fancy equipment. We take these classrooms and pour in $15,000–20,000 to make them sound proof and have these special monitors, cameras, and speakers. I walk by these rooms on campus all the time and see just how underutilized this ubiquitous technology has become. Why? I believe that teaching technology needs to be just-in-time, or nimble.

Bringing expertise into my classroom was what I needed at the time. I didn't need to reserve a physical technology space, I just needed to have the right people to invite. That is the way it should be—the technology should follow teaching and learning needs.

WHAT SHOULD TECHNOLOGY LOOK LIKE IN SCHOOLS?

Dominic

I think technology should look a lot more like the experiences I am having this year in high school. I am able to communicate with teachers after school. I mean, I no longer need to wait to talk to a teacher or to look up what happened in school or assignments that I need clarification on. Even though I have all of that, I still do not have a laptop or iPad. I mean I have access to these things at home, but not all my friends do. I think everyone should have these things.

This is also the first year I have been able to use my Smartphone for school-related things. For example, in Spanish we will be using a map app to learn where Spanish-speaking countries are. And, in my STEM classes we are encouraged to link our Gmail into our phones.

Luke

Right now in my school we don't use a lot of hands-on technology. We mostly use computers for reading tests. I do go online from home a lot to check my class Blackboard sites. This is where my teachers show the homework and due dates. I think we need lots more technology in our classes. I am not saying we should buy all of these iPads, but maybe we could ask for donations so more kids who don't have computers and iPads at home can get one.

We do have some other technologies at school. There is a cool feature in the classroom that saves energy. The lights in classes are on motion detectors so they turn off after 10 minutes.

Matt

Dominic, you cut a lot of videos. Do you think we should do more with video editing and use of video and pictures? Do you think there is place for using videos in schools?

Dominic

Yes, but I think the problem is many people do not know how to cut videos. I think the way you could incorporate that is with presentations. Instead of presenting in the class, you could create a presentation in a different place—a place where you feel more comfortable, where you have more time. Students can then show the video to the class. I think that would improve presentations as well as include important technology skills.

Gabe

At my school we hardly even use technology. We use it mainly for projects. I guess we are using it more now with new apps and since we now can bring an iTouch to class. Last year I went online to practice math using Study Island. We also used the computer to listen to people reading to us. I guess I just like to use more technologies where I do stuff to learn on the computer or with an iPad.

Ron

In 1967, I was on a research committee at Michigan State University on reforming education. At that time we were suggesting distance learning—learning with educational pods which could be carried around. The ideas were to create helmets with learning centers embedded in the helmets. This way, people could wear these helmets while they were travelling on subways, street cars, buses, etc. This was futuristic thinking—way beyond listening to music on iPods!

As superintendent of schools in rural Michigan, I worked with other rural schools to create distance learning labs in each school so that we could share teachers. I had only four students who wanted to take Spanish and three who wanted to take French, so we shared instructors. This saved us an awful lot of money and gave student opportunities that were not possible without technology. I think the schools of the future are going to have to go even further.

We have technology today that we aren't even using. We have enough technology to last us 600 years and it is multiplying exponentially and so I think the whole system is going to have to change drastically. I think the traditional school with the traditional teacher with the traditional classroom is already a thing of the past.

WHY ARE WE NOT EMBRACING TECHNOLOGY IN SCHOOLS TODAY?

Ron

Well I think everyone resists change. No one likes change, and the older you get the more comfortable you get and set in your ways. I think the key is to give the teacher some real hands-on experiences until they feel comfortable with it. I remember when we first encountered computers 20 some years ago, we were all afraid to even touch the keyboard—we were afraid we would break the computer. We were just afraid of the machine. We have to teach teachers to become comfortable. This comes not only with information, but also experience.

Matt

A famous historian in education once wrote that the greatest technology that ever took place in the school was the chalkboard. That it is one of the few technologies and advancements in the school that became interactive. It is used every day and is the focal point of the learning process in classrooms.

Do any of you guys see any other technologies having the capacity, having the ability to change instruction? Maybe it is already in school or maybe it is a future technology.

Gabe

I have a Smartboard in our class. That is like a chalkboard, but it is really cool because you can write on it and it shows up on the computer too.

Luke

We use projectors that display papers or objects. But it is basically to show people things. I think you are right, Dad, the chalkboard is still used more than anything else in our classes. We show work a lot on the chalkboard. I think the chalkboard is basically the design that made everything.

Dominic

Right now in my school I think the only technology that is used on a regular basis is, like they said, the chalkboard, overheads, and LCD projectors. I think the next technology is maybe iPads integrated into your desk so there is no worry of you picking it up and dropping it. Instead of having papers everywhere you just have it on that one thing and every time you go to a new classroom it transfers and then you have all your papers there and you put it on your computer at home. You wouldn't even need a backpack anymore to carry stuff around. So you could go to from class to class and then home without even picking up a book. It would be in your desk and all goes up to a cloud where you could access it from home or any class that you are in.

I think this would work because it is about the student not the teacher. I mean the students already know how to do this. Teachers do not need to learn new things—just put all of their work online—accessible to students.

Ron

I think one of the big problems that we have is the notion that students of the future will have to be reeducated 13 times in their lifetime. I read in the newspaper that people now change careers up to 12 times in their lifetime. That means lots of reeducation. So the traditional classroom atmosphere is not going to work. We are going to have to find more effective ways—distance learning, using modern technologies—to gain new skills and reeducate ourselves if we are going to be able to compete. We are also going to have to be able to make sure that education becomes a top priority in the minds of the public. The old attitude that if working in the factory on the assembly line is good enough for your old man it is good enough for your kids is no longer true because there aren't even any manufacturing jobs available. So if people are going to improve their lifestyle, they are going to have to reeducate themselves on a continuous basis. So the old saying, *learning is a lifetime process,* now has come true.

Luke

As Dominic was saying, the iPads, that is a great idea but what I think what would be less expensive is we go to the computer lab more often. Since we have all of this technology, why don't we take advantage of it? We could use our flash drives more for projects, presentations, even homework, work would be done much faster, less paper, and we would save the environment with less trees we would need to cut down.

ADVICE TO SCHOOL PRINCIPALS

Matt

This book is called *Principal 2.0.* It will be used to help school principals—to give them strategies to incorporate technology in their schools.

What advice would you give to a school principal to help their teachers to become ready and able to use technologies to help their students?

Gabe

Principals should ask teachers to use the technology more. Like the Smartboards—every class should use them every day.

Dominic

Principals should not use paper. Paper gets lost, misplaced. Teachers don't lose their laptops or smartphones. The principal should communicate with these devices. Principals should do things like this so they can show teachers it can be done—and to show teachers how to do this with their own students.

Luke

Principals should work at fundraising so everyone has the right equipment. We need to go paperless—we need to use technology more. The principal can help make sure everyone has the technology, not just kids who are rich.

Dominic

I want to add on to what I said earlier. There is a resistance from teachers and principals from students using their own technologies into class—especially phones. I think the possible uses of these technologies outweigh the negatives like games, texts, etc. I like to type because my handwriting is bad, everything can be submitted electronically, accessed through your phone, automated grading systems. The students who don't have computers would have more access to the school's technology if people could use their own technologies. And like Luke said, if they do not have it we need to find ways to get them technology.

Matt

It seems the communities that surround schools often ask how they can help. One way would be to help the principals to get technology into the hands of all students. But we cannot just stop there with the dissemination of equipment. We must make sure that the technologies are used. I have seen too many Smartboards used as simple data projectors and too many data projectors used as coffee tables. Harnessing technologies will require a new kind of pedagogy—the art of teaching—if the ultimate aim of the educational enterprise—student learning—will be impacted.

Ron

The old paradigm of the teacher of being the fountain of all knowledge is a thing of the past. Teachers have to be aware that they are not going to be that type of educator any longer. They are going to be the type of educator who teaches students how to use available technologies and to become independent learners with the ability to know how to use information and evaluate it. Technology of tomorrow is here today. All educators must be ready, willing, and able, or the kids will pass them up. This will lead to further disengagement in schools—something we cannot afford.

CONCLUSION

Looking around the table I could not help but think about my son who was not present. Oscar is just two years old, not yet able to let us know his viewpoints on technology in schools. Yet, he sits in the other room watching Elmo on an iPad app that he can manipulate himself. In fact, swiping the iPad is more natural to him then turning pages in a book.

In 2019 Oscar will be Gabe's age now, 2022 Luke's, and 2025 he will be in 10th grade like Dominic. What will the world of technology look like then? How about in 2052 when he is 42 like me? Or 2088 when he is my dad's age?

The more important question may be: Will our educational system and educators be able to harness those unknown technologies to enhance his learning experience and to best equip Oscar with the skills he needs? It is hard to say with any certainty that the systems our educators use today are meeting these objectives with Gabe, Luke, and Dominic. This conclusion comes from their dialogue. However, the answers also come from their mouths. How far out there is Dominic's idea of desks that are actually iPads? What is stopping us from engaging in a campaign to give everyone, not just privileged youth like my boys, the technology they need as Luke and Dominic suggested?

Insights offered here are not empirical. They are conceptual views from various generational vantage points. Hearing from youth and elders provides insights into both the problems and the solutions. In this dialogue we learned that the technology we add to schools must be *interactive* and in the *hands of the students and teachers*. Technology's real power lies in the ability for interaction and exchange. Moreover, the accessibility should not be down the hall, but rather on (or, as Dominic noted, in) their desks. In 1968 Phillip Jackson said, "Chalkboards can write, draw, erase, and keep material for days. Given this flexibility it is no wonder that the chalk-smudged sleeve has become the trademark of the teacher" (pp. 3–4). We need to move from chalkboards to the technologies of today and tomorrow. This will take a concerted effort from school leaders and teachers to target professional development for targeted pedagogies (see Mishra & Koehler, 2006). And, most importantly, the end-users, consumers—students themselves—must continue to put unrelenting pressure to bring their technologies into their learning.

The story of educational technology has yet to be told. We can see the aesthetic beauty in the technology—the design of shiny, slim computers and phones with decorative covers. But, we have yet to harness the unseen potential of these technologies in schools. It is indeed the unseen that will unlock the utility—"what [we] don't see that makes it useful." Perhaps creating opportunities for dialogue that is inclusive of multigenerational views will help illuminate potential of educational technology today and tomorrow.

REFERENCES

Jackson, P. (1968). *The teacher and the machine.* Pittsburgh, PA: University of Pittsburgh Press.

Mishra, P., & Koehler, M.J. (2006). Technological pedagogical content knowledge: A framework for integrating technology in teacher knowledge. *Teachers College Record, 108*(6), 1017–1054.

Patton, M. Q. (2002). *Qualitative research evaluation methods.* Thousand Oaks, CA: Sage.

Vidich, A. J., & Lyman, S. M. (1994). Qualitative methods: Their history in sociology and anthropology. In N. Denzin & Y. Lincoln, (Eds.), *Handbook of qualitative research* (pp. 23–59). Newbury, CA: Sage.

PART II

TECHNOLOGY EDUCATORS CAN USE TODAY

CHAPTER 5

DIGITAL STORYTELLING FOR CRITICAL REFLECTION

An Educational Leadership Story

Francisco Guajardo, Miguel A. Guajardo, John A. Oliver, Mónica M. Valadez, and Mark Cantu

PREFACE: STEPPING INTO SCHOOL LEADERSHIP BY MARK CANTU

I began my administrative career as an assistant principal in a rural central Texas school district several years ago. My interview for the position involved a drive around the quiet streets of this sleepy town of about 1,000 residents. The school principal, Sarah, drove the vehicle as she pushed beyond the traditional technical questions of an interview process. She was looking for initiative, intuition, heart, and someone who would understand and bring a place-based knowledge to school leadership in this particular community. As we drove through Waelder, I highlighted my understanding of teaching, learning, and leadership. I shared my enthusiasm for community, youth engagement, and the importance of creating meaningful partnerships with the families we served. That afternoon, we had lunch with the local municipal judge, Luis, and talked about what the community wanted

Principal 2.0: Technology and Educational Leadership, pages 67–80
Copyright © 2013 by Information Age Publishing
All rights of reproduction in any form reserved.

to see in the new school leadership. Marta, a parent of two school children, greeted me with open arms when we stopped at her home to say hello. I got the job offer that day and found the space where I could share what I had learned at the Llano Grande Center for Research and Development as a high school student.

Background: A Leadership Development Story

In the late 1990s a teen-aged Mark Cantu breezed through Edcouch Elsa High School (E-E High) and looked forward to the day he would leave his hometown of Elsa, the quintessential small community, pulled by the lure of bright lights and the big city. But during his senior year, he took a community-based research class taught at the high school by an organization called the Llano Grande Center for Research and Development. Through the class Mark learned about the Llano Grande way, a process that prepared students for college through exercises in self-reflection, deep analysis of family and local history, and the use of technology to make sense of personal identity and community. The last year of his high school career was the first year of his transformation from a youth with the typical anxiety of wanting to leave home, to a young man who gained an awareness of his own personal identity connected to a newfound appreciation for his community. The transformation was triggered through a class assignment: the creation of a digital story, a class assignment that challenged Mark to collect stories from elders and use digital media to build a narrative on the experiences of the storytellers.

Mark's first digital story explored the history and impact of a Mexican labor camp that existed on the outskirts of Elsa, a camp where Mark's grandmother was raised. The camp ceased to exist a few years before Mark was born, but the place represented much of the purpose and vitality of the current social, economic, and institutional context. Growing up, Mark had heard his grandmother's stories about growing up "en el Inglamo" (Engleman Farms), but he didn't quite understand the stories. When he looked at the assignment through the community-based research class at E-E High, he decided to conduct an oral history with his grandmother as a way through which he could not only capture her stories, but also examine the history of "el Inglamo." Mark worked with other high school students and teachers to collect stories of elders and led an effort to produce a digital story that would be shown to some 50 elders at a reunion of those who had grown up at the labor camp. It was a challenging assignment for Mark and classmates, but it was also an emotionally and intellectually arousing experience (see video at: http://youtu.be/JanxH_kg_qk). That high school experience changed Mark's life, as he gained a new awareness of himself through the examination of elders' and others' stories and gained a new appreciation for the struggle and history of his community.

Digital Storytelling, the Llano Grande Way

Digital storytelling at the Llano Grande Center was born out of the long-term oral history project the Center initiated in the mid-1990s. The oral history work intended to reconstruct the history of the rural communities of Edcouch, Elsa, La Villa, and Monte Alto through the popular approach of listening to the stories of elders (Guajardo & Guajardo, 2002; Smith & Sobel, 2010). High school teachers and students worked closely with elders to develop narratives that spoke both to their personal stories and to the stories of the community. Some of the stories were published in a school journal (Llano Grande Journal, 1998). Others were transferred onto VHS cassettes for display in classrooms, in community meetings, or for screening on public access television. Llano Grande experienced a transformation in this work when it hosted a digital storytelling workshop delivered by the Center for Digital Storytelling (CDS) from Berkeley, California. Building on the work of digital storytelling pioneer Dana Atchley, CDS staff trained Llano Grande youth and teachers on how to produce a digital story (Lambert, 2002). The process was simple and exciting. It was all about the story: what's the story, what's the story, was the chorus-like question that guided the experience of crafting a digital story. Once the storyteller finds the story, the essential elements are carefully crafted. Those elements include a script, a recorded voice-over of the script, identifying and dropping still or moving images onto a timeline through digital editing software, and the identification of appropriate music and other sounds to enhance the evocative quality of the story (http://www.llanogrande.org/videos/edcouch-elsa-myrtas-story/).

Through the development of those elements, Llano Grande found a way to enhance the quality of the oral histories. Further, it found a way to strengthen its entire organizational work, including adding depth to teaching and learning processes, to the college preparation program, and to the community engagement initiatives. The use of the elements of voice-overs, pictures, and sound/music took storytelling at the Llano Grande Center to new and exciting places. The newest place is a much more nuanced form of storytelling we call digital storytelling for critical self-reflection (DSCS).

Mark Cantu graduated from high school, went to college, started his career as a teacher, and subsequently enrolled in a master's program in educational leadership in a regional university along the Texas Mexican border. In that program, he deepened his understanding of digital storytelling through the new lens of critical self-reflection. Thereafter, he landed the assistant principal job at a rural school and entered a PhD program at a central Texas university, where DSCS has made its way into school and community leadership development. Today, Mark is the principal of the K–12 school district and continues to build on his evolving personal story as school and community leader.

DIGITAL STORYTELLING FOR CRITICAL SELF-REFLECTION (DSCS): A ROADMAP

In this chapter we provide personal narrative, or the act of storytelling, as a way to chronicle the experience of school leader. We look at the secondary literature, hyperlinks, and theoretical frameworks to serve as markers to illuminate how DSCS is used in the study of self, community, and curriculum. DSCS is useful as a tool to reconnect educators to their purpose for entering and remaining engaged in the educational process of individuals, communities, and organizations. The markers provide the necessary insight required for individuals to engage in an intentional and purposeful reflective process that partners with the technical aspects of digital storytelling. Digital storytelling has also been useful in framing staff development, youth leadership development, and community-building ventures. It has also been effective in community celebrations of student, family, and school accomplishments. School leaders have found this form of public expression useful in building school and community engagement (Guajardo, Oliver, Rodriguez, Valadez, Cantu, & Guajardo, 2011).

The technical and essential digital storytelling elements are important, as readers can see through the Captura digital storytelling toolkit (see first link in the links section at the end of this chapter). They include writing the script, creating a voice-over, identifying appropriate still and moving images, finding the right music and sound, and organizing it through digital media software. But those elements are secondary to the critical self-reflection that leads to discovering, refining, and sharing the personal narrative or "story." The authors of this chapter place a premium on assisting individuals in locating their story and its connection with others in their community and organization. After individuals locate their story, they then use their digital story as a tool to share and make sense of the multiple realities and complex contexts of individuals, communities, and organizations. Ultimately, DSCS emerges as a nexus between developing and sustaining skills, assets, and capacities necessary for educational and community leaders to engage in moral and ethical decisions that lead to successful outcomes, for and with those they serve and lead.

Technical Components of Digital Storytelling

The technical components of the digital storytelling process are presented early in this chapter both to teach and to reduce anxieties associated with the use of technology and its integration in the pedagogic process. While understanding the technical is important, the process of discovering the story is most critical. By presenting the "nuts and bolts" or the "how to" of the digital storytelling process, we leave space to delve more deeply into crafting the personal narrative.

There are numerous resources available to serve as guides in the digital storytelling process, such as the Captura digital storytelling tool kit found through the Llano Grande website, the Center for Digital Storytelling, and the educational uses of digital storytelling at University of Houston. For the purposes of this chapter, we focus on the digital storytelling toolkit by the Llano Grande Center. The center's toolkit presents sections that systematically address each of the technical components associated with the digital storytelling process: technology infrastructure, copyright, consent forms, storyboard layout, editing, and publishing. Each section is accompanied by easy-to-follow text, embedded video examples, and downloadable PDFs.

Personal Narrative

We use personal narrative or story to highlight the journey and the critical self-reflective process of one educational leader who participated in the process of DSCS. This personal narrative provides insight into the journey of Mark Cantu, an educational campus leader in a rural Central Texas school. Mark's narrative serves as a bricolage, or tapestry of life experiences, and our quest to understand those experiences. Prior to understanding others, it is important for individuals to develop a self-awareness of their values, beliefs, and attitudes, particularly as they relate to school and community leadership. We believe the DSCS process assists individuals in exploring and understanding the following questions:

1. What do I value?
2. What is the foundation of my assets, challenges, and self-being?
3. How do my values influence my practices as a leader?
4. What should be the purpose of education?
5. What is the role of leadership in making this a reality?

The chapter weaves literature, hyperlinks, and theoretical frameworks into the fabric of the document.

DSCS helps to move individuals through several stages of leadership development, as it places the student at the center of the learning. The participant becomes the unit of analysis (Guajardo et al., 2011). Learners are invited to privilege their lived experiences and explore the cartography of their lives. They are guided through a critical self-reflective process by examining the following domains: (1) historical, (2) biological, (3) cultural, and (4) political. Each domain is supported by appropriate literature; engaged dialogic processes that involve whole group, small groups, one-on-one discussions; and other dynamic class activities. The above processes reduce the dependence of students on the instructor as the principal purveyor of knowledge. Instead, they are expected to make sense of their lives through an examination and critical reflection of personal experiences.

The DSCS process provides the framework for individuals to gain a new appreciation for their personal, community, and organizational histories. It helps individuals gain a new sense of self, a new awareness of their school, and new perspectives on their community. The process helps display a picture of the multilayered context of feelings linked to teaching and learning. Brookfield (2006) explains the teaching and learning process as one filled with "passion, hope, doubt, fear, exhilaration, weariness, colleagueship, loneliness, glorious defeats, hollow victories, and above all, the certainties of surprise and ambiguity" (p. 1). Successful leadership in organizational settings requires that leaders understand human behavior. That understanding begins with knowledge of self and leads to the understanding of others.

We began with Mark's story and his early exposure to digital storytelling as a high school student in a border town in south Texas. We offer insight into Llano Grande digital storytelling and its impact on the individuals and the communities where the organization works—essentially, we explore digital storytelling, the Llano Grande way. A theoretical framework helps us make sense of the DSCS process. To link the theoretical underpinnings, we return to Mark's story as a school campus leader as a way to connect theory with practice. Finally, we look at how school leaders can implement this process with their school communities and the communities they serve.

THEORETICAL FRAMEWORK

The use of theory as practice has multiple purposes, including: (1) to explain certain phenomena, thoughts, and practices; (2) to project (under other epistemologies, this is called prediction) and inform future actions, outcomes, and impacts of specific practices; and (3) to place boundaries around thoughts, ideas, and practices. Through this frame we put forth a dynamic social-constructivist theory to inform action. This theory helps make meaning of a rich and complex story-making and storytelling process. The story-making process is an opportunity to (re)author one's identity, while the storytelling is the public sharing of one's story. The development of these two concepts is not linear, for the pedagogical process meets participants where they are developmentally. The social developmental work of teaching, learning, and leading helps us get to the sharing stage, while the technical work helps us in the production process. We use the social technologies of relationship, conversation, story, and community building to guide the learning process and to take advantage of the technical skills as we engage in framing the teaching, learning, and development of our selves, students, teachers, and community partners.

Explaining the Work

As we prepared to write this document, a colleague walked into one of our offices and asked curiously:

"What are you working on?"

The response: "The use of digital story and technology for the development of educational leaders."

The colleague responded, "That's already been written!"

Though we have written previously about digital storytelling, the challenge has been to focus on the digital storytelling process rather than to essentialize the concept of digital storytelling into a product (Guajardo et al., 2011; Lambert, 2002), and to put legs on story (Guajardo & Guajardo, 2010) as we practice the catalytic validity of this process (Lather, 1991). This text highlights the action by framing the process, production, and presentation as knowledge creation and as a community-building venture; the process is informed and nurtured when the engagement, production, and presentation of story making are dynamic and dialogical. This dynamic process is critical when practiced in communities and schools that have historically been relegated to the margins, where stories and latent knowledge have not been privileged and have typically not been written by the locals themselves. The theory of action is an instrument to imagine, explore, and act on one's interests for enhancing the human condition in community.

Projecting and Informing the Work

The digital storytelling process, the Llano Grande way, is a pedagogy grounded in place, informed by local history, knowledge(s), and experiences (Maturana & Varela, 1987; Rice, 2001; Spindler & Spindler, 1987). By design, this story making is congruent and responsive to the local values.

It builds on and highlights the skills, assets, stories, and personal experiences of families and institutions in the community. The wisdom of elders and the power of place are privileged, and relationships are honored. The story-making and telling processes are dynamic and shape future actions. In turn, this process of story making is also critical in a community-building and development venture for schools. The actions that emerge from this story-making process include curriculum development informed by the local stories of students, families, teachers, and community partners; actions also include the professional development for teachers, school leaders, and other stakeholders. The process yields transformational change as we use the story making and digital storytelling process to advocate for community actions that impact school bond elections, public health issues such as immunization drives and children's health insurance enrollment, and sundry other matters. The robust nature of this theory of action is evidenced by the impact the actions have demonstrated in our local communities.

Bordering the Ideas

The social-constructivist process we employ to make meaning of the storytelling and story making is bordered by the following organizing ecologies of knowing (Guajardo, Guajardo, Oliver, Valadez, Henderson, & Keawe, 2012) at the self, organization, and community levels. Each story has a purpose and a meaning, and each inspires action.

Self

When a person reflects and shares a story in public, he or she begins to organize values, work, purpose, and relationships in a public manner. The more we practice this story-making process, the more we give clarity to our roles as public people. The movement from a private person to a public educator and leader is a learned process that requires scaffolding for educators and emerging leaders.

Organization

Personal story making is shaped by our roles in organizations and institutions. We serve as members of families, schools, and/or service organizations. The role of teachers and educational leaders in institutions is critical to the social fabric and success of organizations and communities. Schools are mediating institutions that bring and filter the personal assets of individual students, teachers, leaders, and members of the community. Negotiating the individual stories of an institution into a collective school story is important as schools create their public image, their purpose, and their role in enhancing the quality of life for children and their families, while enhancing the vitality of its community organizations.

Community

We view schools as centers of community life, and the identity of schools as a mirror to their surrounding community. For many years, the pride of a community has been its schools, particularly in the rural places where Mark was raised and where he now works; by extension, the school's future is directly connected to the healthy sustainability of the community. The local community provides a familiar and relevant laboratory for schools. The social intercourse of school curriculum into the community's assets, history, and identity is critical for engaging school-age students in framing community stories. When students create community stories, they become stakeholders and citizens in engendering hope for their community. Creating community stories is an engaged process for developing citizens in our communities. We use these ecologies of knowing to organize the learning and sense-making process and are mindful of the unequivocal fluidity and malleability of these ecological and symbolic borders. The different ecologies are interdependent and overlap in time, space, and experience.

Negotiating Theory Building

The ecologies of knowing are filtered through the lens of history, biology, culture, and politics. The story making process is organic and at times messy—and persistently about giving voice to stakeholders, their institutions, and their community. Like the fluidity of the story-making process, the theory-building process sometimes changes, as the stories, the values, identities, and actions of the individuals, organizations, and communities similarly change. We see the story makers as theory builders too, as they work through a process that is dynamic and pedagogical.

In traditional educational settings, storytelling is often akin to the process of telling or retelling an event illustrative of the person's ability to summarize key points. Such stories follow a linear pattern and include a beginning, middle, and end, utilizing the vocabulary necessary to name events. When technology is applied to this understanding of storytelling, the only significant innovation becomes the medium through which the representation of the story is told. But digital storytelling, embraced as art form, can create a unique and critical lens through which to make sense of, reenergize, and reculturize traditional educational settings to become ever more responsive to their members. A digital story connects with broader and divergent audiences because of the eclectic appeal invited by its art form, much of which is fashioned by new digital media and emerging technologies. Through these technologies, traditional storytelling becomes transformed and then transmitted to broader audiences.

In our application of digital storytelling toward the growth and development of educational leaders, we transform this medium into a process where we invite educational leaders to not only tell their stories, but also unpack the various and at times divergent realities interwoven within those stories. In this process, storytelling is no longer marginalized to our singular understanding of a skill set each is expected to master by the end of our primary school career. The singular story told of the traditional educational setting is no longer understood as one-size-fits all. No longer does it make sense that a singular story should inform the creation or sustenance of systems that determine who gets what, when, and where. The digital storytelling process democratizes storytelling, moves storytelling to the masses and away from the modality of the singular master storyteller.

The digital storytelling process in our educational leadership programs invite educational leaders to recapture and harness storytelling as a living learning tool that creates the possibility to identify, acknowledge, and validate the multiple realities that influence their understanding of multiple contexts. These contexts are couched within multiple levels and scaffold from the micro level of self, to the more macro levels of school organization and community. Initiated through an exploration of self, educational leaders are accompanied through the process of making sense of their personal stories, both present and past experiences, as well as generational histories long since masked by meta-narratives that purport to legitimize historically produced power dynamics. Subsequently, the challenging work of exploring a greater understanding of self through digital storytelling by and with educational leaders becomes a generative and dynamic process.

MARK'S REFLECTION ON DSCS IN SCHOOLS AND COMMUNITIES

The craft of digital storytelling that I learned as a high school student over a decade ago has helped me throughout my professional, personal, and academic growth. The digital storytelling process began with the production of my story, and as a principal I have taken that developmental experience to help teachers engage in their own critical self-reflection. Additionally, I utilize digital storytelling to capture the work of the youth in the K–12 rural school I lead by helping students make their story public in a simple, yet engaging way. What began with a conversation among students has developed into an evolving story about the collective power of youth as they journey through high school.

Through digital storytelling, my teachers and students capture the passion high school students have for their school and community. For example, during an interview process to select students to attend a national conference, the idea of a community youth center surfaced. The interview was videotaped, the team of teachers and students reviewed the video, the idea of a community center emerged from that review process, and a digital story based on the community center was produced. The reflective and evaluative process led to the creation of a team of faculty and students who then reframed the concept into initiatives beyond a physical and social space for students. We have committed to establishing a place- and community-based education course at our high school that will lead the way to enhancing the curriculum throughout the school district. This has helped redefine professional development for faculty and staff (Smith & Sobel, 2010).

As a school leader, digital storytelling has helped me engage not only students and faculty on campus, but also many other stakeholders who would otherwise not have the opportunity to engage. I have shared the stories my faculty and students have constructed at academic conferences and community gatherings with the idea that we continue to grow and learn with others. These pieces have become the center of conversations resulting in multiple opportunities for the students, for teachers, and for me. They continue to push us into a space where we examine ourselves in order to draw out the best in us for the collective good. Most importantly, the digital storytelling process has documented the teaching and learning that have occurred over the past couple of years at my school. The process we have participated in could have occurred without any documentation, but we have made a dedicated effort to document the entire process since May of 2011. Having access to hours of footage, pictures, audio, and transcripts of meetings, interviews, and other public events that involve teachers, students, parents, and other community members allows us to reflect throughout and make sense of what we have been saying and doing in order to push the work forward and allow it to evolve as needed.

I have been able to reflect as a practitioner by compiling and editing the footage as my teachers and students craft their own digital stories. The tool has helped me realize who has been part of the conversation and uncover the power dynamics and relationships that might have gone unnoticed. This has facilitated my own understanding of student engagement and helped me reveal how we ask our students to participate in their own learning. The simple acts of writing a script, recording a voice-over, finding images, identifying appropriate music and sound—the essential elements of a digital story—to produce a digital story have helped make my story public through a particular aesthetic, just as it has helped me nurture storytellers in my teachers and students. It has helped me shape instruction across the school district by focusing on the students, the teachers, and the community as a whole. While I honor each of them as individuals, I have come to understand that the deepest learning is a result of all of us pulling together. Sharing the stories beyond the school through participation in conferences has encouraged others to look at our school and collaborate with the district to move curriculum from low levels of engagement and rigor to one that focuses on students and their learning styles—a mode grounded in critical reflection (Freire, 1998).

Beyond the classroom, the use of multimedia encourages teachers to learn about themselves in order to reframe their own teaching and learning practices. Faculty and staff take part in a school- and community-based education class in partnership with a local university educational leadership program. They focus on the self in order to help them understand their own values, beliefs, and assets as they analyze their teaching. Teachers discover what practices work best and become more successful educators by discussing their formative years, as they share some of their most vulnerable moments. Together, we make sense of our own realities and ways of knowing with the intent to enhance our practices. Understanding the power of the process has been invaluable for me as a leader. Through the use of digital storytelling, I have been able to take my staff through a level of analysis and synthesis that we had not experienced together, and we have created stronger relationships and strengthened our organizational ties. This practice has been the best relationship-building tool we have used in my career as an administrator. It has helped us grapple with our organization's underlying culture.

Digital storytelling for critical reflection has been an outlet for my work as principal and for my studies in a doctoral program. I have used digital storytelling to reflect on my own life and the values that shape me as a leader. My leadership qualities are deeply rooted in the core values I learned from my family and which I discovered in high school during the oral history and digital storytelling projects. Continuing the practice of digital storytelling through my academic career has allowed me to develop an engaged reflective practice and to lead in culturally responsive ways. It has helped me challenge my faculty, my students, my community, and myself to facilitate learning through critical self-reflection.

CLOSING STORY

We close the chapter with Mark's digital story not as an ending, but as a beginning to a dynamic and generative process accessible to all school leaders. Mark may be unique in that he grew up in the work of storytelling and story making, but as a school leader, he faces the same challenges every other principal in the state faces. Yet Mark has developed a consciousness by which he understands the process of digital story for critical self-reflection, and it has become foundational in his leadership orientation. He has used it for his own development, as the core for the professional development of his faculty and staff, and for leadership development of his students. The digital storytelling process for critical self-reflection has also catapulted his school to a public space to guide organizational and community development activities in his district. The digital stories repertoire now includes stories of self, organization, and community. This process has engaged the local talents of youth as they practice their digital storytelling skills and as they identify and highlight the local assets in their community. Digital storytelling is a robust, generative, and dynamic process that is grounded in sound social theory, and when utilized within a local context, it can change the world.

USEFUL LINKS

Digital Storytelling Toolkit by the Llano Grade Center
    http://captura.llanogrande.org/index.html

Center for Digital Storytelling
    http://www.storycenter.org/

The Educational Uses of Digital Storytelling: University of Houston
    http://digitalstorytelling.coe.uh.edu/

REFERENCES

Brookfield, S. (2006). *The skillful teacher: On technique, trust, and responsiveness in the classroom.* San Francisco, CA: Jossey-Bass.

Freire, P. (1998). *Pedagogy of freedom, ethics, democracy, and civic courage.* Lanham, MD: Rowman & Littlefield Publishers.

Guajardo, F., & Guajardo, M. (2010). Cultivating stories of change. In K. Ruder (Ed.), *The collective leadership storybook: Weaving strong communities.* Seattle, WA: The Center for Ethical Leadership.

Guajardo, M., & Guajardo, F. (2002). Critical ethnography and community change. In Z. Yali & H. Trueba (Eds.), *Ethnography and schools: Qualitative approaches to the study of education* (pp. 281–304). Lanham, MD: Rowman & Littlefield Publishers.

Guajardo, M., Guajardo, F., Oliver, J., Valadez, M., Henderson, K., & Keawe, L. (2012). A conversation on political imagination and advocacy for educational leadership: Part II. *UCEA Review, 53*(3), 19–22.

Guajardo, M., Oliver, J., Rodriguez, G., Valadez, M., Cantu, Y., & Guajardo, F. (2011). Reframing the praxis of school leadership preparation through digital storytelling. *Journal of Research on Leadership Education, 6*(5), 145–161.

Lambert, J. (2002). *Digital storytelling: Capturing lives, creating community.* Berkeley, CA: Life on the Water, Inc.

Lather, P. A. (1991). *Getting smart: Feminist research and pedagogy with/in the postmodern.* New York, NY: Routledge.

Maturana, H. R., & Varela, F. G. (1987). *The Tree of Knowledge.* Boston, MA: Shambhala.

Rice, D. (2001). *Crazy loco.* New York, NY: Penguin Group.

Smith, G., & Sobel, D. (2010). *Place and community based education in schools.* New York, NY: Routledge.

Spindler, G., & Spindler, L. (1987). In prospect for a controlled cross-cultural comparison of schooling: Schoenhausen and Roseville. In G. Spindler (Ed.), *Education and Cultural Process: Toward an Anthropology of Education,* (pp. 389–400). Prospect Heights, IL: Waveland.

CHAPTER 6

ENGAGING YOUTH VOICE

Collaborative Reflection to Inform School Relationships, Processes, and Practices

Christopher Janson, Sejal Parikh, Jacqueline Jones, Terrinikka Ransome, and Levertice Moses

INTRODUCTION

Principals face tremendous pressure to use data in order to inform practices, processes, and policies in their schools—all with the endpoint of improving student achievement. This pressure has both been caused by and resulted in a proliferation of data, so much so that school principals are often awash in data that flow from various district and state sources. However, school leaders too often underutilize one source of very different, yet invaluable, data: the perspectives and experiences of the students who populate our schools. In this chapter, we describe a process for using digital media to capture reflective conversations between principals and students in a way that can generate a powerful source of informative school data, while also facilitating the development of principals, students, teachers, and other staff. In doing so, we describe how this process provides oppor-

Principal 2.0: Technology and Educational Leadership, pages 81–96
Copyright © 2013 by Information Age Publishing
All rights of reproduction in any form reserved.

tunities for students to voice their perspectives on school practices and the value of casting reflection as a collective process, while exploring a specific case application. We believe that the unique context of every case example and application is important, and ours here is no exception. Specifically, the case example we describe involves reflective conversations between a female African American assistant principal and both a female and a male African American student. We call this process *discursive digital reflection* (DDR) (Janson, Parikh, & Maxis, 2012).

THE NEED FOR DATA THAT INFORMS AND TRANSFORMS

Certainly, the accountability movement in education has brought with it certain standardized metrics in which student and school performance can be measured. We view the emphasis the accountability movement has placed on student achievement data to be necessary, but excessive and unnecessarily exclusionary. We believe that for schools to function at a peak state so that students can thrive as learners, assessment needs to focus on more than simply student learning. Learning in schools involves many complex variables and contexts. Learning is a social event involving relationships between and among school staff, students, families, and communities. Learning is also contained by school processes and procedures both in and out of classrooms. Likewise, learning involves practices exercised by both teachers and the learners themselves. Unfortunately, not only are these pivotal relationships, processes, and practices not informed by standardized student achievement data, but the overemphasis on achievement data too often squeezes out resources and capacity needed to learn more about them. We believe that while it is necessary to know what the data tell us about student achievement, this knowledge of student performance is insufficient to develop high-functioning schools that facilitate deep learning. One way to begin to move beyond our exclusionary obsession with standardized test data about student achievement is to begin developing approaches that allow students to tell us about their experiences in our schools and the practices, processes, and policies they encounter there. A commitment to these types of data can shape our schools so they develop into more effective institutions, and they can also serve to facilitate student and staff development.

WHAT HAPPENS WHEN WE LISTEN TO STUDENT PERSPECTIVES

In the bustle of school life where accountability seems too often to be viewed through the myopic frame of one or two data points, it becomes difficult to maintain a focus on the reality that students in our schools are more than producers of test scores. Rather, they are human beings who are not only learning many things (including their roles in society), but who are also observant and insightful and can teach us about how to collectively build stronger schools. Mostly, though, we haven't been good at listening to what students can tell us.

It is not just principals who too frequently neglect to listen to the students their schools serve. It is neglect on the scales of classrooms, schools, and districts. For instance, some have noted that school personnel in general seldom seek students' perceptions on their school experiences in order to inform practice (Gentilucci, 2004). It may be that the omission of student voices in many local contexts simply mirrors the larger neglect on a national level. For instance, Jonathan Kozol (1991) has long noted the absence of student voices when educational policy and reform is developed, debated, and enacted.

Although we seldom elicit student perspectives with the purpose of informing school practices, those student perspectives have been referred to as "an untapped source" of qualitative data for improving teaching and learning and building more significant student involvement and deeper student participation (Smith, Petralia, & Hewitt, 2005, p. 28). Listening to the voices of students can not only inform and improve teaching and learning, but can also help us better understand the cultural contexts in which schools are situated (Friend & Caruthers, 2012). Beyond student involvement and participation, Levin (1994) suggested that school reform strategies are stronger when they incorporate student voice in purposeful ways and then further enlist student involvement and support while developing school goals and instructional strategies. While the potential benefits of inviting student perspectives regarding pedagogy seem a bit more obvious, still others have found that students' perspectives can provide principals and teaching staff with valuable insights that can be used to design better curriculum (Cook-Sather, 2007).

Of course, the power of structuring opportunities to learn from students is not only contained in how student voices can inform principal and staff practices and school processes and policies. Just as important is the impact on students' development when their perspectives and school experiences are sought out, listened to, and utilized in order to inform visible and positive changes in schools. Students and the dynamic they form with school personnel can change in profound ways when generous and gracious collaborative discourse with the purpose of improving schooling occurs between and among them. Cook-Sather (2006) described three such ways in which this occurs. First and foremost, she wrote that conversations between school staff members and students purposed to explore and address issues of schooling radically alter the "dominant power imbalances between adults and young people" (p. 366). Put differently, these conversations demand that both adults and youth in schools renegotiate their relationships and the power each holds in these relationships so that more egalitarian interactions can occur in the first place. Second, Cook-Sather describes how students begin to feel more respected and empowered by collaborative discourse with school staff, and this empowerment often leads to deeper student learning and feelings of involvement in their schools. Finally, the unbridled participatory nature of collaborative and reflective discourse and inquiry allows for the lived experiences of both students and staff to be voiced. The expression of these lived experiences produces powerful opportunities for transformative experiences through the integration of curricular content with individual and collective experiences and histories (Cook-Sather, 2006).

Finally, all school practices occur within a cultural context and purposeful conversations between students and staff have been identified and described as holding the potential to be among culturally relevant approaches to empowering and learning with African American students (Ladson-Billings, 1995). Examples of conversation-based school practices identified as being culturally relevant to African American students range from sharing circles in which students and school staff (typically teachers) begin to voice and explore their personal histories (Howard, 2001), to storytelling (Howard, 2002), to utilizing song and performance as modes of oral expression (Young, Wright, & Laster, 2003). Importantly, the conversations suggested by both Cook-Sather (2006) and the literature on culturally relevant school practices represent, in part, a paradigmatic shift in *how* we reflect. Specifically, there is power in collective reflection as a social process between two or more people, rather than just one individual.

MOVING TOWARD COLLECTIVE REFLECTION

Few other professions involve the complex and demanding roles, responsibilities, and practices as that of a school principal. In light of that demanding complexity, it is important for principals to engage in professional and personal reflection in order to meet those complex demands (Brooks & Tooms, 2008; Larrivee, 2000). Reflection can provide principals and other educators with a valuable "pause" from the frenetic pace of their jobs and provide the intellectual and emotional space for them to make meaning from the blur of their professional experiences. Notably, reflection has most often been conceptualized as a practice conducted by individuals. We find value, though, in recasting reflection in educational settings as a collective practice, and others have done similarly. For instance, Zeichner and Liston (1996) proposed that we reframe educator reflection as a "collaborative social practice" (p. 77). We, too, believe that a shift toward collective reflective practices holds potential to improve the outcomes of reflection by better informing the construction of more meaningful and effective school processes that can lead to improved learning outcomes for students. At the same time, more collective reflective practices serve to democratize the analysis and meaning-making that often characterizes effective schools. Finally, we believe that collective reflective processes are much more congruent with ideas of collective leadership and culturally relevant school practices. Collective reflective practices like the one described by us below exemplify the conceptual shift in school leadership from the principal as sole container of leadership to more collective models (Guajardo, 2009) involving students, while doing so in a way that resonates with cultural strengths within African American communities.

THE DISCURSIVE DIGITAL REFLECTION (DDR) PROCESS

The discursive digital reflection (DDR) process begins with a principal or other school leader engaging with a student or small group of students in reflective conversation or discourse. Reflection has been described in a variety of ways. For our purposes, we have been working from an understanding that reflection is the process through which we make deeper meaning from our experiences, while also examining our own assumptions and attitudes that inform those experiences. This description of reflection is close to the work of Dewey (1938), who suggested beliefs regarding practice must be a focus of reflection.

The discursive reflections proposed here can focus around topics or practices that members of the school community wish to learn more about. For instance, focus topics could include principal or school practices such as ensuring student safety, building-level processes that include student course selection and registration, school policies related to attendance and discipline, and so on. This collaborative reflective discourse is intended to inform all participants' understandings of the topic through the constructed meanings and understandings that emerge from the collaborative, discursive reflection. The discursive reflection is video recorded and then converted into a digital artifact that is then used as a focal point of further reflection for the principal and possibly other staff. By incorporating other staff members into reflective reviews of the digital artifact, DDR can move reflection from being a purely intrapersonal experience to a collaborative learning experience that can further inform and deepen other staff members' understandings of important school practices, processes, and policies. At the same time, reflective review, analysis, and conversation around the digital artifact also allow for attention to the *reflective process* through which

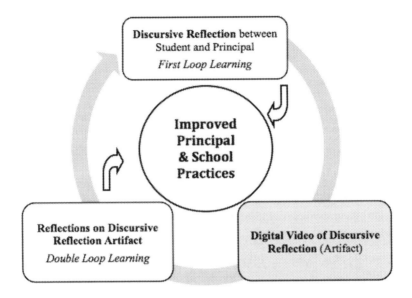

Figure 6.1 Discursive digital reflective process.

understandings are developed (see Figure 6.1). In this way, the practice and process of reflection itself are also subject to reflection and so provide opportunities to build collective school capacity to reflect.

YOUTH VOICE, EMPOWERMENT, AND YOUTH PARTICIPATORY ACTION RESEARCH

As we developed and applied the digital discursive reflection (DDR) process to principal and student collaborative reflection, we became interested in the unmistakable parallels between essential elements of DDR and those of youth participatory action research (PAR). Both place emphasis on collaborative inquiry between youth and adults, the respect and attention paid to the lived experiences of all involved, the shared meaning-making that develops through the process, and the capacity for individual and systems change through their respective processes. For instance, PAR is described as an approach that can "renew the social capital of those practicing the inquiry" (Welton, 2011, p. 1). We believed this emphasis on empowering participants was congruent with the DDR emphasis on youth empowerment through the development of closer relationships with the educators with whom they are partnered. Likewise, youth PAR does not simply examine issues in schools from a detached theoretical stance (Fischer, 2003), but instead it is designed to address those issues and inform solutions (Ayala,

2009). We also found value in the acknowledgement of "insider knowledge that young people bring to an inquiry" (Galletta & Jones, 2010, p. 341) within a PAR approach, which paralleled our intent that the DDR process might lead to enriched understandings of school issues by eliciting and strengthening student voices and allying them with those of the staff. Finally, youth PAR approaches and DDR involve collaborations with youth, so the potential for collective, intergenerational agency emerges (Tuck, 2009). As a result of the philosophical, political, and structural principles they share, we chose to frame our description and exploration of the DDR process through a youth PAR approach.

DDR-IN-PRACTICE: A CASE EXAMPLE

Our exploration of the discursive digital reflection (DDR) process focused on the discourse among three of the authors who, at the time of this writing, had just completed an academic year at the same school. At that school, Ms. Jacqueline Jones was an assistant principal, and Terrinikka Ransome and Levertice Moses had just completed their 12th grade years and had graduated. Their high school is situated in a large urban public school district in the southeastern United States. Like 68% of the overall student population, both Terrinikka and Levertice are African American, as is Ms. Jones. Ms. Jones had worked individually with both Terrinikka and Levertice during that previous year. Before Ms. Jones, Terrinikka, and Levertice engaged in the DDR process, we met as a group and discussed the purpose of these conversations and the need for each of them to try to interact and talk beyond the roles they had inhabited that previous school year. During that meeting Ms. Jones, Terrinikka, and Levertice also decided to focus their conversations around how the importance of relationships between principals and students might better support academic, professional, and personal development for all involved.

As per the DDR process, Jones video recorded a discursive digital reflection (DDR), or collaborative reflective conversation (Janson, Parikh, Young & Fudge, 2011), with both Terrinikka (https://vimeo.com/51038725) and Levertice (https://vimeo.com/51038724). Prior to describing how the digital video recordings of these reflective conversations were used, it is first important to emphasize that any video-recording should occur only after the principal or other school leader engaging in DDR first complies with the school and/or district policy for receiving both informed consent for this process as well as permission to capture and use each student's image and interactions through video. It is also recommended that following each reflective conversation and creation of each accompanying digital artifact, students and their parents or guardians are provided with the opportunity to review the DDR digital artifact in order to provide their consent and permission.

These discursive reflections were subsequently viewed, reviewed, and analyzed by all five of the authors. Additionally, the two university faculty members, Janson and Parikh, also discussed their respective perceptions and analyses with each other. We developed the following thoughts regarding this case example of the use of DDR based on our individual and collective reflections and analyses.

Individual Reflections on DDR

Student Perspective—Terrinikka Ransome

From my experiences in this system overall I have learned that many schools are different, and teachers as well as administration play a big role not only in students' educations, but their personal lives as well. Through the conversation with Ms. Jones and my review of the recording of our conversation through this DDR process, I believe I understand more deeply how administration can build students up, as well as tear them down. For instance, our conversation really brought home the importance of principals getting to know a student before they challenge them or push them to do something they really may be unsure they can do. If a strong relationship is intact between that principal and student, then the student can know that any challenge is coming from a place of concern, respect, and even love. If that strong relationship is not intact, then any challenge might seem like a disrespectful power play.

The most powerful part of this process to me was thinking about and reflecting on how important relationships are in a school. I found it surprising how much Mrs. Jones actually cared about us, the students, and who we

Figure 6.2   Terrinikka Ransome and Jacqueline Jones.

are as complete people. I knew she cared about me before, but this really showed me how much. She really communicated to me that she cares about us mentally, physically, and even emotionally. Just her willingness to engage in this DDR process with Levertice and me spoke volumes. She is so interested in bettering her skills as an administrator and improving the school that she would not only meet with us for conversation about how to do so, but it is important enough to her to tape these conversations so they can be reviewed for even more truth.

This entire experience changed how I see students, principals, and teachers and the roles they play in school. I had thought about these things and observed some of them before, but there was something about the focus of a conversation about them with someone whose job it is to focus on these things. I found it enlightening and only wish I had the opportunity early on in my high school career, rather than the end. Knowing Ms. Jones' and now I imagine all the other principals' commitment to betterment would have made me much more willing and likely to seek help. I know now that administrators also value how important it is to build a relationship and communicate.

I believe all principals could use this DDR process to help them get to know students and teachers better. These reflective conversations also show students that administrators can also open themselves up instead of being too uptight. Relationships require that both sides give a little. Who knows? Maybe some students who haven't had very good examples of how to share appropriately might learn to do so through these conversations with administrators. I can also see how the DDR process could help improve the schools and the curriculum. I realized after watching our videos that nobody really knows how schools are running better than us, the students. Maybe this will make asking those questions part of the school so that we are listened to more commonly. I think there is a lot of upside and feel this process should be considered and started as soon as possible in schools.

Student Perspective—Levertice Moses

What I learned from this overall process was that there are so many things students and administrators can learn from each other if they just take the time to talk and reflect. High school is four years of a student's life, and that is so long that there should be strong relationships between with those people working in the school. How strange is it that these strong relationships are not the standard? Four years of your life with people and there is not a connection? Can you imagine any other type of scenario being around people for four years and there are no deep connections? That makes me wonder why relationships are not more of a priority in schools.

The relationships built in schools should reflect on how that school is performing. Instead we only look at test scores. Just like family at home it

Figure 6.3 Levertice Moses and Jacqueline Jones.

should also feel like family at school. You see these people every day and many have your back and guide you the right way. I feel fortunate because high school was just like another home with a lot more supporters. I learned that building a connection with administrators helped me succeed but this DDR process caused me to start thinking about how these connections and conversations can change things in the school so that all other students can succeed as well.

What I found surprising about Ms. Jones was how much she focuses on developing skills around "that way" she has with her students. I can see now that the connection I felt with her is something partially due to her intentions. Our conversation and reflection made me realize that she values relationships with students and knows that those relationships help them meet their goals. It is not just that she likes people. She likes to see people develop and accomplish. That is why she does it too. Watching our reflective conversation I notice how much I spoke about the importance "personal talk" had for me. After I had those experiences with Ms. Jones it was like we were connected and built a bond that grew. I knew I had somebody there for me to help me get through high school. She knew I had some troubles that were affecting me that might keep me from graduating. The personal talks we had while going over my class work after school were great. Ms. Jones once told me, "We are going to do what ever it takes to make it." She said that in plural. I felt like she had my back from then on. From this DDR process I have learned that she is committed to making the school the kind of place where all the staff can build relationships with all other students so they can feel like someone has their backs too.

Principal Perspective—Jacqueline Jones

Each of my conversation partners provided me with intriguing insights during the discursive reflections. Both Terrinikka and Levertice viewed school administrators as essential to their academic success. They also expressed their need for approachable administrators who see them as individuals and support them with direction and relational strategies. For example, Terrinikka shared that an authoritative administrator who dictates goals for students to achieve is not as effective as an administrator who provides support and guidance towards meeting those goals. While Levertice believed that an administrative team should be diverse in order for students to relate, he also explained the faulty view some administrators may have when dealing with African American students as a whole group rather than individuals. Levertice shared several grass root commonalities that may group African American students together. Students may have grown up in the same neighborhood, they may be related, or school may be the only place they can talk to one another in a safe environment. Therefore, Levertice and Terrinikka believed in the importance of school administrators knowing students by name, having individual conversations and more authentic relationships with students, and collaborating more visibly with teachers to improve student achievement. In these ways, both strongly advocated for administrators forming deeper relationships—something many administrators avoid out of concerns that doing so will cloud their judgment, lead to inconsistent and biased treatment of students and staff, and distract them from focusing on what they too often believe to be more important work tasks.

The DDR process gave me an opportunity to examine the perspectives, confidence, and practices of public school students and administrators. I once believed that students only perceived administrators as disciplinarians. I see now this derived from my belief that they had assimilated broader public beliefs that the traditional responsibilities of administrators are those of bureaucratic deans rather than instructional leaders. However, the conversations with both Terrinikka and Levertice helped me build confidence around my efforts to be a leader who nurtures development through strong and authentic relationships. Students do have a confidence of their own to negotiate their achievement and look for the assistance of teachers and administrators to guide them through the process. As a matter of a fact, it is the administrator that students look for in the hallways, cafeteria, and student services to answer their questions as well as have personal conversations, or as Levertice named them, "personal talk." According to Levertice, speaking to an administrator can sometimes feel like speaking with a family member. He noted that it made the difference in how students opened up and responded to administrators. Terrinikka shared that she saw administrators as her personal coaches. She looked for them to be available and approachable, yet she was able to read their body mannerisms and practices to understand the times they may not be. These insights opened my perspective to students' views and will help me to improve my work as a school leader.

Administrators can use the DDR process in multiple ways. For instance, administrators could use this process as an incentive in schools. One way we might incentivize school participation and involvement (while modeling democracy) might be by allowing the student body to vote once a quarter on the students they would like to represent them for the reflective conversations. Another method might be to select students from the various cultural groups represented in the schools. Regardless of how students are identified and selected for the DDR process, there are many different options for how they might be used more comprehensively within schools. After receiving assent and consent from both students and their families to record and use the videos resulting from this process, the digital artifacts could then be shown during morning broadcasts, student and teacher assemblies, as well as closing of school announcements for student and teacher discussions.

Most importantly, administrators can use the DDR process for both personal and collective reflection. In our district, each public school has an administration team that meets at designated times. The recordings could be displayed and discussed during these times to reflect and examine key issues or improve practices. Individual administrators could also explore their students' ideas and perspectives while determining the next steps they need to take as an administrator. Also, I believe the process would be specifically vital to the development of assistant principals who aspire to be principals. It would serve as a data collection process of building culture, climate, and ultimately student achievement.

Collective Process Perspectives—Chris Janson and Sejal Parikh

Our reflection begins with an acknowledgement of our appreciation for Ms. Jacqueline Jones, Terrinikka Ransome, and Levertice Moses. Our collaboration with them throughout this application and exploration of the DDR process, our shared reflections on their engagement with it, and the co-authoring of this manuscript has been a moving and enriching endeavor. Assistant principals and 12th grade students live demanding lives, therefore we were deeply honored by their enthusiastic involvement in our partnership for this chapter. Their willingness and courage to learn together in this very public way was also very inspiring to us, and we hope this alone provides a strong model to others in both public schools and colleges of education.

Our case example of the DDR process brought to life the literature on the importance of involving and learning from student voices in schools. Whether it was Terrinikka describing and discussing the stagey performance that occurs when principals conduct teacher observations or Levertice expressing his appreciation for the responsibilities principals often have to police school hallways, their insights struck us as alternating between confirming and surprising, but always insightful and informative. In doing so, their contributions to these DDRs illustrated the notion that student perspectives are too often an "untapped source" of ideas (Smith et al., 2005, p. 28) that might inform school practices (Dyson, 2007).

We also believe that this case application of DDR also exemplified elements of Cook-Sather's (2006, 2007) work describing the impact on students' development when school staff listens to them in purposeful ways. For example, Cook-Sather described how staff engagement with students shifts "the dominant power imbalances between adults and young people" (2006, p. 366). Throughout the DDR process and as evidenced through the accompanying videos, the interactions between Terrinikka and Levertice and Ms. Jones are punctuated by a sense of ease and informality in which both Ms. Jones and her conversation partners share and learn together. Cook-Sather also identified a second positive outcome that results from engaging student voices as an increased feeling within students of being respected, which then can lead to more substantial student involvement in their learning and schools. During their DDRs, both Terrinikka and Levertice shared with Ms. Jones the impact their relationships with her had on their motivation to achieve and perform in school. The third positive outcome for students Cook-Sather identified was the generation of opportunities for student and school personnel transformation.

One need only read the individual reflections of Terrinikka, Levertice, and Ms. Jones in this chapter to understand that the DDR process changed the way they view their school experiences, each other, themselves, and the potential application of DDR. We were drawn to Levertice's words when he wrote: "I learned that building a connection with administrators helped me succeed, but this DDR process caused me to start thinking about how these connections and conversations can change things in the school so that all other students can succeed as well." We were moved by Levertice's reflection that purposeful, yet simple conversations can lead to powerful personal changes and insights, but these conversations also hold the potential to lead to broader, systemic shifts in schools.

Finally, the analyses of Jacqueline Jones, Levertice Moses, and Terrinikka Ransome confirmed what most African American students and families have always known, but what many educational researchers and preparation programs have only recently "discovered": that school practices focused around authentic relationships and real conversation are not only valuable, but are also culturally relevant to African American and many other communities. Both Levertice and Terrinikka wrote that Ms. Jones' willingness to engage them and build more authentic relationships through the DDR process was impactful. Jacqueline, in turn, wrote that she felt her interactions with Levertice and Terrinikka affirmed her efforts to lead by nurturing student development by building "strong and authentic relationships" with them. These understandings resonate with the idea that building authentic relationships and engaging in what Lervertice called "personal talk" are essential elements to schools being culturally relevant (Howard, 2001). Given the professional trepidation expressed by Jacqueline Jones regarding her instincts to engage more purposefully in relationship-building with students, a process like DDR might create more support and validation.

CONCLUSION

The discursive digital reflections (DDR) between Ms. Jones and both Terrinikka and Lervertice illustrated the idea that reflection can be expressed as "collaborative social practice" (Zeichner & Liston, 1996, p. 77). As described above, the DDR process supports the literature on the power of reflection when it is utilized collectively (Zeichner & Litson, 1996) in ways that shift toward more balanced distributions of power between youth and adults in schools. When this happens, there is profound and compelling capacity to inform school practices, processes, and policies while also supporting the development of the youth involved (Cook-Sather, 2006, 2007). We also echo Jacqueline Jones' suggestions and recommendations regarding the usefulness of the DDR process for both pre-service and practicing school principals as well as other leaders in schools. We collectively share Jacqueline's belief that the DDR process can serve as a powerful model to staff by encouraging schools to rise above over-reliance on the old metrics used for gathering school and student achievement data. The DDR process involves and invites new metrics built around relationships and the nearly limitless potential and possibilities that lie within our own students.

Just as Levertice asked how strange it is that strong relationships in school are not the standard, we ask now how strange it is that we do not more frequently ask students to help us better understand the processes that govern their experiences and learning in schools. We believe that the DDR process represents one way to render that second question unnecessary. Discursive digital reflection holds great promise as a pedagogical and advocacy approach for principal candidates or principals and the students with whom they work. These reflective discourses can position conversation and relationships as learning tools and mechanisms for individual and systemic change. Importantly, the tools of the DDR process are not agnostic. Rather, because these reflective conversations embody many of the rich cultural gifts of many African American families (and many other cultures) such as skilled orality, rich storytelling, and deep relationships, the DDR process is highly culturally affirming and empowering. By engaging with students in these purposeful, collective reflections, principals can model the importance of listening to students so that they can advocate with them, rather than for them.

REFERENCES

Ayala, J. (2009). Split scenes. Converging visions: The ethical terrains where PAR and borderlands scholarship meet. *Urban Review, 41*(1), 66–84.

Brooks, J. S., & Tooms, A. K. (2008). A dialectic of social justice: Finding synergy between life and work through reflection and dialogue. *Journal of School Leadership, 18*(2), 134–163.

Cook-Sather, A. (2006). Sound, presence, and power: "Student voice" in educational research and reform. *Curriculum Inquiry, 36*(4), 359–390.

Cook-Sather, A. (2007). What would happen if we treated students as those with opinions that matter? The benefits to principals and teachers of supporting youth engagement in school. *NASSP Bulletin, 91*(4), 343–362.

Dewey, J. (1938). *Experience and education.* New York, NY: Macmillan.

Dyson, A. H. (2007). School literacy and the development of a child culture: Written remnants of the "gusto of life." In D. Thiessen & A. Cook-Sather (Eds.), *International handbook of student experience in elementary and secondary school* (pp. 115–142). Dordrecht, the Netherlands: Springer Publishers.

Fischer, F. (2003). *Reframing public policy: Discursive politics and deliberative practices.* Oxford, UK: Oxford University Press.

Friend, J., & Caruthers, L. (2012). Reconstructing the cultural context of urban schools: Listening to the voices of high school students. *Educational Studies, 48*(4), 366–388.

Galletta, A., & Jones, V. (2010). "Why are you doing this?" Questions on purpose, structure, and outcomes in participatory action research engaging youth and teacher candidates. *Educational Studies, 46*(3), 338–357.

Gentilucci, J. L. (2004). Improving school learning: The student perspective. *Educational Forum, 68*(2), 133–141.

Guajardo, M. (2009). Collective leadership: Practice, theory, and praxis. *Journal of Leadership Studies. 3*(2), 70–73.

Howard, T. (2001). Powerful pedagogy for African American students: A case of four teachers. *Urban Education, 36*(2), 179–202.

Howard, T. (2002). Hearing footsteps in the dark: African American students' descriptions of effective teachers. *Journal of Education for Students Placed at Risk, 7*(4), 425–444.

Janson, C., Parikh, S., & Maxis (2012). *Discursive digital reflection: A method for enhanced supervision and training.* Manuscript submitted for publication.

Janson, C., Parikh, S., Young, J., Fudge, L. (2011). Constructing collective understanding in school: Principal and student use of Iterative Digital Reflection. *Journal of Research in Leadership Education, 6*(5). 162–178.

Kozol, J. (1991). *Savage inequalities: Children in America's schools.* New York, NY: Harper Perennial.

Ladson-Billings, G. (1995). But that's just good teaching! The case for culturally relevant pedagogy. *Theory into Practice, 34*(3), 159–165.

Larrivee, B. (2000). Transforming teaching practices: Becoming the critically reflective teacher. *Reflective Practice, 1*(3), 293–307.

Levin, B. (1994). Educational reform and the treatment of students in schools. *Journal of Educational Thought, 28*(1), 88–101.

Smith, P., Petralia, J., & Hewitt, K. (2005). Listening to student voices. *Principal Leadership, 6*(3), 28–33.

Tuck. E. (2009). Re-visioning action: Participatory action research and indigenous theories of change. *Urban Review, 41*(1), 47–65.

Welton, A. (2011). The courage to critique policies and practices from within: Youth participatory action research as critical policy analysis. *Democracy & Education, 19*(1), 1–5.

Young, C.Y., Wright, J., & Laster, J. (2005). Instructing African American students. *Education, 125*(3), 516–524.

Zeichner, K. M., & Liston, D. P. (1996). *Reflective teaching: An introduction.* Mahwah, NJ: Erlbaum.

CHAPTER 7

THERE'S AN APP FOR THAT

50 Ways To Use Your iPad

April Adams and Jennifer Friend

INTRODUCTION

It is commonplace across the United States to see computers in schools (pre-K–12)—a personal computer (PC) on a teacher's desk, student-use computer stations along a classroom wall, a Mac Lab in an art classroom, mobile wireless laptop carts that teachers can reserve for technology-infused lessons. Some school districts are undertaking one-to-one computer initiatives that provide technology for each student to utilize during the school day and beyond, such as checking out a laptop to each student for the school year in the same way that textbooks are assigned for school and home use. In higher education, computers have become ubiquitous in classrooms, libraries, and student unions. This phenomenon is a simple reflection of society, as evidenced by watching people in a park or in line at a grocery store engaged with their many devices.

In addition to laptops and computer workstations for students, educators, and administrators, tablet technology is becoming increasingly adopted as a third device in education. Tablets are flat, portable personal com-

Principal 2.0: Technology and Educational Leadership, pages 97–122
Copyright © 2013 by Information Age Publishing
All rights of reproduction in any form reserved.

puters commonly characterized by wireless Internet access and interface through a touch screen or stylus pen rather than a keyboard. The Online Publishers Association reported that in 2011, 12% of Internet users in the U.S. owned a tablet computer, and in 2012 that number more than doubled to 31% (Moscaritolo, 2012).

It is no coincidence that this rise in tablet computer sales coincided with the introduction of the Apple iPad in 2010. Within one year of its release, the iPad accounted for approximately 90% of tablet computer sales (Gruman, 2011). While the iPad was a new product in 2010, tablet technology was not an innovation. The original vision for a tablet PC is credited to Alan Kay, who described his "Dynabook" technology in a 1972 paper as having the potential to:

> provide us with a better "book," one which is active (like the child) rather than passive. It may be something with the attention grabbing powers of TV, but controllable by the child rather than the networks. It can be like a piano: (a product of technology, yes), but one which can be a tool, a toy, a medium of expression, a source of unending pleasure and delight.... This new medium will not "save the world" from disaster. Just as with the book, it brings a new set of horizons and a new set of problems. The book did, however, allow centuries of human knowledge to be encapsulated and transmitted to everybody; perhaps an active medium can also convey some of the excitement of thought and creation! (Kay, 1972, p. 1)

Thirty years after the publication of his "science fiction" paper, Kay's Dynabook technology became available when Microsoft released its Tablet PC in 2002.

The first tablet PCs used pen and voice recognition and were not widely used. Even with advances in tablet PC technology to include touch screen interface in 2006, it was not until the release of the iPad media tablet in 2010 that sales increased significantly. The iPad made tablet computing more appealing with its user-friendly interface and the iTunes store to acquire any of the 225,000+ downloadable programs known as "apps" available free or at cost to download onto a computer, cell phone, or tablet device. Some of the features of the iPad include a 10-hour battery, sharp graphics, a camera for shooting photos or video, and fast processing speed for playing games or cruising the Internet (Apple, 2012). In Apple's third quarter, they outpaced all competitors in the tablet PC market, selling 3.27 million iPads (Mick, 2010).

This chapter will examine some of the ways in which iPads and various apps for the iPad are used to support student learning and the work of educators and administrators at Liberty High School. This Midwestern suburban school serves an ever-increasing and diversifying population of 2,000 tenth- through twelfth-grade students. The staff includes five administrators, one instructional coach, and over 100 certified teachers with experience spanning first-year teachers with bachelor degrees to 30+-year teachers with doctorate degrees. In this chapter we will share:

- 50 ways to use an iPad in a secondary school setting
- Recommendations for professional development and principal preparation programs
- Methods for technology acquisition and software updates
- Policy development for schools and districts.

IPADS IN SCHOOLS

The use of iPads is on the rise in United States public and private K–12 schools. In 2012 the Indianapolis Public Schools system purchased 2,500+ iPads for use in elementary through high school grades by teachers and students. One Indianapolis school created an online promotional video that "features iPad-toting kindergartners using the tablets to draw and photograph butterflies and edit videos about what they learned about them" (Liebendorfer, 2012, p. 1). Some of the reasons for the popularity of media tablets in schools include the vertical screen display, high degree of portability and interactivity, and speed with which the user can power up the technology and launch applications (see Table 7.1).

Many apps for the iPad are free for educators or inexpensive for individuals to purchase, which is vastly different than software packages and licenses, such as the Microsoft Office Word and Excel programs, which are typically used on desktop or laptop computers in schools. "Free downloading puts the benefits of a learning management system at the fingertips of educators" (Werth & Werth, 2011, p. 15), rather than having the decision-making power for software centralized in a school or district technology department. The vertical screen on the iPad provides an effective layout to read text, which is a desirable alternative to heavy textbooks that have no interactive features to enhance students' learning experiences. One private high school in the Midwest expects each student to purchase an iPad for the 2012–2013 school year as part of their required school supplies (Liebendorfer, 2012). This school previously purchased iPads for teachers and formed a student advisory group known as the "iSquad" to help teachers and the school to effectively use the iPad technology.

The iPad is also becoming more widespread at the post-secondary level. Programs such as AVID utilize iPads with high school students to promote college readiness, and Stanford Medical School purchases an iPad for each student in the program (Warschauer, 2011). In an article that focused on the use of iPad technology at Ryerson University in Toronto, Canada, the

TABLE 7.1   Comparison of Technology Available in Schools

	Desktop (PC or Mac)	Laptop Computers or Netbooks	Media Tablets
Time required to boot up and launch programs	Relatively slow	Relatively slow	Instant-on capability; Fast switching among applications
Screen Orientation	Horizontal	Horizontal	Vertical; Useful as a reading device
Portability	Large size and weight; Stationary, seated work	Medium-size; Portable to different seated-work locations; Must close and reopen screen to move	Lighter weight; Easy to transport inside or outside a classroom; Easy to use standing up to collect data or take notes
Power Supply	Plug into wall	Charge on mobile laptop cart or plug into wall throughout the school day (Battery lasts between 1 and 8 hours)	Charge lasts longer than the school day (Battery lasts up to 10 hours depending on usage type)
Interactivity	External Keyboard and Mouse; Relatively easier to write and edit on; Can add peripherals such as drawing tablets at extra expense	Keyboard and Mouse on device; Relatively easier to write and edit on; External keyboard and mouse available at extra expense	Touch screen provides a high degree of user interactivity; External keyboard available at extra expense
Internet Access	Network plug into wall or Wireless	Network plug into wall or Wireless	Wireless; iPads currently unable to access websites that use Adobe Flash
Software Applications	District, Building or individual computer license for software	District, Building or individual computer license for software	Downloadable educational Apps free or at a low-cost
Purchasing Cost	Relatively less expensive	Relatively less expensive	More expensive to purchase

Source: Adapted from Warschauer, 2011, pp. 38–39.

authors concluded that iPads were "a powerful tool in aiding collaboration, encouraging organization, and assisting learning regardless of field or level of academic achievement" (Eichenlaub, Gabel, Jakubek, McCarthy, & Wang, 2011, p. 17). Higher education students have more self-direction in their use of technology, while in K–12 schools it is important for principals and educators to design learning experiences to teach responsible use.

Students may be autonomous when they interface with iPads during learning activities in schools, but the instructions prior to use and the supervision during use are the responsibility of teachers. Black (2010) observed online social interactions such as "harsh, anonymous criticism, a key element in the growth of online bullying, especially among young adults" (p. 96). With advances in technology in schools, administrators now encounter students referred to the office for disciplinary action for such infractions as computer misuse and cyberbullying. Therefore, it is important to have policies that are clearly communicated to key stakeholders as part of the implementation plan for new technologies.

IMPLEMENTATION OF IPADS AT LIBERTY HIGH SCHOOL

The implementation model used for the infusion of iPads at Liberty High School was limited in its scope during the first year. The decision by building leaders to allocate funds for this new technology was met with questions from both the board of education and the community as to the appropriateness of this expenditure. Through deep conversations about technology and schools, in addition to the need to be a part of the world of the "digital native" student body (Prensky, 2001), funding was approved, and the journey of this team into the 21st century of educational change began.

In August of 2011, iPads were purchased for the entire leadership team, the instructional coach, and the professional development lead teacher. The only expectations communicated by the principal at the time included, "use them," "familiarize yourself with this technology," and "get out in the classrooms with your technology." In hindsight, there could have been a more strategic plan for implementation, but the grand intention was to take the fear out of the device and create a more ambulatory approach to technology usage. Moving from a desktop to a lightweight and highly versatile technological unit was a change. The results of this informal approach proved to be highly successful in reducing anxiety related to new technology, as well as inspiring innovation in its use in a variety of settings. A culture of comfortable inquiry became associated with the iPad, in particular among the leadership team members who embraced branching out and trying new things with technology.

Another change associated with the introduction of the iPad was the introduction of new terminology associated with the device into daily language. Frequent conversations among staff members focused on new apps that were discovered and implemented in the school. The iPad provided mobility, efficiency, accessibility, transparency, visibility, connectivity, all the while heightening accountability and minimizing disruptions. How might a small machine open so many options for learning on so many levels? The applications appeared limitless during the first year of infusion. The iPad impacted leadership capacity, professional learning, pedagogical practices, school culture, and enhanced the self-efficacy of the users.

The relationship that developed with this technology was one of deep connection bordering on affection. Frequent comments included, "I love my iPad," "I don't know what I would do if I did not have this technology," and "Do you know what my iPad did today?" In jest, the idea of titling this chapter in connection to the song "50 Ways to Leave Your Lover" (Simon, 1975) holds an insight into the reality of iPad use at Liberty High School. Within a short time period, this technology proved integral to the learning environment and strong bonds were formed between the user and the iPad. The first challenge, for people to accept the iPad, had been overcome; transference into their pedagogy was a different matter to address. The school purchased additional iPads for the second year of implementation, and a more proactive approach was undertaken by leadership to use the technology to enhance the work of the school.

APPS AND IPADS IN SCHOOLS: THE 50 WAYS

The following is a list of 50 ways to use an iPad in a school setting, compiled from the first year of implementation at Liberty High School. The different usage ideas are grouped according to themes that include communication, teacher supervision, student learning, professional development, curricular supports, pedagogical supports, and extracurricular activities. In some instances, specific apps are named. Some of the apps are without cost, while others do have a small installation fee. The applications mentioned in this section are not touted as the best, just free or low-cost apps that were found useful by the Liberty High School community. Each example is briefly described for administrators and teachers to be able to implement a particular use in their own schools.

Communication

Social networking is increasingly becoming the 21st century manner by which U.S. society engages in conversations and communication. The tools noted below are the ones that Liberty High School educators found to be the most reliable and user-friendly. On a precautionary note, Facebook, Twitter, and other social networking sites should have a standard for operation, be in compliance with the district's social media and communications board policy, and should only be integrated into the classroom when there is a clear educational focus and a standard of conduct for its use.

1. Skype—A free internet connection medium that allows for face-to-face, real-time communication and collaboration through video conferencing and instant messaging. Skyping was used by staff members for collaborative teaming between two high school sites and for conference calling with video imaging capacity. Skype provided connectivity to students who were not located within the classroom, such as students in upper-level courses who were in long-term suspension, homebound, or hospitalized, so they could keep up with the class content. Skype was an important tool within an international language program where Liberty High School students worked in partnership with five sister schools in Taiwan and China. www.skype.com

2. Facetime—Another video chatting app that allows for connectivity. Facetime was also used by classroom teachers to keep students up to date. This app also allowed for two-way communications between home and school when necessary. http://www.apple.com/mac/facetime/

3. Edmodo—This collaboration tool enabled teachers in classrooms to monitor each student's activity and participation within this platform. Many teachers found this tool to be more advantageous than other collaboration apps because of that management feature. www.edmodo.com

4. Facebook—A social networking site that is highly familiar to most. When used in the educational setting, it can be a tremendously effective tool for student-led chats. Although the manner in which students engage in conversation is often informal in structure, teachers used this tool as a learning opportunity for personal Internet safety. Many teachers at Liberty High School established school-regulated Facebook accounts where students connected to the classroom and chatted about novels, classroom projects, or specific topics pertaining to their learning. Some coaches used Facebook, through the school-endorsed administrative oversight, to keep team information up to date, communicate with their athletes, and manage schedules. www.facebook.com

Teacher Supervision

Conducting nonintrusive, informal classroom observations, commonly referred to as "walkthroughs," can be the bane of an administrator's existence. Even though the feedback is timely and formative in nature, entering the classroom with record-keeping tools and trying to discreetly provide positive and supportive instructional strategies can interfere with the teaching and learning process. During the first year of implementation, our team discovered that the iPad was incredibly versatile and inconspicuous in this context.

Creating an environment that allowed for a more effective clinical supervision process was also supported through the iPad. Learning activities could be video recorded using the iPad to help reinforce both best practices and areas of growth; photos could be taken to capture evidence of effective practices; and student efforts and engagement could be collected and compiled efficiently to share within professional learning communities. The video feature that is a part of the basic tools within the iPad, along with the photographing tool, provided immediate pictorial renderings of the happenings within a lesson, experiment, program, performance, or athletic event. This is another area that is important to connect to district policies and legal expectations regarding confidentiality and acceptable use for visual and audio recordings.

The walkthrough format used by Liberty High School was designed by the district. The observation form was constructed by a team of administrators from elementary through secondary settings that researched many different programs, forms, and best practices in order to create a web-based format for consistent implementation. However, there were several apps available for review that administrators and teacher leaders used as a guideline in designing the teacher supervisory program.

5. GoObserve—A tablet-based classroom observation and walkthrough tool was designed through the collaborative efforts of a company called GoKnow and Michigan Association of Secondary School Principals (MASSP). This program operates as a stand-alone observation and walkthrough application, allowing administrators to customize the observation process and generate reports directly from the device. Teacher information can be imported, and the program works in tandem with Outlook for calendar management and organizational features. https://itunes.apple.com/us/app/goobserve/id470340177?mt=8

6. eCOVE Admin—This walkthrough tool comes in multiple editions. Looking specifically at the Administrators Edition, the product allows for customization by the user through the infusion of multiple

tools such as Bloom's Taxonomy, Classroom Learning Time, Classroom Environment, Management Techniques, Questioning Types, and the like. This product does come at an installation cost to the user. https://itunes.apple.com/us/app/administrator-edition-for/id387917575?mt=8

7. SuperVision—This data-collection tool affords the user with options beyond classroom collection processes. This tool includes features for conducting surveys, a process for judging sporting competitions, and appraising items or bidding on the workplace. Some of these features are not relevant to the school environment. This product does come at an installation cost to the user. https://itunes.apple.com/us/app/supervision/id289265774?mt=8

Note-Taking

Note-taking apps abound for the iPad. For the purpose of this chapter, the apps shared are the ones that were used specifically within Liberty High School. One is not endorsed as better than another, for their value truly does depend upon the preference of the user.

8. Evernote—This free app allows to the user to keep track of information across multiple applications. The connectivity it grants allows a busy user to capture information and stay organized. Additionally, users can save ideas and improve productivity. Within this application, the user can take notes, take photos, create lists, and record voice reminders in a platform that has a robust search option. This app also syncs updates if used on a computer, iPad, or mobile device. http://evernote.com/evernote/

9. Pages—This app functions as a word processor and layout tool, enabling the user to create professional-looking documents, newsletters, reports, and more. This application is very similar to having a Microsoft Word product on your iPad. https://www.apple.com/apps/pages/

10. Penultimate—As a handwriting app for iPad, the user holds a stylus to script or print ideas as if writing on paper. Ideas are captured within notebooks that can be organized and labeled to the user's preference. Penultimate allows users to go green without losing the skill of handwriting. http://evernote.com/penultimate/

11. PaperPort Notes—This digital note-taking tool allows users to create and share information. PaperPort Notes affords users with the ability to combine documents, web content, audio, typed text, and hand-

written notes into a single document that can be easily organized and shared with anyone. http://www.paperportnotes.com/

12. Easy Note + To Do—This is a very convenient note-taking app and also a to-do list-making app. https://itunes.apple.com/us/app/easy-note-+-to-do/id382828566?mt=8

13. neu.Notes—This app differs from others as a vector-based app. It allows the user to zoom in close without distorting images through pixilation. An additional feature that makes neu.Notes a highly functional app is that it allows for searching based on tags, and thus the user does not have to spend time looking for items within this notebook. https://itunes.apple.com/us/app/neu.notes+/id433254101?mt=8

14. Noteledge—A notebook that allows the user to capture handwriting, type, photos, videos, and audio. The application then stores the information like a notebook. In the classroom, this can be used for students to create their own textbooks. https://itunes.apple.com/us/app/noteledge-for-ipad/id483101556?mt=8

15. Bamboo Paper—Another note-taking application, it allows the user to sketch thoughts, organize thinking, and capture learning. https://itunes.apple.com/us/app/bamboo-paper-notebook/id443131313?mt=8

16. smartNote—This password-protected note-taking application allows the user to take notes in class, sketch, or highlight text in a .pdf document format. https://itunes.apple.com/us/app/smartnote/id362165952?mt=8

17. WritePad—This application may appeal to those who prefer to compose via handwriting. Users can create text documents, connect to other mobile devices by linking through the built-in HTTP server, and directly convert communication venues to email, Twitter, or Facebook. Additionally, WritePad documents can be synchronized with Dropbox, Evernote, iTunes, and Google Docs. https://itunes.apple.com/us/app/writepad-for-ipad/id363618389?mt=8

18. Notability—This application integrates handwriting, .pdf annotation, typing, recording, inserting media, and organizing features to meet the user's preferences. https://itunes.apple.com/us/app/notability-take-notes-annotate/id360593530?mt=8

19. Sticky Notes—This application provides sticky notes for the user to jot down quick thoughts, keep an ongoing list of to-dos, or pin up a reminder. https://itunes.apple.com/us/app/sticky-notes-for-ipad/id364899302?mt=8

20. abcNotes—Another checklist, sticky note application for organization, reminders, or just ongoing to-do lists. https://itunes.apple.com/us/app/abc-notes-checklist-sticky/id354015291?mt=8

Accessibility

Accessibility is an expectation of this generation of learners. Some of the commonly used applications that allowed users to access documents included:

21a. PaperPort Anywhere—This app provides 24/7 access to all documents on your iPad. It is a free cloud-based file management service that allows users to access, create, and share documents anytime, anywhere, from any web-enabled device. https://itunes.apple.com/us/app/paperport-anywhere/id450834614?mt=8

21b. DropBox is an invaluable tool for teachers that enables students to submit created documents from their iPad that can be retrieved both by a teacher iPad or from a teacher desktop computer. This was a great tool to use when students wanted to print their work, since printing from the iPad was not an easy task, or when large files needed to be shared. www.dropbox.com

Additionally, the iPad applied mobility for special program access for such situations as in-school suspension, out-of-school suspension, long-term suspension, and homebound. This versatile tool provided a venue for instruction to continue in spite of behavior choices, home situations, and medical conditions.

Data Manipulation

Working with spreadsheets on the iPad is somewhat different than working in a Microsoft Office suite. Data manipulation can occur through the use of an application that functions very similar to Excel. Importing and exporting data can now be completed on the iPad.

22. Numbers—This application allows for the creation of templates, formulae, tables, and charts, all within a spreadsheet format. https://www.apple.com/apps/numbers/

Presentations

The iPad has many presentation applications that enabled multiple levels of users at Liberty High School to share information in new ways. From creating to viewing, the applications available to enhance the classroom learning environment or the faculty meeting forum were many and varied.

23. Keynote—A presentation application that allows the user to create, deliver, and share presentations. Keynote melds features from PowerPoint and pushes presentations up a notch because of seamless integration of multimedia. http://www.apple.com/apps/keynote/

24. Prezi Presentation Viewer—Although the Prezi presentation creation process cannot be completed on the iPad at this time, presentations are viewable with the use of the iPad. Users can manipulate the presentation, but editing is not yet an option. http://prezi.com/ipad/

25. Educreations—This application turns your iPad into an interactive whiteboard for instruction. Teachers can also create audio tutorials to coincide with text or sketched instructional processes using this app. https://itunes.apple.com/us/app/educreations-interactive-whiteboard/id478617061?mt=8

26. SlideShark—This application facilitates viewing and sharing of PowerPoint presentations. Creation of PowerPoint is not yet a feature for iPads at this time. www.slideshark.com

27. Splice—This video-editing and audio/video effects system allows the user to capture images and film, edit, import music, and then share the presentation with others. This app can be used in collaboration with other presentation apps to import music or images. https://itunes.apple.com/us/app/splice-video-editor/id386894062?mt=8

28. Explain Everything—As a presentation application, the app allows the user to annotate, narrate, and create throughout the presentation process. This editing and revising feature is a plus, since many of the other presentation apps do not allow creation and revision within with the real-time implementation. This application also works with multiple other apps on iPads, such as Evernote and Dropbox. www.explaineverything.com

Functional Apps to Support Learning

Again in the vein of accessibility and instructional supports, there are many free tools that can be utilized in a variety of content areas. From free calculators to support basic and upper level math classes to word source Apps to support vocabulary development, new Apps continue to be developed.

29. Calculator Pro—A free application provides the features of a calculator for most basic calculator functions and for the more sophisticated functions of a scientific calculator. Functionality includes two modes: (1) basic calculations in Portrait Mode, and (2) advanced in Landscape Mode. The app includes degrees and radians calculations, memory buttons to help with complex calculations, copy and

paste numbers from or into display, swipe feature for editing, and multitasking support. https://itunes.apple.com/us/app/calculator-pro-for-ipad/id398572670?mt=8

30. Free GracCalc—A free graphing calculator to support math instruction. Features include a scientific calculator, graphing capabilities, a unit converter, constants for scientific calculations, tables for capturing the values of any functions created, and reference features to remind the user of formulae. https://itunes.apple.com/us/app/free-graphing-calculator/id378009553?mt=8

31. Office2 HD—This application allows the user to interact within the familiarity of the Office suite. Through this tool, the user can open, view, create, and edit Word, Excel, and PowerPoint files. https://itunes.apple.com/us/app/office2-hd/id364361728?mt=8

32. pdf-notes Free—Reads pdfs and allows the user to mark up texts. Also allows for the organization of .pdf files. https://itunes.apple.com/us/app/pdf-notes-free-for-ipad-pdf/id391487223?mt=8

33. Dictionary.com—Allows the user access to a web-based dictionary and thesaurus for enhancing writing capacity, expanding word choice, and exploring words. https://itunes.apple.com/us/app/dictionary.com-dictionary/id364740856?mt=8

Professional Development

Professional development using the iPads allowed educators access to information at a fraction of the cost generally associated with workshops, traditional professional development materials, and travel. iPads connected educators with professional, reliable, and credible resources with the touch of the screen. From reading recently released white papers from authors such as Bill Daggett and Ray McNulty to linking into podcasts broadcast by thought leaders and practitioner colleagues, professional development changed for the staff of Liberty High School.

34. iTunes U—Unlimited free resources for professional development and growth. Through iTunes U, educators can access professional subscriptions, webinars, instructional resources, and much more. http://www.apple.com/education/itunes-u/

35. TED Talks—Started in 1984 as a conference that merged Technology, Entertainment, and Design, TED has expanded its conference capacity to allow users the option of searching for topics of conversation and presentations. Free to users, sharing in the "Ideas Worth Spreading" provides incredible access and information for educa-

tors, such as talks related to online education and using technology to interface with students with disabilities. http://www.ted.com/talks

36. TED Books—This App functions in tandem with TED Talks. Many of the ideas shared on TED Talks become short original electronic books produced every two weeks by TED Conferences. Like the best TED Talks, these are personal and provocative, and designed to spread great ideas. Typically less than 20,000 words, these narratives provide the reader with quick, interesting thinking points. Additionally, TED Books can be more interactive reading with embedded audio, video, and social features to go deeper in learning and thinking. A recent example is a book and film titled *Brain Power: From Neurons to Networks* by Tiffany Schlain, which applies neurological research on child brain development to ways in which Internet and online networks are formed. http://www.ted.com/pages/tedbooks

   The TED Books app allows the user to embed audio, video, and social features into each book, broadening the depth and detail of each work. These additional multimedia features suit the wide-ranging creative palette of contributors, many who use photography, audio, and video in addition to the printed word to fully express their ideas.

37. ibooks—This tool allows for the accessibility and management of .pdf documents, free books, and the option to purchase books. Genre reading and professional reading are all options on ibooks. https://itunes.apple.com/us/app/ibooks/id364709193?mt=8

38. Textbooks—Many of the prominent and popular textbook companies are now releasing electronic textbooks along with the traditionally published hardcover books. These interactive educational experiences allow students to go deeper in their learning, and to fill in limited background knowledge through embedded audio, video, and interactive links. Students can go on a fieldtrip right in the classroom. http://www.apple.com/education/ibooks-textbooks/

39. Providing reliable resource access in real time occurs in schools through the internet, but this is made more convenient through the iPad, as students can flip back and forth between multiple news worthy sources. Through the Newsstand feature, users can download many free magazines. There is free access for many credible resources such as *New York Times, National Geographic, Time, Money* or more informal teen or fashion magazines. Additionally, users can download news apps such as: CNN, PBS Kids, USA Today, Life, ABC News, and the Weather Channel to name a few. https://itunes.apple.com/us/genre/ios-newsstand/id6021?mt=8

Curricular Supports

As our educational system embraced the Common Core State Standards (CCSS), the iPad provided the teachers and administrators at Liberty High School with greater accessibility to educational supports. Through the integration of apps, the educators got to the point where users regularly stated, "There is an app for that." Apps are available for all content areas within the curriculum. Determining the legitimacy of applications and their impact on learning takes a great deal of time. Along with the fidelity within apps is that of the reliability of website or online access points. The below mentioned items are by no means a comprehensive list, as the amount of information and constant development of additional applications is ever changing and evolving.

40. Common Core—Created by MasteryConnect this application allows the user to view the Common Core State Standards. This K–12 reference tool provides easy to read access for all levels of users in English Language Arts and Math, along with categorization features (subject, grade, subject category–domain/cluster). Teachers can monitor the English language arts standards, explore the eight standards within math, and go deeper within the College and Career Readiness Standards (CCRs). https://itunes.apple.com/us/app/common-core-standards/id439424555?mt=8

41. Math Khan Academy—Not just an app but also a website, this mathematical resource can be used for remediation and acceleration in multiple levels of math classrooms. Students are able to review concepts with the layering of video instruction. Course of knowledge can also be tracked in a scope and sequence, and teachers have the ability to create accounts and virtually interact with student learning. This resource has been used in Liberty High School classrooms, both regular education and special education, and for student learning support for individuals within the long-term suspension program, homebound instruction, and the in-school suspension program. https://www.khanacademy.org/downloads

42. Math apps that can support learning in the classrooms are vast in numbers. When accessing the "Education" icon in the AppStore and selecting a math option, iPad users will be directed to a multitude of resources. Organized by Numbers & Operations, Geometry & More, Algebra, Calculus, Probability & Statistics, Applying Math, and Math Games, educators can seek out applications that will support the area of math needed. Applications include HMH FUSE Algebra I, Algebra Pro—Complete Workbook, Play 123, Video Calculus, Math Concentration, Pick-a-Path, Equivalent Fractions, Sushi Monster,

Motion Math Zoom, Elevated Math, Minds of Modern Mathematics, Skills Tutor Math Fact Fluency, and HMH Math on the Spot. http://www.apple.com/education/apps/

43. Science Apps are located in the AppStore under two separate icons, Life and Physics. The life science options are organized as follows: General Biology, Anatomy & Physiology, Plant & Animal Biology, Applying Life Science, Reference Tools, and Games. The apps noted in this section again are mentioned because they are free to educators. Applications include 3D Cell Simulation and Stain Tool, Science 360 for iPad, Molecules, National Geographic Explorer, NatureTap, Creatures of Light, Fotopedia Wild Friends, Leafsnap for iPads, SPARKvue, Promga, LabTimer, PLoS Reader, Pollen Count HD, Butterfly Farm, HHMI (Howard Hughes Medical Institute) Bulletin, Science WebMD, HumanBody, ISS Live, and NASA Science. There are many more applications, and costs can range from $.99 to $29.99. As a consumer of applications, it is important do some research to investigate the apps prior to purchase. http://www.apple.com/education/apps/

   The physics applications are organized in the following categories: Motion & Forces, Electricity & Magnetism, Heat, Energy, & Work, Lab & Reference Tools, and Games. The following apps are free to educators: Intellective Physics, Particle Zoo, Gas Laws HD Lite, Xperica HD, SPARKvue, Video Science, iBlast Moki 2 HD, and TinkerBox HS. There are numerous applications available at a cost to the consumer. http://www.apple.com/education/apps/

44. English Language Arts—There are many supports in the English Language Arts (ELA) area, from spelling and writing to comprehension and fluency. Educators need to discern the focus of enhancement or support and then determine the applications necessary. Included are suggestions noted due to the lack of cost to the consumer. Within the framework of the five main components proffered by Reading First and Reading Next as to what constitutes a strong literacy program weaving in the phonics, phonemic awareness, vocabulary development, comprehension and fluency, support abounds through apps on the iPad.

   In the areas of phonics and phoneica awareness, free applications include but are not limited to Phonics Genius, ABC Alphabet Phonics–Preschool, Phonics Awareness–1st Grade, ABC Phonics Animals Writing, Phonics Tic-Tac-Toe Interactive, Phonics Vowels, ABC Phonics Sight Words HD, Magic Spell, abc PocketPhonics Lite, ABC Magic Phonics, Phonics and Reading by McGuffey Lite, and 700 hundred more options to date. SparkleFish, Hooked On Words, Words HS

Free, and SWF are all spelling applications that can be integrated into the classroom. http://www.apple.com/education/apps/

Comprehension checking can be assisted with the use of Reflection while Reading, MyPrepPal: SAT Critical Reading, Painless Reading Comprehension, Reading for Kids —I Like Reading, Using I and Me, MELS Reading And Comprehension, Matrix Brain Free, English Reading Test Collections, Kidz Memory Quiz, Go English!, and many more. For fluency support, Dragon Dictation and VoiceThread (vt) are free applications where struggling readers can hear their fluency in an audio recording of their reading. The Michael Tillyer Fluency application costs consumers $2.99 but is a very good tool for the classroom. Reading Apps include Kobo (1 million free books), Unlimited Free Books—Wattpad eBook Reader, Sight Words List, Free Books (23,469 Classics), Scan, Goodreads, Scholastic Reading Timer, and Google Play Books. Additionally, accessibility to e-readers is available through Kindle, iBooks, and Nook Apps. Again, note what the goal of the application will be within the learning objective. http://www.apple.com/education/apps/

45. Social Studies—Because K–12 social studies learning takes on so many different aspects, the applications for this content area are equally vast and can be located within social skills, geography, social justice, law, and civics applications to ancient, European, modern, U.S., or country-specific history, current events, and world news applications. For ease in searches, a few free applications are: History Maps, National Geographic Explorer, Pass the Past, American History Games, Brain Quest, Lincoln Telegrams, Geography Spotlight, CNN, US Citizenship 2012 Edition, Best Banner, U.S. Government, Citizenship USA, Pocket Law Firm, Civic Quotes, Peace, and many more. Again, although repetitive in nature, application acquisition is truly contingent upon educational need and learning outcomes. http://www.apple.com/education/apps/

46. Non-Core Applications—Our public education system supports the infusion of art, music, business, health, physical education, international languages, and practical arts such as family consumer sciences and industrial technology experiences. The integration of educational supports through the use of the iPad spans from drawing and painting to music history and composition apps to foreign language development and financial literacy to health and wellness. Free access to education supports can include: Accounting WhizKid, Safari To Go, Harvard Business School Executive, WFG (World Financial Group, Inc) Essential, World Figures, Art of Glow, Glow Draw!, Draw Something Free, Pic Collage, Spark Art!, SketchBook Pro for iPad, Let's Create Pottery Lite, Epicurious, Food Network In the Kitchen,

Timer+, Tap A Tune, NoteStar, On the Music Path, My Note Games, DJ Mix, LyricFind Lite, iHeartRadio, PIY 4 HD, Piano Free, Drum Kit, Magic Guitar, Learn Spanish Quick, Living Language (Spanish/ French/German/Chinese), Foreign Language Pronunciation, Eat This, Not That!, iHealth Scale, iHealth BMI, Everyday Health for the iPad, CalorieKing Calorie Counter, HealthMap: Outbreaks Near Me, Get in Shape, along with access to free magazines in automotive, carpentry, health, child development, etc. Limitless! http://www.apple. com/education/apps/

Pedagogical Supports

47. Differentiation and individualization of instruction can be time-consuming pedagogical techniques for teachers. This is where the iPad, as a tool for interactive learning, can enhance high-quality teaching. Teachers at Liberty High School who included the iPad in their instruction facilitated tiered assignments that included scaffolded learning based upon level of knowledge, not multiple activities that produced more or less work. Deeper thinking is at the core of true differentiated learning, along with pushing students to explore new knowledge. The iPad enabled teachers to create learning experiences that allowed for flexible grouping to remedy knowledge gaps, direct teaching or modeling, and affording students the opportunity to investigate learning through creation and production of artifacts that demonstrated their knowledge and skills. iPads were tools that provided flexibility, individualization, collaborative production, remediation, acceleration, and much more. It was about the expert teacher making strategic decisions about the curriculum while infusing this access-granting technology into their students' learning experiences.

48. Formative assessment of learning was also enhanced through the use of iPads. Checking for comprehension through the use of Socrative afforded immediate feedback to teachers about the learning gains or needs. Both Teacher Clicker and Student Clicker are needed to make Socrative work correctly. eClicker Client is another program that allows students to provide immediate feedback to a framework of knowledge checkpoints designed by the teacher. BubbleSheet is an application that allows for quick assessment of knowledge. On the Spot, Flash Cards, WorkBook, and Teacher Pal are also free applications through the App Store for educators to weave into their instruction that assist in immediate formative assessment data. https:// itunes.apple.com/us/app/eclicker-client/id329200145?mt=8

49. Individualization for students' unique learning goals was supported through the iPad as strategies within individual education plans (IEPs), English language learner (ELL) programs, and for students with 504 learning plans. iPads provided the one-on-one instruction necessary to meet the needs of diverse learners. Augmentative communication programs, spelling enhancement applications, voice recognition applications, translators, tiered practice designed for specific skill gaps, and the ability to video record lessons or provide direct live feed into classrooms were nonintrusive options. For documentation, using the iPad to access GoogleDocs to capture information or to record video or pictures to assist in learning, and then being able to upload this feed onto other electronic platforms, enhanced learning potential.

Extra and Co-curricular Support

50. Extension of use is another area in which the iPads enhanced educational opportunities at Liberty High School. Using the iPad for the learning that takes place beyond the traditional school day has made it an invaluable tool. Many coaches integrated iPads into the teaching that they do in their sports programs. In football, Liberty High School coaches captured practice and game footage, breaking the footage down using a program called Huddle. This allowed the coaches to drill down to specific athletes and provide one-on-one feedback about performance. This has expedited the feedback process to the point that athletes and coaches can review game footage within minutes after a play as opposed to a delayed review at the next practice session. Additionally, many coaches are using this videotaping and feedback feature to then upload footage on secure BlackBoard sites where the athletes access the film remotely and have pushed out purposeful learning to complete on their own prior to or following a practice or a game. The versatility of the iPad also enhances fine arts with recording students singing, performing, acting, engaged in competitive rehearsals and other venues and then immediately being able to break down performances and upload images to other connected platforms for multiple users to access, critique, and learn from. The iPads have also influenced tutoring and preparation programming in affording differentiation based upon student learning needs and individualization in instructional remediation or acceleration. https://itunes.apple.com/us/app/huddle/id501101411?mt=8

TECHNOLOGY IMPLEMENTATION AND POLICY-MAKING

The iPad became an incredible tool to establish chronologies of learning at Liberty High School. Students loved the opportunity to create pictorial montages of their academic performance. The options afforded with the use of an iPad allowed teachers and students to capture still pictures of learning over time and catalogue these images to demonstrate growth, or to enable a teacher to follow up with individual and small groups of students for greater instructional differentiation. In addition to the image acquisition, there were many apps utilized to support the various aspects of learning in classrooms.

As educational leaders, it does not matter whether we are digital natives or digital immigrants who are new to the language and culture of today's technology (Prensky, 2001). The students who are coming to us know technology in ways that the adults in schools have not yet encountered, and it is our collective responsibility to keep up with this most important stakeholder in public education (Stewart, 2010). We have an ethical obligation to push the antiquated structure of schooling into the 21st century. Before long, brick-and-mortar school buildings may be an artifact of days gone by. Virtual learning and distance education are transforming education at every level.

Many educational electronic news platforms predict that by 2019, half of high school courses will be online. According to Tyson (2010), "When instructional content is delivered through digital media, it no longer must be taught in the physical classroom space at a specific time of the day" (p. 130). Schools must keep up with students, not drag them back into an antiquated system of learning. This means that we, as educators and leaders, need to engage in this technological paradigm shift. Our students want and need more in their learning environment, and as producing consumers, they demonstrate distinct boredom when asked to learn using the techniques of yesteryear. These learners demand and create new knowledge in a linked and embedded virtual world. iPads are only one tool that allows us to connect to that world which is inhabited by these digital natives.

One complication is that the technology is fluid. It is difficult to know what is best, affordable, sustainable, and reasonable—what is a fad versus a long-lasting change in education. Today's advanced technology is tomorrow's outdated or obsolete technology. Technology is a tool that enhances the work of professional educators already capable of facilitating high-quality learning experiences. Thus, having a roadmap that gives guidance but is flexible to embrace change is essential. Jacobs (2010b) pushes educators and leaders to think strategically and to critically plan for the integration of technology in schools by "thinking about new versions of school by asking whom are we serving ultimately, and how can we best meet the needs of our specific learners" (p. 77). We must ask ourselves if the way in which we operate schools is working for the learners in our care.

Schools need courageous leaders and teachers who are willing to model lifelong learning related to technology and to share the benefits that advancements such as the iPad provide for today's learners. Today's schools "need leaders who are versed in the potential and pitfalls of information and communication technologies (ICTs) for our nation's students" (Hughes, McLeod, Brahier, Dikkers, & Whiteside, 2005, p. 51). Principals and district administrators must buffer the criticism associated with resource allocation for new technologies, knowing that the leadership focus is on what is necessary for tomorrow's workforce. Creating partnerships with district office for funding approval and long-range planning is essential. Creative implementation can also include grant writing for technology, professional learning for adults that is digital in nature, allocation of funding resources, policy development to guide the levels of professional conduct necessary for a virtual presence along with the melding of state and federal law, and opening discussions about one-to-one learning in a public school environment. These are all elements that contribute to the journey leaders must take for progressive change through the use of technology in schools.

Infrastructural determinations need to be addressed prior to the implementation of new technology launches. The MILE Guide produced by the Partnership for 21st Century Skills (2009), provided districts and schools with a template for self-assessment to evaluate current structures and determine the implementation processes which are most feasible and fiscally allowable. The professional development process will greatly impact buy-in and follow through. "Professional development is far and away the most important part of the work" (Kay, 2010, p. xxv). Levels of comfort must be developed with the non-digital native adult before the integration of these tools into the classroom can occur. Building up the levels of efficacy is essential, as adults who do not feel confident or competent will not use the technology to its fullest potential. Knowing this, professional learning needs to be tiered for the various levels of proficiency among the adults. School districts must also have regular opportunities for administrators to engage in professional development related to technology in order to effectively facilitate use of innovations to support student learning and the functioning of the educational organization.

Assessing the current reality of facilities is essential for launch success. Knowing wireless capabilities, powering multiple locations for charging abilities, and determining district server bandwidth are all components that must be determined before the devices are installed into a school environment. Working with district technology staff in the process of upgrading facilities to handle the power needs, connectivity capacity, and upgrade or upkeep of the new technology is crucial for responsible sustainability. Ex-

ploring the integration of teacher devices that are for classroom use and
not personal machines takes form in establishing protocols and procedures
for usage. Establishing the regulation of the equipment, the integration of
sustainable upgrades such as scratch-free screen protectors, and heavy-duty
rubberized rhino coverings to protect devices from drop damage all come
at a cost.

Lastly, working with technology staff in determining how to roll out
iPads, which were designed for personal use, in a public domain creates additional challenges. How does the district establish iTunes accounts to push
out applications in mass? How does the district supervise whether a student
downloads a free application on a device while in use that is not regulated
by the district? How does the district manage printing from devices that are
designed for green communication, as iPads currently do not talk to server-
based networked printers?

The facilitators of an iPad pilot project at one higher education institution utilized the same profile and AppStore account when checking out
iPads for an entire semester to individual students. "We quickly learned
that the students needed to personalize their experiences to really engage
with the software and embed the device into their studies, which the initial
configuration would not allow" (Eichenlaub et al., 2011, p. 20). But how
do we do this if there are only classroom sets versus one-to-one technology
integration? The list of questions continues to evolve, and the answers are
sometimes hard to determine. But, they are the right questions to wrestle
with, for if we do not, our students will be at a disadvantage in the context
of a globalized learning community.

This changing horizon of education is thrilling, for as students gain
more accessibility through technology, real-world, real-time learning that
is relevant and rigorous creates limitless learning potential in classrooms.
Learning from someone in another country about their government, economy, history, and culture is just one of the globalized learning opportunities afforded through technology, and iPads were found by Liberty High
School to be an affordable tool that allowed this to occur. In addition to
policy development, technology needs to be a component of district-wide
strategic planning efforts. School leaders collaborated with district technology coordinators to design a plan for building-level implementation, which
was critical for sustainability and alignment.

Liberty Public Schools have been progressive in supporting iPads in the
classrooms and for use by school leadership teams. This support has not
come without criticism and skepticism by factions of the local community.
But staying the course and keeping the focus on the benefits that this technology can have on student learning has further supported adoption of
iPads into schools. Several elementary buildings have partnered with their
Parent Teacher Associations in purchasing iPad carts. All lead and assistant

principals in elementary through high school levels are now using iPads as a daily tool in walkthroughs, presentations, data collection, composition of documents, and various other frameworks of instructional leadership. Apps abound that are assistive and enhancing of and for learning. The integration of iPads into special programs such as gifted, special education, English language learning, and supporting the response to intervention tiered levels of instructional remediation and acceleration has proven to be extremely effective for our students.

CONCLUSION AND RECOMMENDATIONS

To say the Liberty Public Schools or Liberty High School has figured out the best method of integrating technology into schools is presumptuous and would be a misrepresentation of the truth. Educators and leaders are learning daily and making changes accordingly as to what is the best direction to travel with the students. Staying attuned to current research, practices, and technology while working with limited resources, funding, and staffing, feels at times like snorkeling through a tidal wave. The constants that propel these educational leaders and teachers forward and provide the energy to navigate the tumultuous waves include:

- Students are not passive learners. They demand deeper, more dynamic, engaging, critically challenging, problem based learning that connects to the world in which they exist (Jacobs, 2010a).
- Pedagogy has evolved to demand mastery of content and process skills by teachers. With this change comes the reality that students with access to technology become partners in the learning process (McNulty, 2009).
- Educators must keep up with our students in the platform in which they interact. Technology is a part of who they are, and if we do not acknowledge this, our students can and will learn elsewhere (Fisher & Frey, 2010). Education delivery models in post-secondary platforms are changing, and we have a responsibility to acknowledge, adapt, and enhance our standards of learning for the necessary preparation of our graduates (Zhao, 2009).
- Education practices in the United States must stay competitive with a globalized society where barriers of accessibility to information have economic consequences if we maintain an isolated presence (Friedman, 2006).
- Common Core State Standards, currently implemented in 48 states in the U.S., are a leveling mechanism that has created a system

of comparison that informs schools about their current work and pushes the system to be better for all students (Besser, 2011).

- Deeper, more critical thinking that is assessed more frequently to inform instruction is a normal practice as education continues to practice assessment for learning (Costa & Kallick, 2010).
- Accountability systems are challenging educators to look at learning as a process, as opposed to a product-driven experience. The infusion of data that inform instruction in a constant and evolving manner has created demands for methods of data extraction that are efficient and effective for the teacher and the students (White, 2011).
- Technology enables educators to activate and engage diverse learners with different readiness levels and interests in differentiated and individualized teaching and learning.

To be cliché, the only constant is change. Technology is a part of our learners' identities and lived experiences; thus it is a part of education. Teachers and administrators have a responsibility to keep pace with students, as adult learners of technology who often gain the most from listening to and observing the students themselves. Lifelong learning is a norm, not just a catch phrase. The Liberty High School educators chose to adapt to the innovations and enhancements that the iPad provided, and they continue to explore advanced technologies through the support of district strategic planning and resources. As the Liberty High School principal leads these digital immigrants into unfamiliar waters, she is aware that the tides of technology roll in and roll out. The force of the waves changes with environmental influences, causing the adults to monitor and adjust to meet the ever-changing ebb and flow of current reality. Who knows...there probably is an app for that!

REFERENCES

Apple, Inc. (2012). *iPad: Features*. Retrieved November 20, 2012 from http://www.apple.com/ipad/features/

Besser, L. (Ed.). (2011). *Standards and assessment: The core of quality instruction*. Englewood, CO: Lead+Learn Press.

Black, A. (2010). Gen Y: Who they are and how they learn. *Educational Horizons, 88*(2), 92–101.

Costa, A. L., & Kallick, B. (2010). It takes some getting used to: Rethinking curriculum for the 21st century. In H. H. Jacobs (Ed.), *Curriculum 21: Essential education for a changing world* (pp. 210–226). Alexandria, VA: ASCD.

Eichenlaub, N., Gabel, L., Jakubek, D., McCarthy, G., & Wang, W. (2011). Project iPad: Investigating tablet integration in learning and libraries at Ryerson University. *Computers in Libraries, 31*(7), 17–21.

Fisher, D., & Frey, N. (2010). Preparing students for mastery of 21st century skills. In H. H. Jacobs (Ed.), *Curriculum 21: essential education for a changing world* (pp. 221–240). Alexandria, VA: ASCD.

Friedman, T. L. (2006). *The world is flat: A brief history of the twenty-first century.* New York, NY: Farrar, Straus, & Giroux.

Gruman, G. (2011, July 5). The iPad's victory in defining the tablet: What it means. *InfoWorld.* Retrieved August 15, 21012 from http://www.infoworld.com/d/mobile-technology/the-ipads-victory-in-defining-the-tablet-what-it-means-431

Hughes, J. E., McLeod, S., Brahier, B., Dikkers, A. G., & Whiteside, A. (2005). School technology leadership: Theory to practice. *Academic Exchange Quarterly, 9*(2), 51–55.

Jacobs, H. H. (2010a). New school versions: Reinventing and reuniting school program structures. In H. H. Jacobs (Ed.), *Curriculum 21: Essential education for a changing world* (pp. 60–96). Alexandria, VA: ASCD.

Jacobs, H. H. (2010b). *Curriculum 21: Essential education for a changing world.* Alexandria, VA: ASCD.

Kay, A. C. (1972). A personal computer for children of all ages. *Xerox Palo Alto Research Center.* Retrieved August 10, 2012 from http://www.mprove.de/diplom/gui/kay72.html

Kay, K. (2010). Foreword: 21st century skills: Why they matter, what they are, and how we get there. In J. Bellanca & R. Brandt (Eds.), *21st century skills: Rethinking how students learn* (pp. xiii–xxxi). Bloomington, IN: Solution Tree Press.

Liebendorfer, A. (2012, July 11). Indy schools embrace technology with iPads. *San Francisco Chronicle.* Retrieved August 15, 2012 from http://www.sfgate.com/news/article/Indy-schools-embrace-technology-with-iPads-3698974.php

McNulty, R. J. (2009). *It's not us against them: Creating the schools we need.* Rexford, NY: International Center for Leadership in Education.

Mick, J. (2010, July 30). Ballmer admits Apple is beating Microsoft in the tablet sector. *DailyTech.* Retrieved August 15, 2102 from http://www.dailytech.com/Ballmer+Admits+Apple+is+Beating+Microsoft+in+the+Tablet+Sector/article19215.htm

Moscaritolo, A. (2012, June 18). Survey: 31 percent of U.S. Internet users own tablets. *PC Magazine.* Retrieved August 15, 2012 from http://www.pcmag.com/article2/0,2817,2405972,00.asp

Partnership for 21st Century Skills. (2009). *The MILE guide: milestones for improving learning and education.* Retrieved August 10, 2012 from http://www.p21.org/storage/documents/MILE_Guide_091101.pdf

Prensky, M. (2001). Digital natives, digital immigrants: Part 1. *On the Horizon, 9*(5), 1–6.

Schlain, T. (2012). *Brain power: From neurons to networks.* New York, NY: TED Conferences.

Simon, P. (1975). 50 ways to leave your lover. On *Still crazy after all these years* [CD]. New York, NY: Warner Bros.

Stewart, V. (2010). A classroom as wide as the world. In H. H. Jacobs (Eds.), *Curriculum 21: Essential education for a changing world* (pp. 97–114). Alexandria, VA: ASCD.

Tyson, T. (2010). Making learning irresistible: Extending the journey of Mabury Middle School. In H. H. Jacobs (Ed.), *Curriculum 21: Essential education for a changing world.* (pp. 115–132). Alexandria, VA: ASCD.

Warschauer, M. (2011). *Learning in the cloud: How (and why) to transform schools with digital media.* New York, NY: Teachers College Press.

Werth, E. P., & Werth, L. (2011). Effective training for Millennial students. *Adult Learning, 22*(3), 12–19.

White, S. H. (2011). *Show me the proof: Tools and strategies to make data work with the Common Core State Standards* (2nd Ed.). Englewood, CO: Lead+Learn Press.

Zhao, Y. (2009). *Catching up or leading the way: American education in the age of globalization.* Alexandria, VA: ASCD.

CHAPTER 8

STUDENT-OWNED MOBILE TECHNOLOGY USE IN THE CLASSROOM

An Innovation Whose Time Has Come

Tricia J. Stewart and Shawndra T. Johnson

INTRODUCTION

Technology is changing rapidly, transforming the nature of life, work, and communication. The role of technology in PreK–12 schools must also change and evolve in order to reflect the nature of the world that students will engage in as adults. A mobile phone is no longer cutting edge; instead, today's phones serve many functions: phone, camera, computer, calendar, and social network device. Society is continuously incorporating technology into every aspect of life, and it is important for students to acquire essential 21st century technological skills. One way that this can be achieved is by school leaders embracing the technology (e.g., tablets, smart phones, laptops) that students own to advance the learning opportunities.

The ability of schools to embrace technology has evolved from one computer in a classroom to a technology lab to laptop carts to the one-to-one

Principal 2.0: Technology and Educational Leadership, pages 123–132
Copyright © 2013 by Information Age Publishing

initiatives, which all have the goal of providing each student with a device to utilize. All of these levels of access have relied on schools providing the device. However, a paradigm shift is afoot with the advent of the mobile learning initiative, which relies on utilizing technology that students already own. Known also as bring your own technology (BYOT), bring your own (BYO), or bring your own devices (BYOD), the approach is described by Lee (2012) as an:

> educational development and an alternative instructional technology re-sourcing model which relies on the collaboration between home and school in arranging for student use of their own digital technologies to be extended into the classroom to assist in their learning, the organization of their school-ing, and relevant complementary educational experiences outside the class-room. (p. 2)

This type of learning is popularly referred to as "anytime, anywhere learn-ing," which emphasizes students being able to benefit from an ability to be tapped into the larger digital world at their choosing. Regardless of the phrase that is used to capture this type of initiative, the emphasis is on school-supported learning through student-owned mobile devices—smart-phones, tablets, and laptops.

The opportunity to capitalize on technology that students already have access to is important given the financial constraints found in most school districts. Historically, increasing student access to technology has been financially supplemented through the Telecommunications Act of 1996, and through the Schools and Libraries Program of the Universal Ser-vice Fund, commonly known as E-Rate. All of these programs sought to provide technologically rich environments and curriculum experiences, which are still costly today. At the same time that educators have looked to decrease the costs of providing classroom technology, there has been a dramatic increase in the number of individuals who own mobile devices that have many of the same attributes as personal computers (e.g., access to the Internet, word processing applications, presentation development, etc.). This is significant, as the 2010 Census found that a mere 18% of homes in the United States still remain without computers.

To provide further perspective on this, Prensky (2004) estimated that there were 1.5 billion mobile phones in the world—three times more than the number of personal computers. Today it is estimated that there are more than 6 billion mobile phone users and more than a billion comput-ers in the world. Additionally, as the concentration of mobile phone users broadens, the user also becomes increasingly younger, with the initial age of owning a cell phone between 11 and 15 years old that same year (Kolb, 2008). Therefore, schools have an opportunity to capitalize on this exist-ing technology that most high school and many younger students have available. Project Tomorrow and Blackboard, Inc. (2010) found that between 2006 and 2009, the number of students with access to a smartphone (phones that have more advanced computing ability and connectivity to the internet than a traditional mobile phone) more than tripled to from 9% to 31%. Similarly, in just one year (2009–2010), the number of mobile devices in the hands of students dramatically increased yet again, with 44% of high school students and 33% of middle school students having access to a smartphone, which represents a 42% increase from the previous year (Project Tomorrow & Black Board Inc., 2010). These figures represent actual usage, although the Gartner Research projected that Internet-capable mobile devices would outnumber computers by 2013 (New Media Consortium, 2011).

This increase in mobile phone devices necessitates that educators adapt to create learning experiences that harness the availability of these devices so that students are provided education that is relevant. This is particularly important given that many school districts still have policies in place that ban cell phones on school campuses. These outdated policies waste school resources that could support student learning and enhance student engagement by facilitating learning modalities that capitalize on students' status as "digital natives." Recently, school administrators have begun to investigate ways that student-owned technology programs can be utilized as a way to meet instructional goals in a more economical manner (Attewell, 2005; Bonk, 2009; Keefe & Zucker, 2003; Ullman, 2010). With this emphasis, it is also important to consider ways that schools can plan accordingly for students who do not own their own technology, so that these students are not left behind.

PRINCIPAL AS TECHNOLOGY LEADER: STARTING WHERE YOU ARE

In order to embrace opportunities associated with learning via mobile devices, it is important that principals reflect on the current policies in place in their districts. Some school districts have restrictive district policies that ban mobile devices from school grounds or restrict cell phone and other mobile technology use until the end of the school. Changes in these settings will require a well-developed plan to move stakeholders forward when considering learning through mobile devices. In some instances, this will be a shift from mobile device as toy to mobile device as instrument for learning. While for others, it will be a change in policy that is less strict given that in 2011, the Federal Communications Commission decided that social media and networking sites were no longer the danger that they were once believed to be:

> Although it is possible that certain individual Facebook or MySpace pages could potentially contain material harmful to minors, we do not find that these websites are per se "harmful to minors" or fall into one of the categories that schools and libraries must block. (FCC, 2011, p. 4)

This clarifies that schools face less risk should students see something on these sites that was not intended. Schools can encourage the use of social networking sites, including Twitter, without fear of losing funding from constraints previously attached to the Children's Internet Protection Act (Carr, 2011).

This shift in policy provides principals with an opportunity to revisit the existing policies for mobile devices included in their Acceptable Use Policies. However, it may be that some administrators will need to revisit their own feelings about student-owned mobile devices; when 3,578 school/ district administrators were surveyed as part of the "largest collection of authentic, unfiltered stakeholder voice on digital learning" (Project Tomorrow & Blackboard, Inc., 2010, p. 3), a full 65% of them responded "No way!" to allowing students to use their own mobile devices (Project Tomorrow & Blackboard, Inc., 2010, p. 6). In essence, administrators can use these policy changes as a catalyst to internally assess their own attitudes and beliefs toward technological advances. In this way, they can then work in conjunction with the staff and larger community to decide how to move forward with policy revisions that support student learning.

Policies that principals may consider include not only an Acceptable Use Policy for Students, but also an Understanding of Mobile Learning Contract for Parents, as well as Policy Guidelines for Teachers as they work to create meaningful learning experiences for students. Some principals may also find it useful to establish a "coalition of the willing," those teachers who would embrace the opportunity to work with students using a new platform for learning, while others may need to start with full faculty or the Parent Teacher Association to ensure that the opportunity to utilize mobile devices is approached as a win for all students. Regardless of the starting point, the need to strategize the way to broach the modification of or elimination of a ban on mobile technologies will be crucial.

EMPHASIZING LEARNER-CENTERED INSTRUCTION USING TECHNOLOGY

As principals look forward to ways to incorporate mobile devices into the schools, it is important to promote the understanding that utilizing student-owned mobile devices is inherently learner-centered. The ultimate goal of the principal and the teachers needs to be to create learning environments that help students grow in their understanding of how, why, and when to use their mobile devices. There are obvious functional or organizational tools that can be easily accessed through mobile technology such as scheduling, recording tasks, note-taking, emailing, and checking grades (Project Tomorrow & Black Board Inc., 2010). The benefit of students being able to use these agenda and communication features is that they provide students with real-world applications that will mirror the world they will enter as adults.

Beyond serving as communication tools, student-owned mobile devices also make possible a deeper level of learning—the goal of using the devices as a tool that provides a platform for enhancing student understanding of content material. Research suggests that mobile device utilization is believed to be more of a way of engaging students than just as an advanced agenda tool (Attewell, 2005). Principals who embrace the importance of a focus on student-centered, constructivist learning should appreciate how students engage meaningfully with the lesson through the use of their mobile device. Equally important is a mindset shift that encourages teachers to see mobile device utilization as a way to foster student responsibility and self-direction with the content materials. For instance, student learning can be monitored through applications like Poll Everywhere (www.pollevery-where.com), which allows teachers to easily create polls that can be used with students in the classroom. It can also be used as a homework assignment where students can create polls for one another quickly and without difficulty to extend their own learning and to be shared the next day—thereby enhancing the learning of others.

Other applications, like the Kindle app (www.Amazon.com/kindleapp), as well as public library e-lending opportunities, provide students with access to thousands of free or low-cost eBooks. Additionally, publishing companies are also increasing their investments in providing eTexts and working on software specifically to be used in the classroom (Fossum, 2012). For example, Houghton Mifflin Harcourt has offered an app that provides a version of Skillstutor software that provides instruction and intervention in language arts, including writing, math, and science (www.skillstutor.com/hmh/site/skillstutor/Homme/Products_Services/mobile).

Regardless of the specific ways that teachers choose to utilize student-owned mobile devices in their classes, it will be essential that the principal work with them to ensure that the initial professional development offerings explicitly address the creation of meaningful and effective learning assignments. It will also be up to the principal, with the support of curriculum leaders, to ensure that ongoing professional development be provided over time that supports the continuation of the initiatives. Integrating student-owned mobile devices to support learning should not seem like another hastily added professional development topic, but rather an important in-novation in teaching and learning.

REALITIES OF TEACHING THE M-GENERATION AND MOVING BEYOND THE CLASSROOM

Both the educational community and society at large must acknowledge just how "wired" most students are when it comes to utilizing mobile technology. According to Kolb (2008), "the Kaiser Family Foundation (2005) named to-day's youth the M-generation, because of the adolescents' ability to multitask with a variety of media devices at one time, such as talking on the cell phone, instant messaging, and writing an essay all at once" (p. 5), although others have coined the m-generation to apply only to media. Given the character-istics that have been attributed to students aged 8–18, it is imperative that schools integrate tools and strategies that capitalize on students' skills just as easily as pencil and paper are used in order to create a ubiquitous learning environment. Ubiquitous learning or U-learning takes place when a seamless and pervasive connection to learning occurs without explicit awareness of the technologies being relied upon (Keefe & Zucker, 2003).

Through allowing students the ability to bring and use their own digital devices, educators can change the very nature of instruction in the class-room, but ubiquitous learning can only be truly realized when students are allowed not only to utilize the device in all of their classes throughout the course of the day, but also to take it home to continue their learning beyond the walls of the school building. Otherwise, a disconnect between school life (where they are "unplugged") and real life (where they are con-tinuously able to access information) works against enriching their learn-ing experiences. Work is being done to investigate the idea that creating a bridge in the learning divide between home and school will help students be more academically successful (Kolb, 2008). By encouraging students to think of the mobile devices they use outside the walls of the school build-ing as information and research tools, not merely communication devices, students can personalize and extend their own learning.

One of the initial challenges to the success of this model is the reality that not all students have the same access to owning technology; thus schools must put in place mechanisms to address this issue. We recommend that schools that are going to initiate a student-owned mobile device program acknowledge the need for supplemental mobile devices and plan accord-ingly for the students with families that are unable to provide technological devices. One possibility is for the district to partner with local for-profit or-ganizations that might be able to donate new or previously enjoyed devices as they purchase upgrades for their employees. Another possibility is that as the district makes plans to embrace mobile devices, they proactively speak with parents and the Parent Teacher Associations (PTA) about affordable devices that could be purchased and donated to the school.

DISTRICT-LEVEL ADMINISTRATION
AND MOBILE LEARNING

A hard reality is that moving forward with a student-owned mobile device initiative is simply too large of an undertaking for a particular building or administrator to implement without significant support from the district level administrators. However, lessons from one-to-one initiatives can serve as appropriate guideposts for districts that are interested in developing a BYOD initiative. The following recommendations are designed to be action oriented for those at the district level of administration. They include what must be considered when undertaking the specifics of implementing a mobile learning initiative:

- Cultivate district, building, and staff leadership around why and how to include mobile learning.
- Develop short- and long-term financial planning to support mobile learning.
- Plan an infrastructure (bandwidth, software, software support, district provided email for all, etc.), including the ongoing maintenance of the infrastructure.
- Chart technology preparation, rollout, and support with a minimal five-year plan—implementation and financial.
- Engage in communication across stakeholder communities; include teachers, parents, students, and other community members. Monitor stakeholder expectations and address and adapt to concerns as needed.
- Initiate policies and procedures that are research-based, legally defensible, and clearly articulated that will foster the development of mobile learning across grade levels.
- Consider utilizing a pilot program to manage and adapt to learner and teacher needs and to identify successful practices to replicate on a larger scale.
- Provide meaningful and adequate professional development that occurs systematically over time.
- Invest an online learning platform like Moodle, ANGEL, or Blackboard to enhance ease of stakeholder use.

DIGITAL RESOURCES

Increasingly, there is more information available about moving beyond a traditional one-to-one initiative and towards utilizing student-owned mobile devices for the enhancement of student learning. The caveat attached to this is that this information is being provided by organizations who are interested in advancing this movement, and the research community has yet to be able to provide sufficient data-driven results. With that said, websites that provide information on one-to-one initiatives, digital learning, or student-owned mobile devices are located in the appendix. Their inclusion does not suggest support of the individual organization or the information provided; principals are encouraged to utilize their professional discretion.

CONCLUSION

Admittedly, there are obstacles to overcome if schools want to consider implementing a student-owned mobile device learning program in classrooms; however, this initiative can prove to be a worthwhile endeavor. Harnessing mobile technologies has the potential to improve both teacher pedagogies and student learning outcomes. In order for this initiative to work effectively, educational leaders must take the time to develop and communicate detailed implementation plans, clear management policies and procedures, and high-quality professional development to ensure that teachers are integrating mobile devices into instructional activities effectively for all students.

Researchers Norris and Soloway (2011) claim that it is a mistake for districts not to consider a BYOT program, not only because of the fiscal savings it could represent, but more importantly for the improvements to student achievement that it can bring. They suggest that ideally, technology initiatives that have student use at the forefront are at the heart of educational change and must take place to prepare children for the 21st e-Century. The opportunity to enhance student engagement through real-world application that fosters students as self-directed learners and collaborative team players can also be achieved. Utilizing student-owned mobile technology can be at the forefront of the type of educational change that is crucial for students to find success as members of the 21st-century e-workforce, which will be technology dependent. Principals and teachers working to enhance student learning through increasing the use of student-owned mobile technology in the classroom is one way that this vision can come to fruition; for surely this is an innovation whose time has come.

APPENDIX
Websites with Information on One-To-One Initiatives, Digital Learning, and Student-Owned Mobile Devices

America's Digital Schools 2006
http://www.ads2006.org

App.net: A Quickly Maturing Infant Social Network
http://web.appstorm.net

Consortium for School Networking, which includes Leadership for Mobile Learning
http://www.cosn.org/

Digital Learning Environments
http://www.guide2digitallearning.com/

Houghton Mifflin Harcourt
www.skillstutor.com/hmh/site/skillstutor/Homme/Products˙_Services/mobile

International Society for Technology in Education
http://www.iste.org/welcome.aspx

Intel's K–12 Computing Blueprint
http://k12blueprint.com/k12/blueprint/

One-to-One Institute
http://www.one-to-oneinstitute.org/

Partnership for 21st Century Skills
http://p21.org/tools-and-resources/educators

Tech & Learning
http://www.techlearning.com

Note: These websites were viable at the time of publication.

REFERENCES

Attewell, J. (2005). *Mobile technologies and learning: A technology update and m-learning project summary.* Retrieved November 12, 2012 from http://www.m-learning.org/docs/The%20m-learning%20project%20-%20technology%20update%20and%20project%20summary.pdf

Bonk, C. J. (2009). *The world is open: How web technology is revolutionizing education.* San Francisco, CA: Jossey-Bass.

Carr, N. (2011). *FCC opens access to social media sites for e-Rate users.* Retrieved November 12, 2012 from http://www.eschoolnews.com/2011/09/26/fcc-opens-access-to-social-media-sites-for-e-rate-users/

Federal Communications Commission. (2011). *FCC-11-125: Schools and libraries universal service support mechanism and a national broadband plan for our future.* Retrieved November 12, 2012 from http://hraunfoss.fcc.gov/edocs_public/attachmatch/FCC-11-125A1.pdf

Fossum, M. (2012). *eBooks are beginning to replace textbooks in the classroom.* Retrieved November 12, 2012 from http://www.webpronews.com/ebooks-are-beginning-to-replace-textbooks-in-the-classroom-2012-02

Keefe, D., & Zucker, A. (2003). *Ubiquitous computing projects: A brief history* (Technical Report No. P12269). Menlo Park, CA: SRI International.

Kolb, L. (2008). *Toys to tools: Connecting student cell phones to education.* Eugene, OR: International Society for Technology in Education.

Lee, M. (2012). *Technology in Australia's schools: The scene in 2012.* [Web log comment]. Retrieved November 12, 2012 from http://malleehome.com/?p=199

New Media Consortium. (2011). *The NMC Horizon Report: 2011 K–12 Edition.* Stanford, CA: The New Media Consortium. Retrieved November 12, 2012 from http://www.nmc.org/pdf/2011-Horizon-Report-K12.pdf

Norris, C., & Soloway, E. (2011). From banning to BYOD. *District Administration, 47*(5), 94. Retrieved November 12, 2012 from http://www.districtadministration.com/article/banning-byod

The One-to-One Institute. (2012). Developing a 1 to 1 program. Retrieved November 12, 2012 from http://www.one-to-oneinstitute.org/index.php?/becoming-a-one-to-one/developing-a-1-to-1-program/

Prensky, M. (2004). *What can you learn from a cell phone?—Almost anything.* Retrieved November 12, 2012 from http://www.marcprensky.com/writing/prensky-what_can_you_learn_from_a_cell_phone-final.pdf

Project Tomorrow & Black Board Inc. and Blackboard Inc. (2010). *Learning in the 21st century: Taking it mobile!* Irvine, CA: Project Tomorrow & Black Board Inc.. Retrieved November 12, 2012 from http://bbbb.blackboard.com/LP=146?JYQYJRGP6M

Ullman, E. (2010). How it's done: BYOT (Bring your own tech). *Technology & Learning, 30*(6), 12.

U.S. Census. (2010). *Computer and internet use in the United States: 2010.* Retrieved November 12, 2012 from http://www.census.gov/hhes/computer/publications/2010.html

CHAPTER 9

AFFECTIVE LEARNING THROUGH SOCIAL MEDIA ENGAGEMENT

David Ta-Pryor and Jonathan T. Ta-Pryor

INTRODUCTION

The members of a school community—students, teachers, leaders, parents—are active information seekers (Potter & Bolls, 2011). As humans, we are consistently assessing our environment through our senses—whether through sight, vision, touch, smell, and/or taste. Learning is an emotional process (Bradley & Lang, 2007; Bolls & Potter, 2011). Emotions guide our ability to react to the information we receive from external sources. This is the essence of learning, and in order to understand how humans learn, we must have an understanding that emotion and learning are intertwined. In today's educational environments, much of our students' learning comes through media, whether in the form of books or through videos accessed from the Internet. The use of media impacts how students process the message (McLuhan & Fiore, 2005), which in turn impacts how information is stored and later recalled. Teachers, administrators, and parents need to be concerned with the type of information that can come from different com-

Principal 2.0: Technology and Educational Leadership, pages 133–148
Copyright © 2013 by Information Age Publishing
All rights of reproduction in any form reserved.

munication technologies, and also how students use these devices in their everyday interactions.

Today's students have been bombarded with media ever since they were born. In places where there once was blank space, we see media such as print advertisements, messages flashing on electronic billboards, or videos playing on flat-screen monitors in grocery store aisles. Media seem omnipresent in our daily lives. When a new communication technology approaches the border of mass consumption (think iPhone), it is greeted with both excitement and skepticism. For example, when Apple released their iPhone in summer 2007, fans and enthusiasts lined the streets and camped out at stores so they could be the first to own an iPhone. It featured a simplistic icon menu and a home button. It was simple, easy to use, and aesthetically pleasing. It was also viewed with skepticism in the private business industry. Many pointed to a lack of security features that Blackberry had and control from an IT standpoint. However, its rapid adoption led to solutions being built, and its continuing popularity can be cited as one of the causes for the Blackberry's decline in the cell phone market. New technology brings with it efficiency and provides a different way for people to communicate with each other. This becomes problematic when social meaning is attributed to how technology is supposed to be used. For example, our younger generation may use technology more often than the older generations, and the way younger people use technology to communicate may be perceived by members of older generations as threatening or inappropriate.

However, the argument that mediated communication is becoming increasingly prevalent is nothing new. This argument dates as far back as the invention of writing, when Socrates (as quoted by Plato, 2008) lamented that writing will destroy the oral tradition of Greek society (Ong, 1982). Socrates argued that media (i.e., writing) does not provide truth, but only a shadow that is the truth. This argument has been continuously echoed with other communication technologies such as the telegraph, telephone, television, and the Internet (Baym, 2010).

Social media is the latest technological innovation to fall victim to this fear. Boyd and Ellison (2007) define social networks as "web-based services that allow individuals to (1) construct a public or semi-public profile within a bounded system, (2) articulate a list of other users with whom they share a connection, and (3) view and traverse their list of connections and those made by others within the system. The nature and nomenclature of these connections may vary from site to site" (para. 4). Skeptics argue that communication via social media is not as authentic as face-to-face interactions, and the quality of those interactions are greatly reduced because we lose the social cues people use to construct context of the situation (Baym, 2010). However, this viewpoint lacks an understanding of how media functions and the constructive ways in which technology enables people to communicate in new and different ways. Social media complicates how people interact with each other online. When you compare it to older Internet platforms (e.g., IM, message boards, listserv, and chat), people are more likely to communicate with those they have a relationship with offline. The modality gives people the ability to dynamically share content, shape their online identity, and control how they communicate with certain groups from their friends list. Also, social media provide a convergence of different technologies that integrate into their daily habits. Students may check their social media accounts when they wake up and carry the same task throughout the day on their cell phones. Social media allow people to post messages with a variety of modalities. For example, video and audio are integrated into some social media platforms where friends and family can (1) communicate with one another with written messages; (2) watch videos and photos posted on each other's profiles; and (3) communicate in ways that are uncommon or unavailable face-to-face—thus providing a context that may be richer in certain circumstances.

What implications does this have for educational leadership? Many educators approach social media with caution. It depends on the individual school district; however, many have adopted a policy that limits their use in classrooms and between the educators and students. In Missouri, teachers were legally banned from having students under the age of 18 as friends on social media platforms through legislation that was later revoked when challenged by a lawsuit from the teachers' union. Many limit cell phone usage because of the problems it may bring in the classroom, which include lack of attention to instruction, cyberbullying by students, and using it to send explicit pictures to one another (also known as sexting). The fear that social networks will hurt or victimize children is similar to earlier warnings about the impact of film and television. When film and television were initially introduced to the public, many were warned of the negative effects that would come from its use. Now we see these technologies as integrated and normalized in our daily lives and as utilized in teaching practices. In education, many saw the benefits of film and television as a means to deliver content to diverse learners and to inspire interest pertaining to learning objectives. With an increase in the use of video in education, we saw the quality of instruction increase because education became more motivational and interactive than in text-based study. The lesson from this example is that there may be ways to integrate social media with our teaching practices to improve student learning outcomes. These limiting policies hinder educators from developing a healthy and constructive relationship with the platform, and they deny educators the ability to educate students about the features of these technologies and how they can be socially responsible when interacting with one another in social network sites.

Social media marries relational communication with technology. The social cannot be separated from the educational. Many people are attracted to social media because it offers them a way to communicate and maintain relationships with friends, family, and acquaintances across distance and time. Educators with technology proficiency use social media to engage their students in a variety of contexts. Teachers post information about assignments and events that relate to the current course topics, engage students with discussion questions, and use it as a question and answer forum. Social media allows teachers to engage students in learning outside the classroom space and time. This in turn allows students to better apply information to everyday situations in their own lives.

As active information seekers, how might educators better use social media to impact learning and to improve educational outcomes? This chapter will examine the characteristics of new media and the symbiotic relationship younger generations have with new media. The purpose of this chapter is to help educators and administrators understand how students use new media and technologies in their everyday life, and harness the potential of social networks for educational use. A brief literature review on emotion research will be examined, and we will illustrate how this body of literature is used to engage students' motivation, which is a key component to learning. Finally we provide tips for best practice in using social media to interact with students. The chapter does not list specific platforms, but gives a general guideline that can be applied to an instructor's preferred social media platform.

THE INTERNET GENERATION → FUSION GENERATION

The potential the Internet has to offer education is both exciting and complicated. The Internet has given us the ability to efficiently communicate with each other and to streamline how we obtain up-to-date information. Prensky (2001) defines two types of technology users: digital immigrants and digital natives. Digital immigrants grew up without the use of the Internet, cell phones, and the modern communication technologies many people take for granted. They grew up in an age where television was bounded by a few channels, asynchronous communication was done with postal mail, and synchronous communication was conducted over a landline. They are mostly bound by age, but are grouped by their use of technology. Digital natives are those who grew up with computers and had access to the World Wide Web. They used the Internet to access information, communicate with each other via text and instant messaging, and spend time playing online games, watching online videos, and consuming their information from websites rather than traditional books. People have categorized this younger generation as the internet generation, generation ao (always on), igeneration, and net generation (Carr, 2011). Digital immigrants use technology, but many may not see it as natural as a digital native does. This is like the child who is showing his grandparents how to check their e-mail or the teenager showing her dad how texting works. Digital natives are more likely to experiment with technology and figure it out faster than digital immigrants. However, there is one interesting aspect that is not addressed: the social.

The problems that this generation brings are some that change the way people fundamentally communicate with each other. What makes this generation different from those who grew up without the internet is the seamless integration of technology, communication, and applications in their everyday lives. What makes an application like Facebook successful is the social nature that it brings to the scene. No longer are young people bound by a desktop computer or even a laptop computer. If they have a smartphone, they can install Facebook, carry it with them throughout school, and check it in between classes, during lunch, in the bathroom, and on the ride home. Once they are home and are doing their homework, they can check their Facebook on both their phone and on their computer. How many people do you know who check their e-mail on any device they can get their hands on and all points throughout the day? What about those who participate in a media convergence of traditional media and new media? There are many television shows that ask their audience to post messages on social network sites during the show, log into their application, and interact with content that unlocks during the show. We argue that this generation is different because of its communication habits rather than its use of technology. Therefore instead of categorizing this generation by its age, we call it the fusion generation. This is different because of the combination of communication habit and technology, whereas other definitions see how technology is used.

However, in terms of communicating with each other, some have feared that technology and social media have changed our social interactions in a negative manner. Some have argued that technology and digital media have created an ADD generation—one that is characterized by an inability to pay attention; people are more concerned with the online community and are becoming dumber because technology has made it easier to find information (Bauerlein, 2009). The fear lies in the assumption that we will communicate less with each other in face-to-face contexts, or we will lose our ability to appropriately communicate with each other. For some people, these fears may be well founded. There have been cases where students use digital media to send each other inappropriate, explicit pictures; bleed their short-hand communication in their formal writing assignments; and post videos of fights on YouTube or some other video streaming service. In other cases, some people prefer texting to calling someone on the phone. Others may send an e-mail to the person in the next room rather than walk over to speak with that person. One lens through which to view the Internet is as a communication conduit where uses and effects vary depending on the communication technology's features (Metzger, 2009) and the purpose of the communication. Walther, Gay, and Hancock (2005) stated, "Internet use is too broad a category to assess systematically or sensitively potential impacts of various communication channels for which the Internet is a conduit" (p. 650). It is both the type of technology and the people using the technology that will mediate our communication. Research by Walther (2007) examined impression management in a computer-mediated setting. He found that when speaking to more socially desirable partners, people's language complexity increases. This provides evidence that in a mediated relationship, people rely on digital messages as their primary means of expression. Research shows that computer-mediated communication (CMC) leads to more extreme impressions than face-to-face and more positive relationships over time compared to face-to-face. In education, research shows that the type of communication matters in student achievement (e.g., Garrison & Vaughan, 2007; Richey, Klein, & Tracey, 2011). How much a teacher communicates with students, the type of platform used, and what is disclosed matters in the relationship-building process that can motivate students to become more interested in an academic topic.

Communication Technologies

Media convergence blurs the line between what was considered traditional communication technologies and new communication technologies (Jenkins, 2008). The different modes of communication (i.e., one-to-one, one-to-many, many-to-many) on the Internet give educators both the challenge and the flexibility to engage with students. One of the main challenges is the ability to navigate the blurred line between technology/content-focused effects (mass communication) and effects coming through interactions with others (interpersonal communication) and using or developing theories to help explain media effects. Are the messages you send for a mass audience? A group of students in your classroom? Will everybody see it, or will it be available to those select groups of students?

Technology is meant in part to make life and tasks easier for users. A key feature is audience control and selectivity. With social media, users have new ways they can communicate with family and friends. They also have more control over the content they consume. This control and the ability to be selective gives people a unique experience with how information is presented, and being able to select different content challenges the assumption that people are exposed to the same messages at approximately the same time (Dayan & Katz, 1992). People on a social media platform such as Facebook can have the same friends, but they can choose to filter out certain messages from those friends. One user may see where their friends have been in the past 30 minutes, while the other user may only see pictures from the event. Selectivity allows users to access information from different perspectives, which may make it challenging for educators to send the same message out to all students and expect them to see it if students utilize media-selective tools.

The structure of content of information goes back to discussion of flow and how messages communicated through social media may not be organized in a linear fashion. An example is the use of hyperlinks posted in a social network, which goes back to audience selectivity and allowing the audience greater control over the content they consume. Someone may choose to click on a specific hyperlink, which directs them to a different site. Another may choose to click on a different hyperlink, which takes them to a completely different site. The effects due to messages received may be different because each person is exposed to different content. This connects well to Tomlison's differentiated instruction framework (2010), which states that a student's acquisition of content and making sense of it involves the student taking a different avenue and the teacher providing that avenue to the student.

As a communication tool, the Internet has dramatically improved how people communicate with each other across space and time. With the Internet, educators can post information and students can view that information from anywhere they have access to the Internet, such as a mobile device, a home computer, a public library, or a computer classroom that offers open lab time before or after school. Students can solicit and receive information from their peers if they miss class or see the latest announcement from their teacher. However, this also complicates how we prioritize communication during certain times and in certain spaces. For example, would it be considered appropriate for students to text while they were in class? What if students were posting or searching for information on a piece of a lecture they found interesting? Educators need to learn how to utilize students' motivation and direct it toward helping students academically achieve without hindering their propensity to communicate with others through technology.

The idea of media convergence is coupled with media portability. The portability of media content transcends both time and space, and with wireless technology, people have greater access to media content when they are not at home or at work. With mobile wireless technology, people can stream videos and other multimedia using a cell phone. While media effects generally focus on media content, wireless technologies call more attention to the media experience. Is watching a video on a smart phone the same as viewing the video on a desktop monitor? Maybe not if researchers were interested in the emotional arousal and cognitive processing of media (e.g., Reeves, Lang, Kim, & Tatar, 1999). Reeves and his colleagues (1999) examined the effect of screen size on emotional arousal. Their findings suggest that the bigger the screen size, the more emotionally arousing the experience. This in turn suggests that students are more likely to process and store information if that information is presented on bigger screens.

Social Media

While social media speak to a mass audience, many of our communications can be specific and tailored to groups or a select few. They are tools that people use in their everyday lives. We see many students using social media to engage with friends and family and to gather information based on what they are interested in at the moment. Because the technology has become very successful (Brandtzæg, 2012), most members of younger generations no longer see it as novel. Most students use social media, and many adults use it as well. This domestication of technology occurs when we see communication technologies move from being fringe novelties to everyday objects that are engrained in our everyday lives, and life without the Internet becomes unimaginable (Baym, 2010; Haddon, 2006). Rather than find ways to exclude these technologies from the classroom, we need to find ways to maximize their effectiveness to enhance our teaching and learning.

One important feature to be mindful of is the user's ability generate content. With social media, audiences have changed their ability to participate in content creation as well as how they use media in their everyday lives (Metzger, 2009). Specific features that distinguish social media from traditional media are (1) interactivity, (2) diversity of content, (3) audience control and selectivity, (4) personalization, (5) media convergence, (6) structure or organization of information, (7) global reach, (8) media portability, and (9) audience social connectivity (Metzger, 2009). Each of these features facilitates different types of communication. As educators, we must realize that these technologies are becoming deeply integrated into the younger generation's everyday lives. Structuring how we communicate, personalizing our messages, creating policies to set healthy boundaries, and using technologies to increase communication and interactivity in the classroom is important to students' academic success.

When using social media, we should be goal oriented with the purpose of engaging students. Social media is multimodal, allowing individuals and groups to consume media that is textual, auditory, and visual. The diversity of content challenges the way messages are produced and distributed. With social media, content varies in both diversity and magnitude, and the consequence of this variety of selection is that the audience is not provided with a coherent set of messages. Educators can take advantage of social media by giving students up-to-date and diverse information not found in printed textbooks. Social studies teachers can post recent presidential speeches as part of a government class, science teachers can post news reports of scientific breakthroughs or the latest findings from the Mars exploration rover, or language arts teachers can post clips from a movie adaptation of a novel students are currently reading in their literature class.

With new media, there is more interactivity afforded than the traditional mass media, so students could post comments, engage in online discussion, or post links of their own to lead peers and educators to information related to classroom topics. Interactivity is the degree to which communication is two-way instead of one-way (Bucy, 2004). Examples of this are blogs, social network sites, YouTube, and other user-generated content that is characteristic of Web 2.0. Interactivity puts forth a challenge because the ebb and flow of content varies between users and the effects vary from person to person. Interactivity is key in education because it creates online presence. Currently, there is extensive research that demonstrates how presence relates to student achievement (e.g., Garrison & Vaughan, 2007; Gunawardena, 1995; Richardson & Swan, 2003). For now, think of how different types of interaction in social networks establish a certain level of connection between users, and how that can be used to engage students. We will examine the role of presence later in the chapter.

Social Connectivity

The final characteristic of new media discussed in this chapter is audience social connectivity. The Internet has given people more access to content and others than ever before. People are able to extend their social reach to others across space and engage in direct social interaction. Social network sites have enabled users to engage with each other without having to venture far outside the platform, and people can post and discuss media content in addition to text-only communication. By reducing some of the technological constraints put to the user, they might be more motivated and engaged with others online (Metzger, 2009). The potential implication of this shifts the delivery of content more to a user-to-user perspective rather than a media industry-to-user perspective. While people may use the same social network site, content delivered will be different from person to person, and this challenges one of the tenets of traditional media, that audiences are exposed to a limited set of messages in a uniform manner at the same time.

The features of new media have posed many challenges to educators, but those challenges can be seen as potential for education innovation and ways to generate excitement and student engagement related to learning topics. In the next section, we will discuss psychological states that relate to users' experiences in social media, namely emotion and communication.

EMOTION AND COMMUNICATION

Picture yourself at home watching a favorite show on television. During a commercial break, you see a firefighter pull an elderly woman and her grandkids from a burning building. Then the commercial cuts to a crash scene where a police officer gives CPR to an unconscious man. What are you feeling during those moments when you see those suspenseful scenes? More importantly, how do your feelings inform your thinking during the commercial? Are you alert and aroused? Or bored and annoyed because you are waiting for your favorite show to come back? Finally the tagline of the commercial says protecting yourself is the most important gift you can give to your family, and the only way you can do that is to buy life insurance. If you are one of those people who do not have life insurance, do you feel guilty or anxious? That is exactly what the advertisers hoped to elicit when they created that commercial. Those emotions are important to how we react to and connect with the world. They are internal feeling states that function as coping mechanisms to aid us in dealing with the outside environment (Bradley & Lang, 2007). Emotion informs our thoughts about a stimulus object or event, and it aids us in making critical decisions about obtaining resources and about survival.

Emotions may be triggered in a variety of ways within educational settings, and these feelings are essential to the human embodied experience (Bradley & Lang, 2007). It is difficult to imagine a life without emotions because they are integral to our daily lives. The ability to fall in and out of love, to be surprised by family and friends, and to feel grief over the loss of a loved one is essential to living full and rich lives. Indeed, emotion could be "considered the lifeblood of human existence" (Potter & Bolls, 2011, p. 103). It is so essential that many educators consider emotions to be intrinsically connected to consciousness (Bradley & Lang, 2007; Damasio, 1999; Potter & Bolls, 2011) and seek ways to utilize emotion to motivate students to learn content in order to be successful.

As educators, there are benefits that come from seeking to understand social media from an emotional context. One thing that is clear about emotion is that in emotional situations, the body acts (Bradley & Lang, 2007). The heart beats faster, palms sweat, respiration levels change, and the muscles relax or contract. Emotion is a concept that one can recognize intrinsically, but emotion may be challenging to understand as a whole. It acts as a survival and information seeking mechanism. Educators may design social media experiences with the intention to create an emotional connection that allows users to form/maintain relationships and to invest in retaining information presented to them. It is this connection that keeps people motivated to consume social media daily, and educators need to find ways to connect the personal to relevant content and motivate students to consume the content. One way in which educators can motivate students to consume content is to establish presence. The next section discusses how emotions are used to establish presence and the potential that online presence has for learning.

SOCIAL MEDIA AND ESTABLISHING PRESENCE

Presence has been a concern of instructional researchers, instructional designers, and those concerned with online education. Garrison and Vaughan (2007) stated that social presence is an important component to establishing an online learning community, which in turn is essential to learning and student achievement. However, establishing social presence in education can be difficult given the disconnect many educators have with understanding how the personal is intertwined with their professional lives. This is one of the primary reasons some people object to using social media in education.

Presence is the idea that people experience certain stimuli in the natural world, and the believability of those experiences triggers an emotional reaction. With social media, this may be the closeness a person feels to friends or family members while reading status updates or viewing photos posted. A common phenomenon among people who spend a lot of time on their social network sites is to look up at the time and realize that hours have passed by quickly and the day is almost over. Have you been in a similar situation before? If we read a good book that is self-selected, time goes by more quickly than when we are engaged in required readings. Understanding the psychological construct of presence can illustrate how media can transport people from a static location to one that the mind virtually constructs, and the emotional and cognitive feelings that are associated with having that connection with the media artifact. Our emotions mediate the impact of presence, and the intensity of our emotion can motivate people to engage with others. The engagement people have on social media sites helps establish presence, and the motivation that comes from our emotional engagement keeps us coming back for more.

Presence is a multifaceted construct (Lee, 2004). In order to establish presence virtually, a person first needs to be motivated to perceive objects or people as physically present. Media research that has examined presence has demonstrated that presence lies at the heart of people's mediated experience (Tamborini, 2000). It does not matter what type of media is utilized—books, television shows, movies, video games, or the Internet—the concept of presence is impacted most by how people experience it. However, presence is often a convoluted term (Lee, 2004). It has often been confused with attention, flow, immersion, and interacting with the medium. Lee (2004) explicated a definition from his review of the presence research and argued that presence is "a psychological state in which virtual objects are experienced as actual objects in either sensory or nonsensory ways" (p. 27).

Presence is divided into four multidimensional constructs: physical presence, social presence, self-presence, and spatial presence (Jin, 2011). Physical presence is when a user feels like they can manipulate objects as if they were really there. For example, creating aesthetics and videos that allow students to navigate a classroom may create a greater sense of physical presence than if information was presented in mere text-based format. Social presence refers to the extent that you feel presence because of individuals reacting to you. The mere presence of other social entities in the mediated environment can induce a feeling of presence. Students interacting with each other on Facebook can facilitate a greater feeling of social presence than a message board because students have that extra user-generated content to learn about the person. Self-presence is when a player can identify with the avatar, or virtual representation, of the character that he or she is playing in a role-playing video game.

To effectively use social media in education, we must understand how the level of interactivity and media-rich details can impact users' experience, particularly in how they perceive and engage with others. Presence helps students feel as if their mediated experiences are more real and the other students they engage with online are closer. To create a similar connection, a teacher can self-disclose particular events in her social network profile while not violating her sense of privacy (e.g., "It's bowling league night!"), and still allow students to form a connection with the teacher and view her as more credible (Mazer, Murphy, & Simonds, 2009). With an increasing number of high schools offering online courses to their students (Black, Ferdig, & DiPietro, 2008; Picciano & Seaman, 2009), ultimately, our understanding of presence can help us understand how it can mediate other types of behaviors, such as increased motivation in an online course.

To conclude, we present some basic guidelines that teachers and administrators can use to engage with their students through social media. It is important to note that social media are merely a tool used to facilitate engagement and to maintain or strengthen relationships. Educators must also understand that social media provide opportunities for motivation and learning in ways that are more integrated into the lives of students than other forms of media.

BASIC GUIDELINES TO ENGAGE STUDENTS THROUGH SOCIAL MEDIA

Keep Your Messages Short, But on Target

- Post a change to your course (reading assignment or revised homework directions) or updates related to your school calendar of events.

- Create an online assignment or school-wide discussion topic requiring review commentary or peer feedback. If you are using Twitter or other social media that limit amount of characters, use keywords or hashtags to denote important information.
- Post-supplementary materials (sample questions, links to real-world media, etc.).
- Post or tweet events related to classroom topics or school activities in real time.

The Social Is the Personal

People use social network sites to maintain relationships, to build connections, and to gather and share information. Posting information about the course or school activities is only a portion of the work educators need to do. Take some time to post about your day, disclosing information appropriate to your audience. There are some worthwhile benefits that come from this, including promoting students' self-efficacy, creating opportunities for two-way student communication, building trustworthiness, and promoting the feeling among students and school community members that you are more than their instructor or principal.

Know Your Privacy Settings

Keep only one social media account for each platform. Having two separate accounts for one social media platform is confusing, and most people will find that managing two Facebook sites can become overwhelming. Another consideration is the signal you are giving your students if you don't post on a regular basis. Here are some tips to help:

- Set your privacy settings to the highest in your profile.
- Categorize people into friends, acquaintances, co-workers, and the like. It doesn't matter how many lists you have. Set a default category list for when you post.
- If you choose not to allow your students to add you as a "friend" on Facebook, edit your settings to allow them to subscribe to your feed, allowing them to view your activity and still engage with you in a more limited fashion. There are some social network sites that use the term *friend* to mean add to your list of people you wish to be associated with. Facebook allows people to friend each other, but it also allows people to subscribe, which means that only one person is following the other person and not the other way around.

Use Social Media as Supplementary Communication

Don't use social media as your primary means of communication. Students and other school community members have expectations that they will receive e-mails, newsletters, and other traditional forms of communication from the school. Educators need to communicate important information in class, face-to-face settings, or via telephone conversations.

CONCLUSION

The fusion generation is about how students communicate with each other with their devices and the seamless integration technology has in their everyday lives. Rather than taking a stance against social media and keeping it out the classroom, administrators and teachers are better off with a positive policy that integrates its use in official school communication and learning. Social media and technology are neutral at best. Social media are only negative when students are not educated in how they should be used. Instead of hindering their use in school, students need to be socialized in their use because the consequence to letting them figure it out for themselves will bring on negative behaviors like cyberbullying. If teachers and administrators have a presence in how social media is used, the potential for students to learn around the clock may come closer to reality rather than fantasy.

REFERENCES

Bauerlein, M. (2009). *The dumbest generation: How the digital age stupefies young Americans and jeopardizes our future (or, don't trust anyone under 30)*. London, UK: Tarcher.

Baym, N. K. (2010). *Personal connections in the digital age*. Cambridge, UK: Polity.

Black, E. W., Ferdig, R. E., & DiPietro, M. (2008). An overview of evaluative instrumentation for virtual high schools. *The American Journal of Distance Education, 22*(1), 24–45. doi 10.1080/08923640701713422

boyd, d. m., & Ellison, N. B. (2007). Social network sites: Definition, history, and scholarship. *Journal of Computer-Mediated Communication, 13*(1). Retrieved October 1, 2012 from http://jcmc.indiana.edu/vol13/issue1/boyd.ellison.html

Bradley, M. M., & Lang, P. J. (2007). Emotion and motivation. In J. T. Cacioppo, L. G. Tassinary, & G. G. Berntson (Eds.), *Handbook of psychophysiology* (3rd ed., pp. 581–607). Cambridge, UK: Cambridge University Press.

Brandtzæg, P. B. (2012). Social networking sites: Their users and social implications: A longitudinal study. *Journal of Computer-Mediated Communication, 17*, 467–488.

Bucy, E. (2004). Interactivity in society: Locating an elusive concept. *The Information Society, 20*(5), 373–383. doi: 10.1080/01972240490508063

Carr, N. (2011). *The shallows: What the internet is doing to our brains.* New York, NY: W. W. Norton & Company, Inc.

Damasio, A. R. (1999). *The feeling of what happens: Body and emotion in the making of consciousness.* New York, NY: Harcourt Brace.

Dayan, D., & Katz, E. (1992). *Media events: The live broadcasting of history.* Cambridge, MA: Harvard University Press.

Garrison, D. R., & Vaughan, N. D. (2007). *Blended learning in higher education: Framework, principles, and guidelines.* San Francisco, CA: Jossey-Bass.

Gunawardena, C. N. (1995). Social presence theory and implications for interaction and collaborative learning in computer conferences. *International Journal of Educational Telecommunications, 1*(2), 147–166

Haddon, L. (2006). The contribution of domestication research. *The Information Society, 22*(4), 195–204. doi: 10.1080/01972240600791325

Jenkins, H. (2008). *Convergence culture: Where old and new media collide.* New York, NY: New York University Press.

Jin, S.-A. A. (2011). "I feel present. Therefore, I experience flow:" A structural equation modeling approach to flow and presence in video games. *Journal of Broadcasting & Electronic Media, 55*(1), 114–136. doi: 10.1080/08838151.2011.546248

Lee, K. M. (2004). Presence, explicated. *Communication Theory, 14*(1), 27–50. doi: 10.1111/j.1468-2885.2004.tb00302.x

Mazer, J. P., Murphy, R. E., & Simonds, C. J. (2009). The effects of teacher self-disclosure via Facebook on teacher credibility. *Learning, Media and Technology, 34*(2), 175–183. doi: 10.1080/17439880902923655

McLuhan, M., & Fiore, Q. (2005). *The medium is the message.* Berkeley, CA: Ginko Press.

Metzger, M. J. (2009). The study of media effects in the era of internet communication. In R. L. Nabi & M. B. Oliver (Eds.), *The SAGE handbook of media processes and effects* (pp. 561–576). Thousand Oaks, CA: Sage.

Ong, W. J. (1982). *Orality and literacy: The technologizing of the world.* New York, NY: Routledge.

Picciano, A. G., & Seaman, J. (2009). *K–12 online learning: A 2008 follow-up of the survey of U. S. school district administrators.* Needham, MA: The Sloan Consortium.

Plato. (2008). *Phaedrus.* Charleston, SC: Forgotten Books.

Potter, R. F., & Bolls, P. (2011). *Psychophysiological measurement and meaning: Cognitive and emotional processing of media.* New York, NY: Routledge.

Prensky, M. (2001). Digital native, digital immigrants. *On the Horizon, 5*(9), 1–15.

Reeves, B., Lang, A., Kim, E. Y., & Tatar, D. (1999). The effects of screen size and message content on attention and arousal. *Media Psychology, 1*(1), 49–67. doi: 10.1207/s1532785xmep0101_4

Richardson, J. C., & Swan, K. (2003). Examining social presence in online courses in relation to students' perceived learning and satisfaction. *Journal of Asynchronous Learning Networks, 7*(1), 68–88.

Richey, R. C., Klein, J. D., & Tracey, M. W. (2011). *The instructional design knowledge base: Theory, research, and practice.* New York, NY: Routledge.

Tamborini, R. (2000, November). *The experience of telepresence in violent video games.* Paper presented at the 86th annual convention of the National Communication Association, Seattle, WA.

Tomlinson, C. (2010). What is differentiated instruction. *T/TAC Telegram, 14*(4), 3–4.

Walther, J. B. (2007). Selected self-presentation in computer-mediated communication: Hyperpersonal dimensions of technology, language, and cognition. *Computers in Human Behaviors, 23*, 2538–2557. doi: 10.1016/j.chb.2006.05.002

Walther, J. B., Gay, G., & Hancock, J. T. (2005). How do communication and technology researchers study the Internet? *Journal of Communication, 55*(3), 632–657. doi: 10.1111/j.1460-2466.2005.tb02688.x

CHAPTER 10

THE CENTRAL TEXAS COMMUNITY LEARNING EXCHANGE DIGI-BOOK

Fostering School and Community Engagement Through the Creation of a Digital Book

Lee Francis, IV, Mónica M. Valadez, John A. Oliver, and Miguel A. Guajardo

INTRODUCTION

The Community Learning Exchange (CLE) is a nonprofit organization, encompassing a network of over 40 community-based organizations from across the United States. These include organizations that represent a critical part of the nation's social fabric, including members of PK–12 and higher education institutions, healthcare services and wellness programs, youth engagement and leadership development programs, community organizing networks, and others. Grounded in the practices of collective leadership, the CLE creates opportunities for existing communities to host

Principal 2.0: Technology and Educational Leadership, pages 149–171
Copyright © 2013 by Information Age Publishing
All rights of reproduction in any form reserved.

learning exchanges in which participants not only gain an understanding and appreciation for the hosting community's local history, collective wisdom, and story of change, but also experience new ways of approaching their own challenges and identifying and harnessing the power of their own communities' members and resources for the greater good. Through the utilization of social networks, the CLE continually seeks to invite new members and communities to explore collective leadership methods towards the healthy development and sustainability of partnering communities.

During the first week of January 2012, a group of educators from Texas State University–San Marcos accepted the CLE's invitation to host the ninth learning exchange. Community leaders, activists, and youth gathered at the Lyndon Baines Johnson (LBJ) Museum in San Marcos in central Texas to spend three days engaged in conversation regarding the intersections of politics, education, and community development. Not the first gathering of this sort, nor the first to be hosted by a Central Texas community, this gathering was the first to engage the participants in a new emerging framework. Over the course of three days, participants discussed their work, communities, and the various places where those areas diverge and intersect. Participants also captured the spirit of the gathering through narrative, photos, artwork, songs, and digital stories. The CLE host planning team was very purposeful in the planning and guiding of this chronicling of the gathering. Historically, at the conclusion of each gathering, the CLE host planning team produced a newsletter or report that described the event and specifically prescribed suggestions for the sustainability of the work of the CLE and future gatherings. The Central Texas CLE planning team discussed alternative report formats that could capture the essence of the gathering in ways that would illuminate the work and energy that surrounded it. The planning team discussed the possibilities of making the report an interactive digital book with hyperlinks. The team agreed to develop an iBook.

During the month of the event, Apple released iBooks Author, free software that allowed anyone to create digital books for distribution on iTunes. After a bit of conversation, we realized the potential of the new technology and software and made the decision to create a digi-book summary of the gathering. This digital text contains written stories, digital video, graphics, images, and documents, combined to create a new medium that would allow participants to reflect, remember the experience, and give a sense to new Community Learning Exchange (CLE) members of the activities and intent of the gatherings. This text will focus on the use of a specific technology to chronicle the CLE experience and will highlight the content of the CLE as the focal point of the documentation process.

In this chapter we explore four areas in creating a digital book primarily focusing on the rationale and development process. The first section lays the groundwork, including a brief review of the work leading up to the design of the digi-book and the nature of the developmental process in the creation of the digi-book. The second section provides the framework, or backbone, of the digi-book as we look at the use of digital technology, its position at the intersections of educational practices, and the process for developing the CLE digi-book. In this area, we also discuss the necessity of digital technology, when it should be used, and in what circumstances and situations a digi-book can be most effective. The third section looks at the organizing of the data collection and selection of the content needed for the digi-book as well as how to create a narrative structure for the book. The fourth section focuses on the digi-book itself and will include a brief guide to iBooks Author and examples from the CLE digi-book. We hope to provide a grounded guide for educational leaders to develop their own digital texts and highlight additional ways in which digital media can be used to deliver dynamic and engaging content and pedagogy. Subsequently, we conclude this chapter with examples of how educational leaders can use the technology to further their work in communities, including the intersections of educational practice, policy development, and school and community engagement. Finally, we have developed this chapter in order to share the context of the Community Learning Exchange and what takes place behind the scenes in the preparation and development of a dynamic curriculum in which the digi-book serves as yet another product of the Exchange.

Throughout this chapter, we deliberately utilize the term digi-book rather than ebook in order to create a clear distinction between our work and the mass media's understanding of an ebook. The CLE CenTex Digi-book is available through a link to iTunes on this website: e4educationalconsulting. com/cle-ibook.html. We encourage you to download our digi-book free of charge for use on your iPad and follow along with the examples presented in this chapter. You can also download iBooks Author for free from the Mac App Store. Currently, iBooks Author is only available for use on the OSX (Mac) operating system.

LAYING THE GROUNDWORK

The Central Texas CLE planning team was deliberate about the intended outcomes of the community learning exchange. The team insisted that that the event not only serve as a catalyst for change for the individuals that attended, and they were also purposeful in considering ways of extending the experience beyond the gathering, while also creating a connective link of the experience for future attendees. The team opted for the creation of a digi-book. Creating a digi-book is, by no means, a quick process. Indeed, one of our purposes for this chapter is to create a clear understanding of the process and time required to create a product (i.e., digi-book) that is representative of a community. An authentic representation illustrates the diverse hands, hearts, and minds of the community members that produced, felt, and originated the work encompassed in the digi-book. The necessity of being intentional and deliberate is important in ensuring quality and thoughtfulness around the narrative. In fact, the planning of the digital concept was built into the event as it relates to documentation, release forms, lighting of recording and pictures, and the securing of quality video and audio equipment and staffing each camera recorder.

Over the course of approximately eight months, we planned for the data collection; structured, sorted, and edited video and resource media; wrote introductions and sectional pieces; reviewed, tested, and re-calibrated our digi-book; and finally distributed our digi-book. Depending on the nature of the process and resource availability, this may require more or less time; the amount of time will be unique from community to community and digi-book process to digi-book process. Acknowledging that the development work takes time will allow the space for a more fluid and generative process to guide the production of the digi-book. The framing of this chapter to focus on the documentation and production process is important from a teaching, learning, and leading perspective. How we capture the local experiences, the knowledge creation process, and the action of local communities must be congruent with the content; indeed, the documentation must be dynamic, inviting, and provocative in its form and process. The section below captures the intersections of the main foci of this weekend's exchange: politics, education, and community development.

The Framework

Before we discuss the steps necessary in the production of a digital book, we feel it is important to discuss the impetus for choosing this technology. So rather than looking at this as an amazing breakthrough in technology, which it is, and jumping right in, we feel that there first must be a clear understanding of why this technology is so powerful and how it falls within the intersection of educational leadership, policy development, and school–community engagement (see Figure 10.1). This becomes critically important as each of these areas plays an important role in shaping the resources needed, the content of the digi-book, and the function of the final product. It is also important to first understand the rationale. There are numerous how-to books in the market that can easily show the amazing things that you can do with iBooks Author, but none of them will highlight how this can function in an educational setting, especially one that looks to engage multiple stakeholders through its design and delivery. As evidence, we use

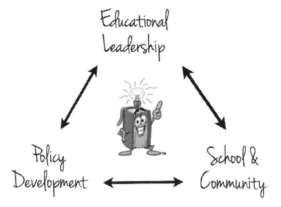

Figure 10.1 Digi-book and the intersections of educational practices.

the three-day CLE engagement process as the material to highlight this point. Thus, we use the digi-book as a tool to share the knowledge, energy, and actions that came about because of the curriculum and engagement process created during the CLE weekend. The screen shots were taken directly from the CLE Central Texas digi-book (see Figure 10.2, Figure 10.3, and Figure 10.4). To access the content you can utilize the following link: e4educationalconsulting.com/cle-ibook.html.

Figure 10.2 Screenshot of iBooks author and the introduction chapter of the CenTex Digi-book.

After lunch, the hunt was on! The digi-hunt, that is.

The idea for this began from an activity at the Minnesota-Wisconsin Community Learning Exchange, where we explored the grounds of the retreat center in teams, found or constructed responses to the clues and photographed the results. Upon the return, we showed our photos to the whole group and explained our rationale.

For the CenTex Digi-hunt, we wanted to utilize as much of the digi as possible and guide people to the CLE website. We created a instruction and clue sheet

Movie 2.14 Digihunt teams return and present their findings to the group

After an afternoon of hunting, the teams return to share their journey and the photos they took to address the clues. (2min 21sec)

The Digihunt instructions and clue sheet.

CENTRAL TEXAS CLE DIGI HUNT

(too the right) and that was all the groups received. Each group had a specific location to try and find and they were to check in on the website for additional instructions. Each group would use whatever camera/cell phone they had at their disposal. When the groups returned, they would present their photos/videos in a creative manner and highlight some of the learning that took place based on the clues. Our idea was to have groups make meaning, as individuals and groups, out of the clues they received. We also wanted to create an activity that wold take advantage of the beautiful weather in Central Texas in early January and get folks outdoors to see San Marcos and the campus of Texas State.

27

Figure 10.3 Screenshot of Section 5: On the Hunt. This page shows the types of media (video and pdf) that can be embedded in an iBook.

Day Two: The Agenda for Day two included: Gracious Space, Q-Sort, Digi-hunt, and home team collaborations.

As our second day began, we once again convened at the LBJ Museum. The altar was in place and so was the living museum we had installed on the second floor, an interactive representation of the CLEs and ourselves.

Over the course of three years, each CLE had a different flavor, but the core elements remained the same. Community engagement, collaboration, and time to reflect. Yet this CLE was also slightly different; site visits and more technology created moments to explore San Marcos and Central Texas and realize other methods of engagement and development. The day would provide more than enough activity to keep everyone engaged and exhausted by days end.

Our work was laid out before us and we offered blessings to Creation for good thoughts, good intentions, and good hearts.

21

Figure 10.4 Another screenshot of a page from Day Two. Blending text and images creates a powerful narrative experience for the audience/reader.

In creating our digi-book, we looked at how the work could parallel the conversations at the gathering and at the same time serve as a representation of the intersection of educational leadership, policy development, and school–community engagement. Simply, the digi-book combines multiple media in a narrative package for portable distribution. This allows educational leaders the opportunity to generate, collect, and share stories from their school and community through multiple forms of digital technology. Educational leaders can utilize these stories to develop a community narrative that helps to shape policy considerations and decisions. Understanding the story of individuals and communities helps to expand the discourse on teaching, learning, and accountability by focusing on the academic and community work facilitated by an educational community. The use of the digi-book process aids in understanding the historical context, both in macro and micro terms, as it relates to discourse on educational policy and the development of schools, particularly public schools. The power comes in the aesthetic of the intersection as well as the power to construct our own local stories of learning, organizing and celebrations. Creating a book that collects the stories, images, and documents on a specific topic, gathering, or theme and translating these artifacts into a narrative format, is an act of art making; in essence, you are creating a collective story of stories. The digi-book format allows for concurrent meaning-making and art-making, and is a creative expression that, when intentional and deliberate, creates an elegant synthesis of educational leadership, policy development, and school–community engagement.

DIGI-BOOK PROCESS

Why a digi-book? Why an ereader or tablet? What's the benefit? First, it's fun; it's new; it's exciting! These technological devices have been able to tap into the creative energy and dynamism of a younger generation and create products that are elegantly designed and intuitive. Apple has put the same energy and simplicity into software and hardware that makes designing a digi-book enjoyable. This excitement and newness can be used to engage stakeholders who might otherwise not be interested in perhaps another brochure, flyer, or report. The fresh nature and new possibilities inherent in this new technology provide it some cultural energy and provides another vehicle to engage with digitally native youth who consume information through increasingly digital platforms (Palfrey & Gasser, 2010).

Second, it's portable. One of the great advantages to tablet computers and ereaders is the fact that you can load a lot of books and information in a tiny space. Whether an iPad, Nook, or Kindle, the largest measurement is 9.5" in diagonal. The size of the device alone makes it an easy fit into a purse, backpack, or other small bag. In developing a digi-book, the same holds true: you can load a lot of information into an electronic format, allowing your content to be portable and allowing your audience the opportunity to view that content at their leisure. You can add videos, audio, text, images, PowerPoints, and other artifacts that have been formatted for the iPad. All of this content does not need to be connected to the internet because it can be downloaded for mobile storage. This is an incredible asset for a world on the go.

Third, the iBook provides a synergy between the written word, images, and video. Digital technology has come so far in such a short time from the first digital computer that was built in 1945 to the iPad in 2010—a span of 65 years. By contrast, it was roughly 1,000 years from the printed text to the first eReader. But the written word continues to provide an intangible quality that functions to help clarify and enable a different sort of aesthetic expression and artistic imagining. The digi-book integrates and unifies multiple artistic forms into a compact and elegant package.

Fourth, it promotes multidimensional thinking and engagement. When you combine writing, images, video, and audio all in one space, you are drawing upon multiple forms of cognitive engagement and development. The tactile experience of manipulating multi-touch objects on the iPad enhances kinesthetic learning and reflecting on the content, which promotes deep thinking about the issues and topics presented in the book. The process of creating the digi-book is even deeper as you have to think across different platforms and presentation areas when making decisions on how to engage readers and the potential audiences that may download and read the digi-book.

Fifth, it draws on multiple forms of creativity and creates paths for deep artistic collaboration and collective leadership. The work of editing and engaging multiple stakeholders is a critical space for developing collective and collaborative leadership, especially in our young people.

Sixth, creating a digi-book helps cultivate and develop agency of meaning making. The digi-book process invites students and teachers, as well as parents and community members, to become authors of their own reality. This opportunity and process moves in a dynamic and proactive manner for the learner and teachers and positions them as creators of knowledge. This pedagogy elevates the learning process into a critical and dynamic process where the learners and teachers become the researchers and authors of a reality and knowledge that is grounded in the local/micro and informed by a global/macro. This meaning-making and authoring process has the ability to inform knowledge production in a different way that is generated and grounded in practice.

Of course, there are some critiques of using this method. First, not everyone has access to the iPad, as the expense of the device can be prohibitive to some families. Also the time for professional development may not be a priority when there are so many other issues and responsibilities for educational leaders and teachers. These critiques really boil down to a cost–benefit analysis and the need to be intentional in utilizing new technology. There are some effective ways to overcome many of these obstacles, such as grant writing for technology funds. Perhaps the school could invite community members to share one of the iPads while visiting the school. Another option would be to create a process for checking out the iPads for community use. Equally important is engaging teachers in using the technology by allowing them to play with and explore their own iPads in their classroom. Lack of infrastructure is always a big concern, but if we refuse to even entertain the technological possibilities then we are doing a disservice to our youth and communities by making decisions for them rather than with them.

DIGITAL CONTENT

As they say in the television industry, "content is king." Before embarking on any digital project, it is important to have a wide selection of content upon which to draw. Otherwise, you will certainly struggle to fill the space and will either have to collect more resources or end up with a final product that did not quite capture what you had intended. Also, knowing what content you have available will certainly make it easier to outline your digi-book, assign tasks, and ensure a coherent narrative. In designing the CLE CenTex Digi-book, we had incredible content to draw from. This was primarily due to the experience of the host team in working with digital storytelling and the necessity of digital imagery when creating video and digital story reflections of gatherings, workshops, community events, and community engagement pieces.

The available artifacts for this project included hours of video, ranging from general wide shots of the entire learning exchange proceedings to specific interviews with numerous participants. We had hundreds of photos from multiple cameras, and we solicited additional pictures from the participants online to add to ours. We had pdf versions of all the documents that were a part of the gathering, and we had excellent graphics that explained various concepts during the gathering. Many of these would not see inclusion in the final digi-book. That is also the role of the editor(s), to sort through all the collected media and distill the data in a way that captures the voice of the community and the essential narrative in the most direct and elegant fashion. Although it seems as if more content will make this job more difficult, when there is not enough content, creating the digi-book can seem unbearable—it's like a painter who has only one color to work with. Sure, they can create something great (depending on their skill level), but it would be so much greater if they had all the colors to work with. The lesson is to capture as much media as you can. Interviews, shots of action and activities, photographs, people, conversations, faces, documents, graphic design, and PowerPoint presentation slides can all have a potential space in the final digi-book.

It is also important to be aware of the quality of the content. You can have hours of video, but if the audio is distorted or the lighting is poor, that video becomes worthless, especially if you are capturing an event (as opposed to an interview) or some other activity that cannot be replicated or reshot. The audio component bears repeating as voices and reflections are key pieces of data that are critical for developing, assembling, reflecting, and creating a digi-book. You also will want to try to frame shots, photographs, and interviews so that they will be aesthetically appealing; at the very minimum, the content should be clear, clean, and easy to view and hear. An eye toward the aesthetic will also go a long way in doing much of the work prior to the construction of the digi-book.

Listed below are a number of considerations regarding content selection. These are important considerations when educational leaders utilize a digi-book to engage staff, students, and community.

Hardware

Once again, it is important to note that for the CLE CenTex Digi-book, we were designing specifically for the iPad; however, the content requirements are pretty standard for all forms of tablets or ereaders, save for the 7" mini readers. However, your dimension ratios will be roughly the same. For the iPad, the screen size is 9.5" × 7.3"; this equals 1250 pixels × 1000 pixels. We mention this because DSLR cameras don't often scale images. In other words, you have only so much screen, and you don't need 10,000 pixel images to fill that screen. High-resolution digital images around 1000 pixels will suffice. Knowing the size also allows you to understand how to design the pages for readability and aesthetics. Some great templates are available online, we prefer a designer who has collected a number of templates for the iPad: http://emilychang.com/2010/03/ipad-templates-and-stencils/. These are mostly for folks who want to design apps, but the blank template is great to be able to conceptualize your digi-book as well.

Another hardware consideration is the computer and operating system. iBooks Author is only available on OSX (Mac), but if you are using Windows or Linux, you can utilize a drive partitioner (Bootcamp, etc.) to allow for multiple operating systems. In working with digital video, you will also need a fairly fast computer in order to edit the media effectively and efficiently; the specifications will most certainly continue to climb as our technological capacity builds upon itself; however, at the time we composed our digi-book, 4 to 8MB of RAM and 2.8Ghz Dual or Quad Core processor worked very well for our purposes.

Storage and Access

Another consideration is where you intend to store your content and how team members and collaborators will have access to that content. For the CLE CenTex Digi-book, we purchased a 3TB external hard drive to store all the video for the gathering, as well as upcoming gatherings and projects. Digital video will be the largest user of memory, and this will only increase as the quality of digital video continues to get better. When you are purchasing storage, keep in mind your future needs. As for access, there are two ways to go about allowing for access. First is a shared computer and second is a shared drive. Either option will allow for multiple editors; however, there is no way to track who changed what in iBooks Author, so if you have multiple editors or collaborators, it might serve well to assign various sections and chapters and have someone who is serving as an editor-in-chief to oversee the whole project. For our work, we had one designer/editor, and the team would then review each section for corrections, ideas, enhancements, and necessary changes. Finally, public access for the finished product is pretty simple: you can only offer iBooks Author multi-touch books designed for the iPad on iTunes, and iBooks Author can only be run on OSX. The iBooks Author software makes publishing a fairly easy process. You do have other options, such as saving the book as an EPUB, but this will not transfer the features, widgets, or embedded media. The best approach for this is to copy the link to your iBook and distribute in various forms—web, email, print, QR code—for folks to access: for our CLE CenTex Digi-book, you can find us at the link listed earlier in this chapter. You can also keep the final digi-book on the iPad hard drive for easy reading.

Software

The main piece of software necessary is iBooks Author. This is free software and can be downloaded from the Mac App store (http://www.apple.com/ibooks-author/); however, it is only available on the OSX operating system. You will also need video editing software, photo editing software, and if you wish to get fancy and use the full capacity of the widgets available, 3-D editing software (http://usa.autodesk.com/) and Xcode (https://developer.apple.com/xcode/) for XHTML effects, such as enabling email functions from within the iBook or creating graphical scrolling effects for a timeline. We did not use the last two features for our digi-book but felt it would be good to include some links for those who wish to pursue more advanced aspects of the digi-book.

For video editing software, both Windows and OSX come with video editing software as a standard feature. There are several other higher-end options for video editing that are worth investigating. Our top selections are: Sony Vegas (http://www.sonycreativesoftware.com/vegaspro), Adobe Premier (http://www.adobe.com/products/premiere.html) and Final Cut Pro X (http://www.apple.com/finalcutpro/). You will need to take into consideration cost, learning curve (some software is more advanced), and user interface in making your decision if you choose to purchase one of these applications.

For photo editing, there are very limited apps that come standard with each OS. For our work, we used Photoshop. It can be costly, although there is a great education discount. A fantastic alternative, though, is the open-source application GIMP (http://www.gimp.org/), which is very similar in output to Photoshop. And best of all, it is free for some powerful software.

Video and Audio

In order to add video to the digi-book through iBooks Author, it needs to be encoded in the correct format. The program uses m4v, which is the standard format for any video that iTunes uses. If you have downloaded a video from iTunes, it is in the m4v format. iBooks Author does not automatically generate an m4v movie and will not allow you to embed video that does not fit this extension. When you render your video, remember it must be encoded with m4v. If you have already rendered or would like to use video you already have, you can use iSkysoft conversation software iMedia Converter Deluxe (http://www.iskysoft.com/imedia-converter-deluxe-mac.html?icn=index1), which handles video, audio, and DVDs. Handbrake is also a great free solution for video conversion (http://handbrake.fr/). There is an audio embed feature for iBooks Author, and a standard mp3 file works fine. Your video editing software can double as an audio editor, although if you have more audio than video, you could use Garage Band for OSX or Sony Sound Forge Audio Studio (http://www.sonycreativesoftware.com/audiostudio).

Photographs

We have covered photo editing software previously, but one thing to note when adding photos (and videos) to your digi-book is the unintended hazard of too much data, caused by the perception that you have unlimited space and the ease of dragging and dropping. Photos are great, but as with all good editing, you must be selective. Additionally, there is a size and memory issue. iBooks Author will resize photos to fit the space you allow for the widget, but if you are not resizing, in order to fit that box you will be pushing oversized photos into that space, slowing down processing and loading of the book on an iPad. Remember: Resize your photos and keep your videos as short as possible. If you want a photoshow or a movie, there are other places to demo those. The digi-book must be created with the total content in mind.

Additional Source Material

Pdfs, PowerPoint, 3d, XHTML all have a widget through which they can be embedded in the digi-book. We included two pdfs and a PowerPoint (Keynote) in our CLE CenTex Digi-book. You can find much more information on the latter two links online about how to include 3d and XHTML (http://support.apple.com/kb/HT5093 and http://www.w3schools.com/html/html_xhtml.asp, respectively).

THE DIGI-BOOK

As we have noted previously, the final output for this work is in an iBook form. You may also consider an eBook format. For our CenTex CLE Digi-book, we chose the iBook form due to the usability of iBooks Author, the access to an iPad, and the desire to engage with new software and new development possibilities. In many ways, iBooks Author makes the process of book creation a fairly easy process. The downside is the proprietary nature of Apple and their iProducts, which means that work created in iBooks Author can only be read on an iPad and can only be downloaded from iTunes. What makes iBooks Author so powerful is the fact that the learning curve is not very steep, which makes the software and the output that much easier to adopt and utilize in educational environments. Almost everything in iBooks Author utilizes drag-and-drop options, built-in widgets for adding content, and advanced design and programming capabilities to expand upon the templates and existing platform in order to create something incredibly dynamic.

As with the content section, there are numerous texts describing how to use iBooks Author; what we list below are a few of the considerations we came across in creating the CenTex CLE Digi-book, and we include some further ideas of how this can be used by educational leaders.

Outline/Storyboard

A solid concept of the story or narrative before moving forward is essential. The first step is to decide the approach. Will it be linear, thematic, conceptual, or something else? iBooks organizes material by chapter and section, but you are, by no means, bound to a rigid structure in telling your story.

For the CLE CenTex Digi-book, we chose a chronological narrative that moves the reader from the beginning to the end of the conference. We chose this narrative style because we wanted something that would allow those who had never attended a CLE conference the opportunity to understand how we structure the gatherings and how the events and activities build and intersect upon one another. Figure 10.5 gives you a chapter listing detailing the activi-

Figure 10.5 Screenshot of iBooks Author and our CenTex CLE chapter list.

ties of each day. The titles are reflective of the activities and highlight the ways in which you can let your creativity permeate the work.

We could have also used a thematic approach and spent some time discussing the themes that emerged from the gathering, though, ultimately, we settled on the chronological approach. You need to think broadly in terms of collecting content, but establishing the narrative style allows you to begin to sort, separate, and manipulate how you want to present that content. This decision also has implications for how the data are organized, coded, and analyzed.

Orientation to iBooks Author

Here is what it looks like when you first begin with a basic template. You will add your content to this and subsequent pages (see Figure 10.6).

Portrait and Landscape

All tablets and eReaders have the capability to be read vertically and horizontally, so you need to be aware of how each layout looks and changes

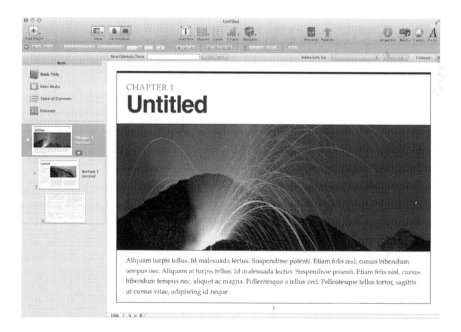

Figure 10.6 Screenshot of generic template for textbook creation in iBooks Author.

Figure 10.7 Orientation buttons for iBooks Author. Be aware of how your content will be presented in each direction.

the arrangement of your content. You can access this function at the top of the menu bar (see Figure 10.7). We are pointing this out because we were several pages deep before changing the orientation and realizing that several of our content positions did not transfer. As we stated earlier, part of the reason for creating and utilizing a digi-book format for delivering information is to enhance the connection and impact by utilizing the aesthetic qualities that the digital book format affords. Realizing how the positions and structure will change from landscape to portrait is important in understanding and addressing the audience you wish to engage. Some folks are more partial to portrait, some to landscape. Moving back and forth and keeping an eye on the design quality will help guide the process of content selection, writing, editing, and designing supporting graphics (see Figure 10.8).

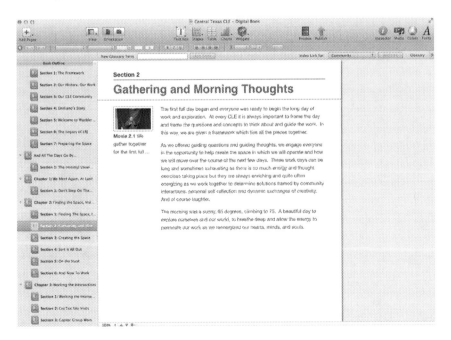

Figure 10.8 Section 2 from the CenTex CLE Digi-book in Portrait Mode.

Chapters, Sections, Pages

iBooks Author allows you to sort your work by chapter, section, and page. This helps create an internal document structure that is then turned into an automatic table of contents. As you have formulated your outline, keep in mind how the chapter can be broken down into sections. The sections are then numbered, and your content is also numbered to align with the chapter and section. For example Chapter 1, Section 1 is listed as 1.1 followed by the title of the section, which you are able to determine. Corresponding content will be numbered the same way, by chapter, then by section number. This allows readers to access chapters, sections, pages, and content through the main menu. For our CLE CenTex Digibook, our broad chapters were organized by day and then by the individual activities like the Q sort that took place during the day. The purpose of Q sort or Q methodology is to better understand the relationships of subjective statements by a group of participants in an objective/quantifiable manner. This methodology helps researchers explain the relationship of statements with a particular group. Understanding these statements is invaluable in the development of the individual and community story. We embedded numerous videos for each section of the CLE, including an internal assessment and organizing tool referred to as the Q sorts in Chapter 2, Section 4 of our Digi-book. The chapter also grounds this process in context, including detailed information about the process and specific explanations of how it worked for this specific gathering. The videos have corresponding chapter and list numbers. iBooks Author also allows for manipulating the order of chapters, sections, and pages and will then reorder the numbers of each of the sections and the media embedded in each section. This is very useful if you find yourself needing to move things about during your development process (see Figure 10.9).

Adding Content

The best feature and the primary reason for using iBooks Author in creating a digi-book is the ease in which you can add content to create the book. We have already covered the types of content and format you can add, but we wanted to highlight the widgets feature and also advise on remembering the aesthetic quality. There are currently seven widgets available, though with time, Apple may choose to add additional features. The gallery widget allows editor to add photo slide shows. The media widget brings in movies, which must be rendered in an m4v format. The review widget creates editor-defined multiple-choice tests to self-check on content. Keynote widget inserts a keynote file. The interactive image widget allows

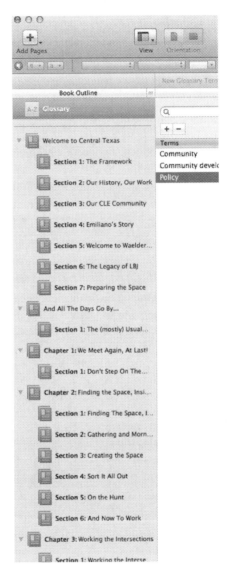

Figure 10.9 Using the Book Outline feature. This helps in navigating your digibook and moving sections, pages and chapters as necessary.

the editor to import an image over which multi-touch text can be added. And finally, we have already mentioned the 3-D and HTML widgets for the more advanced users.

One final item of note relates to adding images. If you drag and drop images without using a widget, they will only be available in landscape mode.

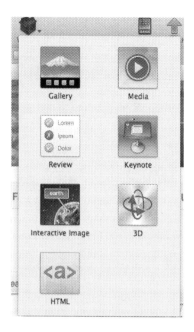

Figure 10.10 The Widgets menu. The best feature on iBooks Author is the ability to embed multiple forms of content and multi-touch media.

When you switch to portrait mode, they will not be there. This is another reason to be aware of the orientation of the device and to remember to switch back and forth.

Testing

Any time during the development process, you can test to see what your work will actually look like and perform like on the iPad. You simply press the preview button, open iBooks (free app) on your iPad, and wait for the book to sync. It will open a preview copy that is only available on that device. You can remove the preview at any time, but if you leave it there, when you look to preview again, it will simply update the copy on the iPad (see Figure 10.11).

Figure 10.11 Preview and publish buttons for iBooks Author. Simplifying the process of editing, reviewing, and publishing your digi-book.

Uploading to iTunes

You can very easily upload to iTunes through iBooks Author. Of course, you need to have an iTunes account and iBooks Developer account. It is free to join, and if you distribute your book for free you are not subject to any charges. However, if you do wish to charge for your digi-book, you will be responsible for the terms of the agreement you sign on to with Apple and iTunes. For more information on this process, you can visit: http://www. apple.com/itunes/content-providers/book-faq.html. Once you are ready, you simply press the publish button, sign in, and your digi-book will be uploaded (see Figure 10.11). Be aware, though, once you publish to iTunes, this work is now out in the world for anyone to download. Therefore, it is important to secure all possible permissions for the content and images that you publish. More specifically, you need to be very careful about image and video rights, citations, and copyrighted material. Best practice is to have participants sign an audio/video release form prior to any photography or recording. We have included our form from the CLE, although your school or district may have a template or you can create your own. Keep in mind that students under 18 must have an adult also sign the release. The issues surrounding digital rights continues to evolve at a rapid pace, so make sure you are informed of your rights and responsibility of what you may or may not publish. Make sure you review your book one final time to ensure all your media is original and the rights are clear.

Additional Formats

We covered only the iBooks Author format in this chapter; however, that does not mean that you should not investigate and explore other potential digi-book platforms. Adobe InDesign has some great features that allow for eBook and digital magazine publishing with the same interactivity (video, audio, pictures) as iBooks Author. The learning curve for InDesign is much steeper but allows for a great deal more customization. Other programs include Scrivener, Calibre, and Pages. Our advice is to try many different forms and see which will suit your needs best and will also give you the flexibility to find that space to create something dynamic and engaging.

EXPLORING CRITICAL INTERSECTIONS: EXAMPLES FOR EDUCATIONAL LEADERS

It's all well and good to show you how we put something together, but it may be of no use if the situation is not the same. So we wanted to include a brief section on how the digi-book format could potentially be used by educational leaders in their work. Below are four examples we thought might be of use: A History of the School, Community Gathering, Community Assets Mapping, and School Needs Assessment.

A History of the School

A great way to engage all stakeholders of your school and community is to create a digi-book about the history of the school itself. Shoot video in and around the school. Interview current students and staff. Interview alumni. Interview community members who may have gone to school there years ago. Find news articles and clippings about the school. You can frame this many ways: overcoming challenges, diversity efforts, a call for funding, or an orientation digi-book. You can work with teachers to include components of this work in their lesson plans, and you can work with students as part of the development team. Students can contribute reflections on the school and poems about their lives at school. Ask your staff members to write pieces as well. Engage your artists in designing the cover and original drawings for the internals. Have students search for archival photos of the school from community members, the library, and the city/town planner's office or records office. Think about how the school has impacted the community and perhaps include a historical overview of the community itself (see the CLE CenTex Section on Waelder Texas).

Community Gathering

Just like the CLE CenTex Digi-book, you can capture a community gathering though video and interviews. Using those data, you can generate a digi-book that explores the themes that the community has determined are worth investigating. Students can do additional research regarding the issues from the community gathering, and the digi-book can be made available at the school and online for community members and students to read.

Community Assets Mapping

Community assets mapping as a project has the incredible potential to engage the entire school and community. The assets mapping work is currently being piloted in Waelder, Texas at the Waelder Independent School District. This digi-book would involve recording interviews with community members, staff, and students. The interview footage would be used to create short videos that share personal reflections of their strengths and what they bring to the community. Students could design and create an interactive map of their community, which would highlight the resources available in and around the area. Students could create art, music, poetry, fiction, and essays about themselves and encourage their parents and community members to do the same. Teachers could create lessons that look at cartography, timelines, and digital storytelling projects that could be included in the final digi-book. The book could be organized around the core assets, the map of the community (sections/quadrants), or other themes that arise. All stakeholders could be a part of the process of developing their own work and stories and could also serve as the editorial board.

School Needs Assessment

Much like the community mapping, this final digi-book could be utilized as a tool to demonstrate the need for some service in the community that would help strengthen the school and instructional delivery, such as a community center or afterschool tutoring. The digi-book could create a compelling argument with interviews pointing to how students and community members would be better off with the need being met. The digi-book could be something community leaders read on the go and subsequently use in making their case for supporting community-based initiatives. As mentioned earlier, the digi-book aids in understanding the individual stories and community narratives at both micro and macro levels. It is essential to the discourse on educational leadership and the development of public schools. Essentially, the process becomes collaborative; it is action-oriented and informed by practice as well as local ecological forces that impact the lives of students, teachers, educational leaders, and communities. Individuals share their connection to place and local contexts. The digi-book process can create a community of learners and educators that help facilitate a school and community change process that will potentially transform the community's vision of itself and the expectations of its schools and students.

CLOSING THOUGHTS: INTERSECTION OF EDUCATIONAL LEADERSHIP, POLICY DEVELOPMENT, AND SCHOOL COMMUNITY

To be clear, the use of technology is a tool in the education and development process, but it is only effective as a lever to move educational concepts and political processes. This process must be grounded and framed within a pedagogical process. Devoid of this careful planning, it will become an elaborate and aesthetically pleasing activity, but tragically miss the opportunity to learn. We caution educators to think, plan, and engage the learners in the construction of this knowledge. At the end of the day, the learning, teaching, and leading is our craft, and the production can be framed in multiple ways. This is a tool that is readily available, and we should take advantage of it for the educational and developmental process.

We have highlighted and elaborated on multiple stages and uses of digi-books as an education and development strategy; an additional element inherent within this concept that must be planned, articulated, and negotiated is the political process. The function of politics in this rapidly changing technological society is critical for school and communities. School districts have begun to explore and create policies for technology, and we recommend you begin there as you are exploring your own development of this process. However, we do want to highlight an issue that is a cornerstone to moving this work forward. We consider this work to be innovative and at the cusp of exciting future products, but in order to get to this point we must explore within our schools and communities the politics and policies behind this work at the forefront of learning and development. This process must be conceptualized, planned, and presented in both an educational framework and a developmental vernacular that will make sense to stakeholders and policy boards within our schools. We must consider how this work is inherently pedagogical and developmentally necessary for our students and communities to be at the cutting edge of learning, teaching, and leading. To explore the mechanics and process for this requires collaboration, education, and multiple conversations with community partners, and we recommend you start now.

Issues of teaching, learning, and leading during a technological age are exciting, but they must also be considered, discussed, and developed in a public and collaborative manner. It is within this context that we present this chapter. The role of educational leaders in schools, in communities, and in cyberspace is to facilitate the development of the next generation of thinkers and innovators. Simultaneously, this process allows us to bring the technology to life. The digi-book process includes creating the opportunities to build skills and knowledge of place and local context. This chapter is an invitation for students, teachers, community partners, and principals to create vehicles for telling their own stories and documenting their experiences while also sharing them with the world. Students can be innovators as they share their learning with the world in route to becoming citizens of the 21st century and the global community. What is your first digi-book?

CHAPTER 11

LEADERS ONLINE

Enhancing Communication with Facebook and Twitter

John B. Nash and Dan Cox

INTRODUCTION

Electronic mail, or email, has been the staple of communication tools for school leaders for the better part of two decades. One of its greatest advantages is that it allows asynchrony, or the capacity of parties to have a conversation with each other on their own schedule. This, and email's other affordances, such as its ability to allow a user to transmit personal messages, send links to websites, distribute mass mailings to stakeholders, and attach files, makes it a tool of efficiency and effectiveness for administrators.

However, email has its drawbacks. The affordances of efficiency and effectiveness can have unintended consequences for school leaders. This is especially true when it comes to fostering conversation in a school. Email, as a medium, does not do a good job of mimicking the conversations and group discussions that might occur in the hallways of a school or at a school function. These informal or non-canonical communications are critical to successful leadership. However, two advancements in technology may

Principal 2.0: Technology and Educational Leadership, pages 173–182
Copyright © 2013 by Information Age Publishing

mediate this problem: Facebook and Twitter. These technologies offer the asynchronous advantages of email with the added benefit of adding a sense of place and community.

In this chapter we look at Facebook and Twitter as tools school leaders can use to improve communication with stakeholders. In doing so we look at why Facebook and Twitter are important communication tools for school leaders, who the tools are impacting, and specific examples of how principals are applying them in their settings. We close with implementation steps and suggestions for district administrators to encourage principals to develop their social media skills.

FACEBOOK AND TWITTER

Facebook is a social networking website that allows users, once registered, to add friends as contacts within the site and provide updates to them in the form of text-based posts, photographs, or links to other websites of interest (see Figure 11.1). In return, a user's friends can comment on the material a user posts on Facebook (Facebook, 2012, n.d.).

Figure 11.1 Facebook's homepage.

Figure 11.2   Twitter homepage.

Twitter is an instant messaging system in which a person may send a message of 140 characters or less, called "tweets," to a list of followers(see Figure 11.2). Twitter belongs to a class of Internet tools known as microblogs, providing users with a way to update people with short messages as opposed to long posts (PC Magazine Encyclopedia, 2012).

WHY FACEBOOK AND TWITTER ARE IMPORTANT

Email communications among school leaders and stakeholder groups are effective at conveying information. However, principals who use Facebook and Twitter find that they can engage those stakeholders in a two-way dialogue, which was not possible through standard forms (e.g., mass emailings or a school newsletter). As such, principals now have the ability to carry out conversations that they previously could not. One of the greatest advantages of tools such as Facebook and Twitter is increased interactivity among participants. This increase in the interactions among principals and their stakeholders is spreading the inclusion of social media tools as part of a comprehensive communications approach for schools (Cox, 2012).

Thanks to the emergence of tools like Facebook and Twitter, principals can now leverage the collective intelligence of their stakeholders in ways never before possible. As Weinberger (2012) notes, the smartest person in the room is no longer a person but the room itself. In other words, in the current era where connectivity via the Internet allows access to knowledge and people in new ways, the role of the lone expert is fading from prominence. And the "room," as Weinberger refers to it, is all the people who are connected to the Internet. For school principals, the implication is clear: leadership can no longer be defined as one person anointed as the sole person in the organization, commanding from above. Rather, leadership must be defined, in large measure, by one's ability to consult the people in the room; synthesize the web of knowledge, opinion, and expertise contained therein; and deliver direction that advances the organization such that everyone in it can learn. Facebook and Twitter offer a handle for school leaders to harness the diversity of perspectives and skill sets in the virtual room represented by a school's community.

A Preexisting User Base

Take, for instance, the way in which Twitter can be viewed as a place where people go to find out what others are saying. There are over 100 million users of Twitter, 40% of whom visit merely to see what other people are saying (McMillan, 2011). And these numbers pale in comparison to Facebook's. In October 2012, there were one billion monthly active users on Facebook, with an average of 552 million people actively using Facebook every day (Facebook, 2012).

With such high user numbers, Facebook and Twitter are destinations where school leaders are likely to already find their stakeholders. Of all adult Internet users in the United States, 66% use Facebook. School principals whose parents are Internet users can expect that 72% of those between the ages 30–49 are using Facebook, and of Internet-using parents ages aged 50–64, 56% are on Facebook. Seventy percent of all adult women Internet users are on Facebook versus 63% of all adult men (Hampton, Goulet, Marlow, & Rainie, 2012). Furthermore, Facebook is "sticky." This means that once a Facebook user subscribes to the feed from a friend or organization, less than 5% hide or unsubscribe to that feed. The same study reports that there is little evidence of Facebook fatigue. In other words, the more time that passes since users started using Facebook, the more frequently they are likely to engage with content on Facebook. That means they were more likely to comment on a school's posted photos, use the "like" button on messages from the principal, and comment on issues discussed by other users.

As for Twitter, of adult Internet users in the United States, 16% use Twitter. Fifteen percent of those in the 30–49 age range are Twitter users, an age range that encompasses a majority of adults with K–12 age children. A telling statistic about both platforms is the prevalence of young adult use:

83% of online adults aged 18–29 use Facebook and 27% use Twitter (Smith & Brenner, 2012).

Sense of Place

A useful metaphor for distinguishing the difference between email and tools like Facebook and Twitter is the notion of *place*. We generally don't think of email as a place we visit to see what others are doing. On the other hand, it's easy to envision sites like Facebook and Twitter as places we would go to see what people are talking about. Email, Facebook, and Twitter rely heavily on the asynchrony of their platforms, yet from a communication perspective, they're more like a *destination* that people visit than a *tool* they use.

Benefits to Principals

Engebritson (2011) notes, "principals want to communicate and need a format to reach their intended audience(s) without it taking a lot of time from their already busy day" (p. 71). As such, a shift is beginning to take place in the way that school officials interact with their stakeholders. Many are choosing to embrace Facebook and Twitter in order to increase the interactions with stakeholders. Principals who embrace the use of Facebook and Twitter tend to find that such tools:

- allow for greater *interactions* between school principals and their stakeholders
- provide stronger *connections* to local stakeholders, to fellow educators, and to the world
- create a significant *impact* on a school principal's personal and professional growth
- extend the dialogue between themselves and stakeholder groups, providing deeper, richer exchanges that foster stronger solutions to questions at hand
- contribute to higher levels of transparency that lead to higher levels of trust between school leaders and stakeholders. (Cox, 2012)

In the next section, we discuss examples of how Facebook and Twitter are impacting the practices of school leaders in their everyday work.

WHO IS IMPACTED BY FACEBOOK AND TWITTER?

Herein we draw upon the findings of a recent study conducted by one of the authors (Cox, 2012) to tell the story of how Facebook and Twitter are impacting principals. This qualitative, multiple case study, titled *School Communications 2.0: A Social Media Strategy for K–12 Principals and Superintendents*, was conducted as a doctoral dissertation project at Iowa State University. Four themes emerged regarding principal and superintendent use of social media. Social media tools: (1) allow for greater interactions between school administrators and their stakeholders; (2) provide stronger connections to local stakeholders, to fellow educators, and to the world; (3) can have a significant impact on a school administrator's personal and professional growth; and (4) are expected to be used; it's no longer optional.

Facebook and Twitter impact principals in myriad ways that have a positive impact on communication and interaction with stakeholders. Consider the following vignettes and their accompanying tips for implementation:

- A principal held a parents' coffee where he answered questions from junior high parents for 90 minutes. A colleague used Twitter to post the parents' questions and key conversation points so that other faculty and parents who couldn't attend could follow along virtually. You can do this in meetings at your school, too. Establishing a Twitter account for your school is the first step. Then ask a colleague to join you at a meeting with a laptop or tablet computer. Sign into the school Twitter account and ask your colleague to post the key questions raised in the meeting and even read back responses from your Twitter followers. In doing so, you enlarge the room for your meetings and expand the ways stakeholders can participate.
- Another junior high principal shifted the majority of her school's communication to Facebook, having realized that it is one of the most readily accessible forms of communication for parents in the district. Having seen a substantial increase in the number of parents on Facebook, this principal obtains rapid responses to information she posts online. Use of Facebook also cut down on the amount of paper sent home with students. She is meeting parents where they already are. You can obtain similar results. After establishing a Facebook account for your school, you can direct the efforts of those who previously contributed to the school newsletter to provide the same information online, as it happens. There is no need to collect a week's worth of stories to publish in a paper newsletter. With a Facebook account, stories go out the day they are ready.
- An assistant principal found himself struggling to find creative ways to communicate with the approximately 650 students in the school, knowing that even on one's best day, it is impossible to talk to everyone. Using Twitter, the students could follow the assistant principal online. You can communicate with your students in the same way. In addition to establishing a school Twitter account, as a principal you

can establish your own account that you use for professional purposes. Once you have an account, encourage your students to follow you.

- Some school leaders are able to use Facebook and Twitter to branch out beyond the school community to advance their own professional development. In one case, a principal has been able to use Twitter to connect with other educators, administrators, researchers, and professors on the topic of educational administration, motivating him as never before due to the direct contact the platforms provide. The very same Twitter account you use to communicate with students is ideal for reaching out to colleagues and leaders in the field. Use your Twitter account to pose short questions to professors and researchers, or to join online chat sessions that occur via Twitter on education topics.

As principal Eric Sheninger (2011) notes, "Quite simply, social media tools such as Twitter and Facebook have improved my effectiveness and efficiency as an educational leader" (n.p.). In the next section, we provide some practical advice and tips on how to communicate using Facebook and Twitter.

TIPS ON COMMUNICATION
WITH FACEBOOK AND TWITTER

How best can one get started communicating with a school Facebook or Twitter account? Here we provide some tips on the kinds of content that are well suited for these media. In the next section, we provide a list of ways to establish Facebook and Twitter accounts for your school.

School principals who have not yet begun using Facebook and Twitter as part of a communication strategy with their community may believe that stakeholders only would want to read about the really innovative activities taking place in the school. However, many principals find that parents are very interested in receiving news on commonplace activities. Therefore consider posting everything, even the humdrum stuff. Post about the buddy reading going on in 5th grade. Talk about the new bulletin boards in the 4th grade wing, and so on.

Eric Sheninger has blogged extensively about his own use of Facebook and Twitter as a leader in his school. He created an official school Twitter account on which he communicates the following kinds of things (2011):

- School events (concerts, art shows, Back to School Night)
- Meetings (PTO, PTA, Athletic Boosters)
- School closings
- Live athletic scores, updates, and final results

- Student honors
- Teacher innovations
- Emergency information
- News

Sheninger also developed an instruction sheet that was disseminated to all parents. In spite of Twitter's growing use, it's not as popular as Facebook, and some parents may not know what Twitter is for or how to use it. The sheet provided an explanation on how to sign up, tips for using their smartphone (if they had one), and expectations for what kind of information they might receive.

He also created an official school Facebook page on which he posts all links to articles in the media that are important to the school community, pictures of events at the school, and videos that show what's going on at school. He also posts any information that goes out through the school's Twitter account.

CONCLUSION

As an increasing proportion of our world's population logs on to the Internet, it is becoming ever more obvious that our school children will thrive online. It is incumbent upon school leaders to be in that space, setting a positive example for how Facebook and Twitter can be a productive part of a school's strategy to communicate with students, parents, and the community.

What is our advice to principals who are not using Facebook or Twitter and are considering it? Review your district's social media and electronic communication policies, then just get started. Not only will you expand your ability to relate to your community more effectively, you will open up new channels that can humanize you in the eyes of your students. A principal in the study by Cox (2012) summed it up well:

> I think that that's been a benefit for me and for the students as a way that we could connect, and I think that sometimes the students, because you're not a teacher, they think you don't communicate. They see you as very different when you could kind of come out to the open and say, "I'm on Twitter, too!" and "I participate in social media just like everybody else." I just think it makes you a little bit more relevant. I think it makes you somebody that they can relate to a little bit better hopefully. (p. 95)

RESOURCES TO GET YOU GOING

The following websites provide information on the importance of social media, setting up Facebook and Twitter accounts for your school, tips from administrators on their use, and other useful resources. These resources were viable at the time of publication. Their inclusion does not suggest support of the individual organization or the information provided. Principals are encouraged to utilize their professional discretion.

Social Media and Two Way Communication
A blog post summarizing the key advantages school leaders accrue through the use of social media.
http://connectedprincipals.com/archives/5710

Why Public School Leaders Must Embrace Social Media Now
Key reasons why school leaders should use social media.
http://www.forbes.com/sites/dorieclark/2012/08/23/why-public-school-leaders-must-embrace-social-media-now/

Setting Up a School Twitter Account
Tips, tricks and terminology needed to successfully set up Twitter for your school.
http://www.teachprimary.com/learning_resources/view/setting-up-a-school-twitter-account

A Simple Guide to Set up Your School on Facebook
A no-nonsense guide on how to put your school on Facebook.
http://www.makeuseof.com/tag/a-simple-guide-to-set-up-your-school-on-facebook/

How to Use Twitter to Grow Your PLN
Advice on how to turn your Twitter account into a powerful personal learning network.
http://www.edutopia.org/blog/twitter-expanding-pln

Social Media is Not Just for Students
A blog post by Eric Sheninger on why social media is a valuable tool for educators.
http://esheninger.blogspot.com/2011/12/social-media-is-not-just-for-students.html

3 Principals Promote Learning with Mobile Devices and Social Media
A profile of three school leaders and their use of social media in their schools.
http://www.centerdigitaled.com/policy/Principals-Promote-Learning-Mobile-Devices-Social-Media.html

Humanizing Our Organizations Through Social Media
A perspective by George Couros on how social media can add a humanizing
     element to the work inside schools.
http://connectedprincipals.com/archives/6061

School Principals and Social Networking in Education: Policies,
Practices, and Realities in 2010
A research report with findings on how school principals use social media.
http://www.edweb.net/fimages/op/PrincipalsandSocialNetworking
     Report.pdf

REFERENCES

Cox, D. (2012). *School communications 2.0: A social media strategy for K–12 principals and superintendents.* Unpublished doctoral dissertation, Iowa State University, Ames, Iowa.

Engebritson, B. (2011). *Principals and blogs: In what ways does blogging support the practices of school principals.* Unpublished doctoral dissertation, University of Minnesota, Minneapolis, Minnesota.

Facebook. (2012). *Key facts.* Retrieved September 12, 2012 from http://newsroom. fb.com/content/default.aspx?NewsAreaId=22

Facebook. (n.d.). In *Wikipedia.* Retrieved September 12, 2012 from http:// en.wikipedia.org/wiki/Facebook

Hampton, K., Goulet, L., Marlow, C., & Rainie, L. (2012, February 3). *Why most Facebook users get more than they give. The effect of Facebook 'power users' on everybody else.* Pew Internet and American Life. Retrieved August 31, 2012 from http:// www.pewinternet.org/Reports/2012/Facebook-users.aspx

McMillan, G. (2011, September 9). *Twitter reveals active user number, how many actually say something.* Retrieved August 25, 2012 from http://techland.time. com/2011/09/09/twitter-reveals-active-user-number-how-many-actually-say-something/#ixzz26iABbgCh

PC Magazine Encyclopedia. (2012). *Definition of: Twitter.* Retrieved December 10, 2012 from http://www.pcmag.com/encyclopedia_term/0,1237,t=Twitter &i=57880,00.asp

Sheninger, E. (2011, December 21). *Social media is not just for students.* [Web log post]. Retrieved December 10, 2012 from http://esheninger.blogspot. com/2011/12/social-media-is-not-just-for-students.html

Smith, A., & Brenner, J. (2012, May 31). *Twitter use 2012.* Pew Internet and American Life. Retrieved September 12, 2012 from http://pewinternet.org/Reports/2012/Twitter-Use-2012.aspx

Weinberger, D. (2012). *Too big to know.* New York, NY: Basic Books.

PART III

SOCIOPOLITICAL CONTEXT
FOR TECHNOLOGY IN EDUCATION ·

CHAPTER 12

BALANCING EFFECTIVE TECHNOLOGY LEADERSHIP WITH LEGAL COMPLIANCE

Legal Considerations for Principal 2.0

Justin Bathon and Kevin P. Brady

INTRODUCTION

For today's reform-minded principals, especially those interested in utilizing some of the modern technologies profiled in this book, there loom roadblocks of rules that threaten to significantly limit or eliminate reform opportunities. These rules, in forms such as statutes, case law, or even district-level policy, are frequently perceived as substantial barriers to change. Sometimes, this is so. More often, however, when examining law and policy broadly through the eyes of digitally minded principals, the law actually encourages substantial reform in our schools. This is especially true of school leaders who are willing to understand the many nuances found inside legal structures and the increasing avenues available for change.

This chapter has three purposes. First, we examine the subtlety of school law and how that affects the modern building-level principal, both in terms

Principal 2.0: Technology and Educational Leadership, pages 185–209
Copyright © 2013 by Information Age Publishing
All rights of reproduction in any form reserved.

of challenges and opportunities. Second, this chapter provides a brief overview of some of the more contemporary and commonly asked-about legal issues that today's school leaders face involving technology in their schools. Finally, this chapter concludes with a series of practical approaches and best practices for dealing with legal issues in technology-rich schools.

LEADING TECHNOLOGY IN LEGAL ENVIRONMENTS

Our law in the United States is open to, and on the whole quite encouraging of, technological innovation and it frequently adapts itself to new technical realities. There are many examples of legal adaptability, but one often used to illustrate the point concerns property law. Before air travel, one who owned property owned it both infinitely downward and infinitely upward. Under this traditional definition, airspace was a patchwork of small plots and any air traveler would undoubtedly trespass many times even on a short flight. When this policy was brought before the Supreme Court in 1946, Justice William Douglas said this policy "has no place in the modern world.... Common sense revolts at this idea" in striking down what was up to that point an unquestioned element of property law (*United States v. Causby*). Even our Constitution, now well over 200 years old and written at a time when livestock were the primary means of travel, still serves as the foundational legal document in the age of artificial intelligence and space travel. It has been remarkably technologically adept.

Even schools, systems that have been notoriously slow to adapt, change their policies constantly to adapt to changing and emerging technologies. Today's digital principals are pushing on the same boundaries stretched many times before by earlier reformers. This reform trait is valued so highly in today's school leaders that legislatures across the country have enacted standards to require principals to view themselves as leaders of school change (ISLLC, 2008). Some states have even codified technological adaptability of school leaders into many state preparation laws through regulatory incorporation of the National Educational Technology Standards for Administrators (ISTE, 2009). The current 2009 NETS-A state the following five aspects of technology leadership standards for today's school leaders:

1. *Visionary Leadership:* Educational administrators inspire and lead development and implementation of a shared vision for comprehensive integration of technology to promote excellence and support transformation throughout the organization.
2. *Digital Age Learning Culture:* Educational administrators create, promote, and sustain a dynamic, digital-age learning culture that provides a rigorous, relevant, and engaging education for all students.

3. *Excellence in Professional Practice:* Educational administrators promote an environment of professional learning and innovation that empowers educators to enhance student learning through the infusion of contemporary technologies and digital resources.
4. *Systemic Improvement:* Educational administrators provide digital-age leadership and management to continuously improve the organization through the effective use of information and technology resources.
5. *Digital Citizenship:* Educational administrators model and facilitate understanding of social, ethical, and legal issues and responsibilities related to an evolving digital culture (NETS-A, 2009).

As adaptable as our legal system has proven over time, at any given moment the system is frequently many months or even years out of date with the leading edge of technology. For example, the courts are just now resolving the MySpace cases related to student Internet speech (*Barnett v. Tipton County Bd. of Educ.,* 2010). Law may find its way, but frequently only after trying several alternatives and waiting several years while the impact of the technology has time to mature. While there are cases where the policy toward adoption has outpaced the usefulness of the technology, smartboards for instance, most often potentially useful technologies are hindered by existing policy built for the previous technology. Thus, as examples in this book demonstrate, there are many new digital technologies over which the law has yet to have full control. Microblogging platforms such as Twitter have yet to manifest themselves in most formal school law either in an encouraging or discouraging way. This is not to say the law forbids their use, only that the law has not yet fully contemplated their use.

In fact, this distinction, between yet to regulate and regulation that either encourages or discourages, is an important one for legal purposes. Twitter is still largely unregulated; texting has been regulated in a highly discouraging way, but using email for basic communication has been regulated in a highly encouraging way. These three technologies, Twitter, texting, and email, represent three different stages in the somewhat standard adoption cycle. Any new technology is unregulated for a period of time while only early adopters explore the boundaries. Some of these trials end in calamity and find their way to newspaper headlines, thus generally sparking a discouragement cycle. Then, if the technology proves overwhelmingly useful, such as email, the law actually reverses itself into an encouragement cycle, even if a new technology has come along to supplant it in the interim.

Yet, we also see different regulatory aims between the local and state or federal level. Local policies, which may react more quickly to new technologies, frequently seek to regulate the technology itself. For instance, many schools have adopted cell phone bans or regularly seek to prohibit particular websites. At the local level, there has been a far more strident approach to Facebook regulation. At the state or federal level, typically laws are aimed at regulating human activity, not particular technologies. Recent legislation has sought to limit bullying, as an example, not the social networks on which it happens. Not surprisingly, when behavior is regulated rather than a particular technology, it has to be updated much less frequently. For instance, acceptable use policies that frequently mention specific technologies are regularly updated to account for changes, while the 1969 standard for student disruption, a behavior, is still controlling in the courts (*Tinker v. Des Moines Independent Community School District*, 1969).

The following section provides a short overview of the law on a variety of topics that have been impacted by recent technology changes. The impacts of these new technologies have been vast and have affected many different areas of law, of which we provide just a sample. Further, this chapter does not permit a full investigation of these issues, and school administrators are encouraged to do their own research when facing technology implementation concerns. Investigating these legal issues when considering new technologies is significant because the school leader is in a unique and solitary position of understanding both the learning opportunities and the legal ramifications. Teachers may underestimate the legal issues, and school attorneys may underestimate the learning opportunities. Thus, it is imperative for today's school leader to be the decision maker after considering both the opportunities and the concerns of emerging technologies.

LEGAL ISSUES FOR SCHOOLS IMPACTED BY TECHNOLOGY

To assist technology leaders in making these crucial decisions as instructional leaders, in this section, we attempt both to answer questions that are frequently asked of us when speaking with school administrators in both a legal and technology advisory role as well as to offer a few additional legal issues that might be under most principals' radar. This list emerges from years of consulting with local school leaders about the everyday challenges they currently face and is by no means exhaustive. In fact, from a legal standpoint, some of these questions are probably even a bit distracting from the more central and challenging technological concerns in schools. However, because some of these issues have a tendency to instill a negative perception of technology in schools, we answer them in this chapter to encourage school leaders to find a degree of comfort in responding to these issues in schools. In calming some fears on these less legally challenging questions, we hope to give principals the confidence to respond to the more challenging instructional areas necessary for providing our students with the 21st-century education that they deserve.

Students: Free Speech and Expression

Perhaps the question that we receive most often, in some form or another, is one related to students engaging in misbehavior online. This happens frequently in schools; therefore, as a principal, you will have to address the issue of student online speech eventually. The potential for students to misbehave, of course, exists across nearly all communication technologies mentioned in this book as well as on the telephone, the chalkboard, and on paper. The issue is not new and as a result this is one of the easiest questions to answer as the law in this area has been generally settled for decades. The technology used, perhaps surprisingly, is actually a somewhat irrelevant question in this analysis. Broadly, principals should regulate as if the behavior were not online, as long as there is a strong relationship between any out-of-school conduct and the school environment. If, in an offline environment, the speech would be protected, it is likely protected speech online as well. To determine whether speech is protected for students, we ask a fairly standard and hopefully rote series of questions first articulated by the *Tinker v. Des Moines* (1969), *Bethel v. Fraser* (1986), *Hazelwood v. Kuhlmeier* (1988) and *Morse v. Frederick* (2007) analysis.

Again, this analysis is applicable no matter the technology used in expressing the speech. The only additional question in this standard equation is simply whether the speech that occurs outside of school substantially affects the school environment. If it does not, then the school has no legal authority to regulate the out-of-school conduct. New communication technologies, of course, have increased the amount of out-of-school speech that becomes public. Thus, there has been a rise in the amount of litigation on the topic of regulation of off-campus speech in recent years (Brady, 2011; Daniel, 2011; McCarthy, 2012). For school leaders who seek to regulate off-campus Internet speech, and certainly there are instances that warrant regulation, they must be prepared to defend their actions both in the relationship to the school and the actual disruption that occurred (*Layshock v. Hermitage School District*, 2010; *J.S. v. Blue Mountain School District*, 2011).

Students: Searching Cell Phones

Do today's students have an expectation of privacy on their cell phones while at school? The rapid and extensive use of cell phones by school children led to the enactment by some school districts of school board policies designated to regulate student possession and the use of cell phones in today's schools (Russo & Mawdsley, 2012). This everyday legal issue depends on many factors. As it relates to student searches, the prevailing legal standard involving student searches is that of reasonableness. According to *New Jersey v. T.L.O.* (1985), students are legally protected by the U.S. Constitution's Fourth Amendment against unreasonable searches and seizures. The United States Supreme Court held that "maintaining security and order in the schools requires a certain degree of flexibility in school disciplinary procedures, and we have respected the value of preserving the informality of the student–teacher relationship" (*New Jersey v. T.L.O.*, pp. 340–341).

Emerging technologies, including cell phones, personal digital assistants, tablets, and smartphones all raise important legal questions regarding the authority of educators to seize, search, and inspect the contents of these devices. The central issue is whether students have an expectation of privacy that outweighs the authority of educators to search, seize, or even ban their possession and use in schools. There is certainly a strong argument for school administrators in prohibiting or searching cell phones in schools with the primary objective of eliminating student disruptions and harassment, or to discourage cheating on exams. On the other hand, there is also a strong case for students having access to their phones in the event of an emergency either at school or at home.

Under the U.S. Constitution's Fourth Amendment, legally permissible searches in a school environment must be deemed "reasonable." The U.S. Supreme Court ruled in *New Jersey v. T.L.O.* (1985) that "[t]he accommodation of . . . the substantial need of teachers and administrators for freedom to maintain order in the schools does not require strict adherence to the requirement that searches be based on probable cause" (T.L.O., 469 U.S. at 341). Instead, the rules governing student searches require a two-step inquiry. First, school officials must determine whether the decision to search a student was "justified at its inception"; second, school officials must determine whether the student search "was reasonably related in scope to the circumstances which justified the interference in the first place" (p. 341).

First, principals should understand the distinction between searching for possession of a cell phone and searching the contents of a cell phone. Searching for possession of a cell phone in violation of school rules is the same as searching for possession of any other banned object. The more unsettled legal area is how far an educator can go in terms of content searches of student cell phones. To date, there have been a total of five legal cases cited specifically involving student cell phone searches in K–12 public education. Three of the five legal cases upheld a school's right to enforce policies that prohibit cell phones and other technological devices on school premises (*Price v. New York City Bd. of Education*, 2008; *Lancy v. Farley*, 2007; *Requa v. Kent School District No. 415*, 2007). The two remaining legal cases, *Miller v. Skumananick* (2009) and *Klump v. Nazareth Area School District* (2006) address the decision of officials to search the content of cell phones, and in both, local officials potentially overstepped constitutional bounds. In *Klump*, the legal case most often cited on the subject of student cell phones, a teacher confiscated a student's cell phone because it was visible during class, a violation of school policy. Both a teacher and an assistant principal searched the student's cell phone's number directory and attempted to call nine other students at the school to determine whether they too were in violation of the school's policy. The teacher and assistant principal also accessed the student's text and voice mail messages and communicated with the student's brother without telling them they were school staff. The Court held that school officials were justified in seizing the cell phone but should not have used the student's cell phone to catch other students in violation of the school's cell phone policy. In *Miller*, a district attorney prosecuting a case of "sexting," the common name of the practice of sending nude or sexual images via cell phone, had a temporary restraining order granted against him by the girls who were the nude subjects of the texts because of the likelihood of a viable free expression claim in the content of the photos (2009). While these cases do not always result in findings against school officials (see, for instance, *S.B. v. Saint James School*, 2006, where school officials were found to not invade the privacy of students investigating sexting by demanding copies of the offending files), the situation is uncommonly risky from a legal standpoint.

As these cases illustrate, the potential for school administrators to cross constitutional boundaries while searching the contents of a student's cell phone is relatively high. Thus, school officials should seek to craft specific policies for student cell phone searches and to err on the side of caution in conducting these searches. If legitimate criminal action is suspected, such as sexting or drug use, it would be wise to involve the police, district attorney or other criminal law authority to conduct the searches. These same cautions also apply to other student- or parent-owned devices such as laptops in bring-your-own-device districts. Given the growing presence of cell phones and other technological devices in schools, school leaders and their lawyers should regularly review their student search policies. Equally important, when student search policies are updated, school leaders need to keep parents and students informed of the modifications in policy in multiple venues, including newsletters, student handbooks, and on the school's web site. An additional value of regularly reviewing and updating student search policies is evidence to convince courts that school administrators are doing their best to be up-to-date while simultaneously safeguarding the rights of students given rapid changes in both the law and technology.

Students: CyberBullying and Online Harassment

One of the more frequent issues that arises anytime there is a discussion of technology and legal issues is cyberbullying. This issue has received many headlines, and there have been many sad stories of bullying in electronic environments, especially from anonymous sources. Stories like those of Rachel Ehmke, a Minnesota seventh-grader who committed suicide after months of bullying (Post, 2012), are too frequent. Rachel was bullied at school, but could not even find a reprieve at home as students sent text messages with inappropriate name-calling. Although the school had a policy against online teasing or bullying, the parents of the deceased student still felt they should have done more. These shocking headlines have generated a considerable amount of literature on the subject, including some entire books dedicated to the issue (Daniel, 2011; Hinduja & Patchin, 2009; Shariff, 2008; Trolley & Hanel, 2010).

While there has been a considerable amount of attention to the specific issue of cyberbullying in society and schools, there has only been minor treatment of the specific issue in case law. Elected officials, though, have been somewhat more responsive. Quite a number (45 of 50) of states have formally enacted anti-bullying educational legislation. Of those, 31 states have anti-bullying laws that include electronic harassment, and six states have anti-bullying laws that specifically mention cyberbullying. Although this legislation is a step in the right direction, problems do exist. Most important, such legislation lacks consistent language between states that would uniformly recognize the authority of educators to regulate student conduct that takes the form of cyberbullying. In addition, there is little uniformity of language in general and a great disparity of what behavior is actionable or protected. Thus, even among those laws that address electronic harassment, like most anti-bullying laws of the past decade, they serve mostly to simply encourage schools to adopt policy on the topic. This policy adoption requirement thus does not create a more substantial legal analysis or remedy, such as a student or parental private right of action against the school for failure to address cyberbullying.

Even if these recent laws are mostly a paper tiger, schools still have broad capacity to regulate student misbehavior in both digital and traditional formats, and the awareness raised by the legislation has drawn further attention to this power for school officials. This regulatory ability easily covers the kind of misbehavior that we commonly call cyberbullying. Teasing, hazing, name-calling, and other behavior that affects students in the school is, as it always has been, subject to regulation and punishment by school authorities, whether digital or not. Thus, school administrators confronting incidents of cyberbullying that implicate students in school should immediately stop the offending behavior and discipline the offending student appropriately. Paying close attention to, and acting aggressively to stop, incidents of bullying and harassment not only satisfies the baseline legal requirements (see Dayton, Dupre, & Blackenship, 2011), but also is just good practice for a school leader.

Teacher: Free Speech and Expression

Teacher expression in online, off-campus environments is related to student expression, but has an entirely different legal analysis. Of late, these questions always seem to involve the social networking platform, Facebook. The digital archive of most people, including teachers, is increasingly extensive, and the likelihood of something inappropriate in that history is substantial. The default position of existing conversations on the Internet is both open and always recorded, while the default position of conversations in the teachers' lounge is both private and fleeting. Because of some of these technical differences, schools have had to deal with much more of their teachers' personal lives than ever before. Unlike student expression, there has been a substantial legal change in the teacher expression analysis in support of even greater regulatory flexibility on the part of the school. First, if teacher expression does not qualify as protected by the Constitution, it can be regulated through the various teacher discipline mechanisms, long established. First, as an employer, the school has the authority to regulate the non-protected behavior of its employees. Schools, especially, are provided wide latitude on this issue because of the "higher standard" that teachers are held to. This regulatory authority stems also from teacher discipline and termination statutes that typically allow for termination for insubordination, inadequate performance, incapacity, immorality, and the other state-specified grounds for dismissal. Immorality, in particular, provides wide grounds for regulatory authority. In regulating teacher expression, though, school leaders must keep the substantial procedural requirements in mind, particularly if the teachers in the district collectively bargain or have tenure rights.

The constitutional analysis is a complex one only if the conduct is outside of the scope of employment of the teacher (Bathon & Brady, 2010). In other words, if the employee expression occurred in their role as an employee, there is no constitutional protection (*Garcetti v. Ceballos*, 2006). Only conduct outside of the scope of employment is potentially protected. If it relates to a matter of public concern, the *Pickering v. Board of Education* (1968) balancing test asks whether the public interest served by the expression outweighs the school's interest in efficient administration. Finally, as in cases related to student speech, courts have employed a de facto analysis of whether the teacher's off-campus conduct bears any relationship to the school environment before permitting the school the ability to regulate.

School Devices

An issue of increasing relevance for school districts is student and teacher usage of school-owned devices. Recently, with the large-scale implementation of one-to-one (1:1) student computing initiatives, schools have begun to provide both their teachers and students with school-owned devices to support teaching and learning, respectively. This has brought with it some new legal issues that schools must contemplate in addition to the burgeoning research on program effectiveness (Fleischer, 2012).

First, teachers, like most people, do not do a good job distinguishing between professional and personal uses of a device. If teachers have been given an iPad, they are going to use it both for lesson plans and for Facebook, both during the school day and at home. While doing so, they will not distinguish between the two different uses, or the appropriateness thereof. This mixing of professional and personal is simply the nature of the Internet. While our modern lives may be structured in this very ill-defined way, the law still uses roles as a distinguishing characteristic. Thus, if a teacher is using a publicly owned device, that device is subject to federal or state open records request; it is creating discoverable electronic records, and there are some purposes for which it cannot be used. For instance, teachers should not be making personal political donations on publicly owned devices. While this issue is less legally troublesome for students, the potential implications for bullying and other misbehavior with public devices should be obvious.

Schools have chosen to deal with this issue in a number of ways. First, some schools have eschewed the 1:1 device distribution concept in favor of a "bring your own device" concept, where although the devices use the public network during school hours, the private activities remain private. This relatively new concept has yet to be fully vetted, but obvious legal issues such as equitable access to technology are immediately apparent. The equal protection clause of the 14th Amendment, for instance, is very harsh on school policies that have a discriminatory impact on particular classes of students. Thus, with any policy like this relying on private wealth to support learning, the school must provide a mechanism for low-income, limited English proficient, or disabled students to have access to the same device and information.

Another technique that schools use to limit liability is to require all school owned devices to continue to use the school or state filters before accessing the Internet. While what must be filtered is constantly changing and students continue to find proxies around such filters, at minimum it shows that the school did not ignore the issue. Further, as with students, schools distributing devices to their employees should also require that employees sign a responsible use agreement that articulates some of the prohibited uses and passes personal liability, or at least attempts to, onto teachers for any misuse. Finally, a specific and regular education program on acceptable device usage, for both students and teachers, is mandatory. Not only does this fulfill new federal legal requirements (Protecting Children in the 21st Century Act, 2008), but it also provides some shield from future legal liability when the inevitable issues surrounding improper device usage emerge.

Filtering and Acceptable Use Policies

Acceptable Use Policies (AUP), a standard first-week document sent home to parents for their signatures, are now heavily engrained into the school's policy and technology infrastructure. These documents arrived in the late 1990s after the passage of the Telecommunications Act of 1996 that, for the first time, provided schools and libraries part of the Universal Service Fund, known as E-Rate. To receive E-Rate discounts on technology purchases, schools had to adopt policies providing for the safe use of these technologies. The particular law that requires such safety regulations is the Children's Internet Protection Act (CIPA, 1996), which has been upheld by the Supreme Court (U.S. v. American Library Association, 2003). This federal mandate has manifested itself both in the broad use of filters by schools but also in the form of the AUP. In recent years, there has been some reconsideration of how best to implement the aims of CIPA as the filters have been somewhat relaxed and AUPs have been rewritten. Even the federal government has shifted a bit from a pure safety mentality to more of an education mentality. This is a result of the passage of the Protecting Children in the 21st Century Act (2008), which was scheduled for initial implementation in the fall of 2012. Many state laws that require schools to regulate in specific ways have supplemented these federal laws, which are rather broad and ambiguous. These state laws are further supplemented by local policy that dictates the specific device, software, and Internet policies applicable in the school. Thus, if one feels these policies are too restrictive, the restriction is likely either a state or local decision and not a direct result of the federal laws.

Technology leaders of schools, particularly instructional designers, do typically grate against both the filters and the district or state versions of the AUPs, as they can sometimes restrict legitimate technology tools. The specific elements of the AUP are a decision for the school board. To change the local policy on either of these issues, a school leader must convince the school board, probably the school attorney, and perhaps even a lawyer at the state school board's association or other state policy guidance body that relaxation of these standards is appropriate. School leaders should also encourage these bodies to implement policies that have inherent flexibility at the discretion of the school leader as to which technologies teachers and students may use.

Assistive Technology

Over the past decade, evolving technologies and their integration into the classroom have unquestionably changed previous teaching approaches and methods by which students with disabilities and special needs were educated. Although not a new concept or practice in the educational community, assistive technology, often referred to as AT, has made a notably dramatic impact toward increasing the functional as well as educational capabilities of students with disabilities. The type of assistive technologies available to students with disabilities is extensive, including not only computer hardware and software, but also relatively low-cost technology applications, commonly called "apps" on Apple iTunes or a host of other open-source application-based websites for use on mobile technology devices, including smartphones or tablet-based computers, such as Apple's iPad.

From a legal perspective, AT is defined under federal law in the Individuals with Disabilities Education Act (IDEA, 2006) as any piece of technological equipment that can be used to support or enhance individuals as they achieve, improve, or continue the skills necessary for learning, daily living, and recreation. AT results from a process that is highly individualized, comprehensive, and self-validating. AT, as it is addressed by the federal mandate, allows for the individualization, comprehensive design and implementation, and data collection and analysis necessary for ensuring an effective method of technology integration.

With respect to the use of AT by students with disabilities, the IDEA contains a number of relevant legal provisions that address these very issues and should inform school principals of their proper use and application. Thus, the AT provisions in the IDEA are yet another example of how the law calls specifically for individualized instruction and the collection of supporting data that document the effectiveness of this instruction to ensure that a student with a disability realizes meaningful benefit from the special education services he receives. Concerning AT, these provisions include proper evaluations, comprehensive program design and implementation, and validating data collection and analysis. In summary, any decisions regarding the provision of assistive technology to students with special needs or disabilities should be based on the comprehensive data associated with a student's needs (Osborne, 2012). While it is not necessary to conduct a formal assistive technology evaluation on any student with disabilities, an evaluation should be completed any time the issue is raised by parents or the Individualized Education Plan team feels that the assistive technology may be required to fulfill the legal obligation of a free and appropriate education (FAPE) for the student. While providing assistive technology to students with disabilities may be expensive, it can often be an effective tool in meeting the IDEA's FAPE legal obligation, and school leaders need to monitor the emerging legal compliance laws involving the provision of assistive technologies to students with disabilities.

Moreover, as states have developed assessment systems for the purpose of addressing relevant parts of the No Child Left Behind (NCLB) Act of 2001, they have created lists of allowable accommodations that can be used by students with disabilities when they participate in statewide assessments of student achievement. This includes protocols for the use of these accommodations on a daily basis in the classroom. Accommodations do not enable a student to alter the content standards she is required to master but do allow her to use different ways to demonstrate mastery of the content (e.g., orally state rather than write responses), or to demonstrate mastery of the content during different, yet acceptable, testing conditions (e.g., complete the exam in a small group arrangement rather than a large group arrangement or take additional time to complete the material).

While the details of these special education assistive technologies are frequently the responsibility of the special education director, it is still your job as the principal to ensure that your school is providing the best learning options to your students and that your school is informed of the latest technologies. While knowing each assistive technology is beyond the scope of your position, requiring your special education staff to attend technology-based professional development sessions certainly is within your responsibilities.

Copyright

A continuing issue with technology and schools is the difficult application of copyright law. In recent years, technology continues to enable greater copying ability of nearly everything digital. In her book, *Copyright Clarity,* Renee Hobbs (2010) provides one of the more extensive treatments of the issue, ultimately concluding that fair-use protections for users of copyrighted content provide enough protection for teachers to be effective in the digital age. The fair use guidelines state that educators and other users can use a copy of a protected work when after considering these factors: (1) the purpose and character of the use, (2) the nature of the copyrighted work, (3) the amount of the work used, and (4) the market effect—on balance, the use is not overly offensive to the copyright holder (Silberberg, 2001). There is further definition for educators provided by the Copyright Office that provides definition to the additional determinates of brevity, spontaneity, and cumulative effect. The definition of brevity, though, is somewhat brief in the level of detail that it provides: A poem of less than 250 words or less than two pages is the extent of the definition of brief (U. S. Copyright

Office, 2009). Copying anything longer, assumedly, does not meet the definition of brevity.

To institute these fair use guidelines, schools have taken different approaches. Some districts seek to articulate, with an amazing level of detail, their policies on copyright of each particular type of media. On the other hand, some districts choose to adopt a fairly broad copyright policy that places the general onus on teachers or students for copyright violations. As a practical matter, especially for smaller districts, the latter approach seems more reasonable as the technology is changing so rapidly that a district could spend a considerable amount of time every year just modifying the copyright policy. Further, technology leaders who understand the general purpose of copyright, to protect and encourage the creation of new ideas, will have a better sense of those instances in which making unauthorized copies substantially violates the aims of copyright or exceeds the flexibility of the Fair Use Guidelines. This advice comes with the caveat that the one type of copyright violation that will lead to the most disputes is in copying material produced by companies that sell materials directly to schools. Because unauthorized copying of their products will result in potential lost revenue, they are more likely to sue the school under copyright law. This includes both learning content companies, such as textbook publishers, and technology companies that sell software to schools.

Electronic Records

The maintenance, storage, and production of electronic records are an underappreciated area of technology law that implicates schools, especially as more and more information becomes paperless. While a deep understanding of this area is beyond the scope of this chapter (see Fatino, 2003), the simple fact to understand is that things stored on school computers or other devices are both public information capable of state and federal Freedom of Information Act (FOIA) requests (keeping in mind the FERPA exception for students) and potential evidence in lawsuits, thus subject to e-discovery under the Federal Rules of Civil Procedure (U. S. Supreme Court, 2010). What this means in practical terms is that school email and other data, including the metadata about all this digital information, is public and, especially if involved in a lawsuit, discoverable. It is a lesson that some, such as the former superintendent of Des Moines and Omaha City Schools who resigned after sexual emails were requested (Robb, Ruggles, & Dejka, 2012), have learned the hard way. Each school should have an established policy and procedure for making a FOIA request of the district and should also have an established policy and procedure for the maintenance and, more importantly, the dumping of data after the required period of storage is completed. State and local policies on the length or necessity of data storage vary considerably, and the school district attorney is a good source for information on these regulations.

From a practical standpoint, school leaders need to heavily reinforce with both staff and students the public nature of their actions in electronic environments. Both students and staff have a false sense of security in these digital technologies. While only one person may be in the address line of an email, every public employee should also consider the whole world included in the email. Tell your staff that every email they send from school accounts carries with it an additional "wcc" line that is always present: the "world carbon copy."

Open Meetings

Another underappreciated area where technology has impacted school law is in the open meeting requirements for schools (sometimes called sunshine laws). The issue centers on the new communication outlets for various school officials, but particularly for school boards or local school councils. School leaders cannot engage with these boards as groups in digital environments, even including email, because this violates the public notice and access requirements for all such meetings (*Johnson v. Metro. Government of Nashville and Davidson County*, 2009; also see Texas Attorney General Opinion GA-0896, 2011). Thus, when working with board members in particular, principals and superintendents must be cautious that they are not working in a quorum or otherwise triggering the open meetings laws. These open meeting laws have also come into question as the public increasingly seeks to record, and subsequently post to the Internet, these officials during the meetings. There are generally no prohibitions against this type of recording, and school leaders should encourage board members and other officials to be patient and forgiving with such attempts as a natural byproduct of an open democracy. How deeply these laws will impact school leaders in the future is an open question as technology facilitates ever greater opportunities for sharing with the public (Sherman, 2011).

Online Schooling

A rapidly developing area of schooling that is facilitated by technology is the proliferation of online schooling, either as a supplement to the traditional educational program or through full-time online schools called cybercharters (Brady, Umpstead & Eckes, 2010). In 2011 it was estimated that there were more than 40 states permitting supplemental course enrollments with over 536,000 enrolled students and more than 30 states authorizing online, full-time education with 250,000 students (Watson, Murin, Vashaw, Gemin, & Rapp, 2011). In a national report by the Sloan Consortium titled, *K–12 Online Learning: A Survey of U.S. School District Administrators*, online and blended courses, or those courses that combine online and face-to-face course delivery, grew 47% between 2005–2006 and 2007–2008 (Picciano & Seaman, 2007). In fact, blended courses, or those courses that combine both online and traditional face-to-face, has emerged as the model believed to be the most effective in merging the best instructional practices from both online and traditional face-to-face instruction (Horn & Staker, 2011).

Increasingly, schools are offering online learning options to their students, and there are a variety of new legal issues that principals must contend with when students are working online. Because this new educational option does not rely on many of the traditional assumptions of the legal system, such as student location in a school building, much of the school law we have come to know in the United States does not fit neatly. For instance, our system of teacher evaluation that includes classroom observation, does not easily apply, and principals who supervise teachers in online environments must either improvise a new evaluation system or write a new policy with which to conduct this necessary part of the principal's role. Legislatures, to this point, have been of little help to school leaders on these issues as most online schooling-enabling legislation is merely concerned with issues of funding, teacher qualifications, and student testing (Glass & Welner, 2011). Thus, on most issues related to supplemental online education, principals are asked to apply the existing laws, policies, and standards to the online environment to the best of their abilities.

For principals who are hired into newly created online education programs, such as cyber-charter schools, there is a further challenge. Because these new entities are typically created from scratch, there are no existing policies in the district upon which to base everyday decisions. In these unique circumstances, principals must create new policy regularly in the course of the first few years of existence of the new school. When creating these policies, principals first need to understand and keep in mind the state cyber-charter authorizing legislation, as it is substantially different in each state (Brady et al., 2010). If multiple districts combine to form a new cyber-charter school such as is the case in Colorado (Colorado Revised Statutes Annotated, 22-30.7-105, 2012), while neither of the authorizing district's policy applies directly, principals may choose to borrow from one or the other authorizing district in establishing new policies for the school. On the other hand, in a state like Pennsylvania (24 P. S. 17-1743-A, 2012), the paperwork requirements are much more stringent and must be delivered to the districts in which a student resides upon request. As a result, working as a school leader in these new virtual environments frequently demands more detailed policies in an environment in which there is less existing policy upon which to rely.

As should be apparent, online schools represent a deeper challenge to the legal infrastructure underlying schools. Online schools are an example of the much more fundamental changes to the educational infrastructure that many have predicted will be facilitated and accelerated by technology (Christensen, Horn & Johnson, 2010; Vander Ark & Wise, 2011). This type of change to the education system will have many more profound legal consequences and generate a great deal more litigation in the future. For principals exploring these spaces, the opportunities are immeasurable, but so too are the legal concerns. In these situations the best advice may be to proceed boldly, with a very healthy dose of common sense.

GUIDANCE FOR TODAY'S SCHOOL TECHNOLOGY LEADERS

Amid all of this turmoil in the law, and assuredly there is much more to come, principals face a difficult task in the everyday implementation of technology-rich learning. To attempt to fully understand all of the applicable laws or predict the legal outcomes in the various novel cases happening each day in the school would not only be impossible, but a distraction from the instructional leadership role so desperately needed from principals. Thus, principals must act practically. The following paragraphs provide some practical advice for working with new technologies and learning environments in schools.

Old Standards, New Applications

New technologies do not emerge into a legal vacuum. Instead, until new law takes effect, the existing standards applicable to old technologies are still the laws. Thus, principals must apply these standards to new circumstances. Sometimes this is easy, such as with student speech, and sometimes this is complex, such as with copyright law. Such application, though, must be a part of the overall process. District boards of education, regulatory oversight panels, and the courts will tolerate a certain degree of new interpretation of old standards, but they will not tolerate ignoring what is still, unquestionably, applicable law. A certain amount of creativity is required of principals in applying the old standards to new applications. The meaning of *disruptive* in terms of student cell phones, for instance, might change as the technology advances and pedagogy changes. Generally, the courts will support the schools in these new applications if there is documented evidence that the legal standards were considered and interpreted differently within the new context. Without documented evidence of a new interpretation, though, the courts have little choice but to rule that ad hoc new interpretations are at best inequitable and at worse a blatant disregard for the law.

Change the Law

Perhaps surprisingly, this might be easier than most initially think. The vast majority of the law that affects an average school day takes the form of district, school, and classroom policies. These are not especially difficult to change from a bureaucratic standpoint. The larger challenge in changing these policies is usually political in nature, but convincing a reluctant school board or working with teachers to see new possibilities is what we expect of our education leaders. Further, changing state regulations is also, likely, easier than the average principal believes. In fact, we have found state regulators to be usually quite open to changes, and pleased to receive practitioner or scholar feedback as well. The following represent some keys to changing policy and regulation, in our experience.

1. *Do your homework.* People are reluctant to take a chance on your ideas if you do not already know the basics such as: (a) what other laws are implicated, (b) what is the exact bureaucratic process from start to finish, and (c) what people need to be involved in this conversation, among others. Your homework shows your seriousness and dedication, traits that are attractive to policymakers.
2. *Work the backchannels.* Every person who has decision-making authority about your policy change should have already been aware and had an opportunity to ask questions about the policy. To have these conversations will require you to expend some effort to understand what other individuals can facilitate these conversations. Typically, there is an individual that both you and the decision-maker know and trust. Approaching decision-makers in this way allows them to provide you critical feedback through a safe backchannel so that you can meet their needs in your policy changes.
3. *Go in with a draft.* It is not enough want change; you have to articulate, clearly and precisely, what policy should be changed, and how. Think of your draft as a prototype. It is not perfect or polished, but it has to convey the basic idea, and it has to work at a rudimentary level. If the prototype is decent, impossibility is off the table as an option, and the debate must then center on the value of the traditional policy against the new alternative.

4. *Sell it.* Perhaps you prefer to think of it as "advocacy" instead of "sales," but the bottom line is that no one will make the pitch for you, which is good, because no one can make the pitch as well as you. In advocating for the change, though, be sure to employ tactics other than just the sheer force of your reason and a PowerPoint. For instance, let a child talk about how the change would help students or bring an expert to help you answer questions. Creativity can be critical as you advocate for change.

Regulate the Activity, Not the Technology

Schools have a tendency to react to new technologies by attacking the technology. This rarely works over time. Technologies such as texting, smartphones, and Facebook are simply tools and will inevitably find their way into schools whether or not they are sanctioned activities. This type of reaction to any new particular technology can eliminate the benefits while encouraging the detriments. Teachers told not to use texting as a tool likely will not. Students told not to use texting likely will use it more. The potential educational benefit is sacrificed to address technical concerns often stemming from a lack of familiarity with the tool. This eliminates both instructional and disciplinary flexibility, the very flexibility needed to navigate the tricky new terrain. Instead, policies designed to regulate the activity provide the option of educational benefit while retaining an even broader ability to regulate any misbehavior. This approach has the added benefit that policies do not have to be updated as frequently as Friendster changes to MySpace that changes to Facebook that changes to Google Plus, with Twitter, Tumblr, Posterous and Pinterest along the way, among many others. Trying to regulate specific technologies is simply not an efficient use of your time as a school leader.

Ask Your Friends and Neighbors

It is shocking how little principals know about the policies in surrounding districts. They hold not only one of your best arguments for change, but frequently a how-to guide as well. In all likelihood, your school or district is not the first to implement a new technology or operational method. Other districts have already struggled, tried alternatives, and have the lessons you need. One of the first places you should turn when struggling with a law or policy in your school is to your friends and neighbors. Once you find a neighboring policy that seems promising, the second place you should turn is deep into their district or school policies. In our experience, the most technologically adept schools and school leaders are constantly borrowing ideas and policies from other places. There is no need to reinvent the wheel. Find one that works somewhere else, and you might find that most of the hard work has already been done.

Do Not Forget or Ignore Special Populations

From special education to socioeconomic status to linguistic differences, there are real and important implications for all special populations within the school when new technologies are adopted. The varied implications of new technologies can have both beneficial and detrimental effects on diverse students, especially in large, school-sponsored installations such as 1:1 or bring-your-own-device programs. In these installations, the potential for discrimination is very high. This potential lies deeper than just making sure students have a device that is useful to them. As schools come to increasingly rely on the Internet for learning, there is a real issue with the predominantly English nature of the platform for non-English speaking students. Also, in our rush to publish new content to the Internet, schools are sometimes ignoring ADA compliance guidelines (U.S. Department of Justice, 2010; see also U.S. Department of Justice, 2003 on state and local government websites) so that disabled students can access the information. Because of the complexity of these issues, schools may have a tendency to overlook the needs of these special populations. Doing so not only opens the school to liability but also is bad ethical practice for a school leader.

The School Attorney Works for You, Not the Other Way Around

School attorneys have a lot of influence over schools, but they are not educators. Principals are tasked with leading schools, and attorneys are tasked with advising them. Ultimately, learning decisions rest with you, not your attorney. School attorneys are frequently in a difficult position because most school leaders rely on them to make some of the hard choices easy. Because they work for the client school district, they want to make the client happy and frequently assume that providing schools with an easy, safe legal answer is best for their bottom line. If, however, you make clear that your bottom line, student learning, is what is best for their bottom line, school attorneys can be wonderful partners that provide advice to school leaders, including school boards, that facilitates greater technology support for student learning. If your school attorney is not comfortable with this arrangement or is entrenched against technology generally, recommend that the school board find a different one.

Partner with Colleges and Universities

The ivory tower frequently is just that, and it can be frustrating trying to reach individuals in higher education. But take advantage of what universities can offer. There are uses for a tower: They can see things you cannot on the ground, as universities frequently can make connections with similar schools or experts both locally and globally. Further, there is a great deal of respect in the ivory. When a university is involved in the implementation of a pilot project, vets a new policy proposal, or evaluates a new technology tool, it provides a trusted third party upon which to improve the project. Also, universities function within a broader circle of influence and can make connections not available to local practitioners. For example, a school in Delaware might have just dealt with an extremely similar issue to your school in New Mexico. University scholars are more likely to make and exploit that connection. Further, colleges of education are rapidly changing to a more practitioner-friendly approach (Williams, Atkinson, Cate & O'Hair, 2008). Colleges such as both the University of Kentucky and North Carolina State University, our employers, are even developing new well-funded units to work exclusively with local schools and leaders on technology driven change initiatives.

Pressure Leadership Preparation Programs

As university preparation programs open their doors to educators and their current needs, a new opportunity has arisen for principals to influence preparation programs to prepare school leaders for next generation schools, rather than the previous generation systems from which the instructors might have emerged. Because of market forces, employee inertia, and other factors, universities can be slow to adapt to changing learning conditions. Ultimately, though, principal candidates and alumni are the primary customers of leadership preparation programs and thus hold a lot of influence over their activities. If we are to have technology-savvy school leaders, their preparation must have an explicit focus on elements of technology leadership, and the instructors must be technology leaders themselves. This is particularly true in the area of school law since, as this chapter has demonstrated, there are so many legal issues currently impacted by new technologies. Unfortunately, most school law instructors in the United States are anything but technology leaders. Many school law instructors are still advising against technology in schools. They confuse the most legally *safe* learning policies for the most legally *sensible* learning policies, teaching black letter school law from textbooks, which, by necessity, report stable law rather than innovative trends or new technologies. Many leadership preparation programs are preparing leaders for school conditions that no longer exist and, surely, will not exist in the career cycle of young educational leaders. Preparation programs must do better, and you must not only hold them accountable, but, more importantly, help them to reform.

CONCLUSION

This chapter started with an eccentric proposition, that the law actually encourages innovation in schools on the whole. After an examination of some of the many changing legal issues in schools, one cannot be blamed for seeing roadblocks, or, at minimum, mass confusion. But to see only the roadblocks or the confusion is to focus too narrowly. The broader picture shows that there are full-time cyber-charter schools now operating in over half the states. Districts are rapidly adopting 1:1 or bring-your-own-device policies. Students with special needs are increasingly overcoming disabilities with new communication technologies. Teachers are now using a multitude of new applications in classrooms to support their teaching. Students are sharing their work and participating in global conversations. This entire book, actually, is a testament to the fact that our schools can, do, and will continue to change. The law is happy to see them do so and encourages you to try the new technologies mentioned in this book in your schools while working within the broad legal confines outlined in this chapter.

There are so many difficult legal issues currently facing our schools that one can quickly be overwhelmed by the challenge. There are so many new technologies that one can quickly be incredulous of the next latest and greatest innovation. Both the law and the technology may seem insurmountable. Like all challenges, though, only therein lies the opportunity. The leaders who choose to boldly push forward into the challenges of the information revolution are the ones who provide their students with the greatest opportunities to thrive in it. Each generation before has faced new technological challenges and adapted legal and policy systems to compensate. The law is now asking you, encouraging you even, to write it anew for another generation. You are to find learning opportunities never before available and to give kids an education relevant to the digital, global world which they so boldly enter. This is the primary challenge. The law can be confusing and unclear, but for technology-savvy and supportive school leaders, it should never be an insurmountable obstacle.

REFERENCES

Barnett v. Tipton County Bd. of Educ., 601 F.Supp.2d 980 (W.D. Tenn. 2009).

Bathon, J., & Brady, K. P. (2010). Teacher free speech and expression in a digital age: A legal analysis. *NASSP Bulletin 94*, 213–226.

Bethel School District v. Fraser, 478 U.S. 675 (1986).

Brady, K. P. (2011). Online student speech rights and the uncertain disciplinary reach of school officials in a digital age: A U.S. jurisdictional dilemma. *Education and the Law, 11*(3), 203–217.

Brady, K. P., Umpstead, R. R., & Eckes, S. E. (2010). Unchartered territory: The current legal landscape of public cyber charter schools. *Brigham Young University Education and Law Journal 2010*, 191–230.

Children's Internet Protection Act, 47 U. S. C. 254 (1996).

Christensen, C., Horn, M. B., & Johnson, C. W. (2010). *Disrupting class: How disruptive innovation will change the way the world learns.* New York, NY: McGraw-Hill.

Colorado Revised Statutes Annotated, 22-30.7-105 (2012).

Daniel, P. T. K. (2011). Bullying and cyberbullying in schools: An analysis of student free expression, zero tolerance policies, and state anti-harassment legislation. *West's Education Law Reporter, 268*, 619–642.

Dayton, J., Dupre, A. P., & Blackenship, A. E. (2011). Model anti-bullying legislation: Promoting student safety, civility, and achievement through law and policy reform. *West's Education Law Reporter, 272*, 19–37.

Fatino, J. F. (2003). Public employers and email: A primer for the practitioner and the public professional. *Northern Illinois University Law Review, 23*, 131–186.

Fleischer, H. (2012). What is our current understanding of one-to-one computer projects: A systemic narrative research review. *Educational Research Review, 7*(2), 107–122.

Garcetti v. Ceballos, 547 U. S. 410 (2006).

Glass, G. V., & Welner, K. G. (2011). *Online K–12 schooling in the United States.* Boulder, CO: National Education Policy Center. Retrieved from http://nepc.colorado.edu/publication/online-k-12-schooling

Hazelwood v. Kuhlmeier, 484 U.S. 260 (1988).

Hinduja, S., & Patchin, J. W. (2009). *Bullying beyond the schoolyard: Preventing and responding to cyberbullying.* Thousand Oaks, CA: Corwin Press.

Hobbs, R. (2010). *Copyright clarity: How Fair Use supports digital learning.* Thousand Oaks, CA: Corwin Press.

Horn, M. B., & Staker, H. (2011). The rise of K–12 blended learning. San Mateo, CA: Innosight Institute. Retrieved from: http://www.innosightinstitute.org/media-room/publications/education-publications/the-rise-of-k-12-blended-learning/

Individuals with Disabilities Education Act, 20 U. S. C. 1400 (2006).

International Society for Technology in Education (ISTE). (2009). *National educational technology standards for administrators (NETS-A).* Eugene, OR: Author.

Interstate School Leaders Licensure Consortium (ISLLC). (2008). *Standards for school leaders.* Washington, DC: Council of Chief State School Officers.

Johnson v. Metro. Gov't. of Nashville and Davidson County, 320 S.W.3d 299 (Tenn. App., 2009).

J.S. v. Blue Mountain Sch. Dist., 650 F.3d 915 (3rd Cir. 2011).

Klump v. Nazareth Area School District, 425 F.Supp.2d 622 (E.D. Pa. 2006).

Lancy v. Farley, 501 F.3d 577 (6th Cir. 2007).

Layshock v. Hermitage Sch. Dist., 593 F.3d 249 (3rd Cir. 2010).

McCarthy, M. (2012). Student electronic expression: Unanswered questions persist. *West's Education Law Reporter, 277,* 1–20.

Miller v. Skumananick, 605 F.Supp.2d 634 (M.D. Pa. 2009).

Morse v. Frederick, 551 U.S. 393 (2007).

New Jersey v. T.L.O., 469 U.S. 325 (1985).

No Child Left Behind (NCLB) Act of 2001, 20 U.S.C. § 6301 et seq. (2003).

Osborne, A. G. (2012). Providing assistive technology to students with disabilities under the IDEA. *West's Education Law Reporter 280,* 519–533.

24 Pennsylvania Statutes Sec. 17-1743-A (2012).

Picciano, A. G., & Seaman, J. (2007). *K-12 online learning: A survey of U.S. school district administrators.* Needham, MA: Sloan Consortium.

Pickering v. Board of Education of Township High School District, 391 U.S. 563 (1968).

Post, T. (2012). Family mourns suicide death of bullied teen. Minnesota Public Radio. Retrieved from http://minnesota.publicradio.org/display/web/2012/05/04/rachel-ehmke/

Price v. New York City Board of Education., 51 A.D.3d 277 (N.Y. App. Div. 1st Dep't, 2008).

Protecting Children in the 21st Century Act, 15 U. S. C. 6551 (2008).

Requa v. Kent School District No. 415, 492 F.Supp. 2d 1272 (W.D. Wash. 2007).

Robb, J., Ruggles, R., & Dejka, J. (2012). Sexual emails led Sebring to resign in Des Moines. *Omaha World-Herald.* Retrieved from http://www.omaha.com/article/20120601/NEWS01/120609979

Russo, C. J., & Mawdsley, R. D. (2012). Constitutional issues surrounding student possession and use of cell phones in schools. *West's Education Law Reporter, 280,* 1–17.

S.B. v. Saint James School, 959 So. 2d 72 (Ala. 2006).

Shariff, S. (2008). *Cyberbullying: Issues and solutions for the school, the classroom and the home.* New York, NY: Routledge.

Sherman, B. (2011). Your mayor, your 'friend.': Public officials, social networking, and the unmapped new public square. *Pace Law Review, 31,* 95–145.

Silberberg, C. M. (2001). Preserving educational fair use in the twenty-first century. *Southern California Law Review, 74,* 617–655.

Texas Attorney General Opinion GA-0896 (2011). Austin, TX. Retrieved from https://www.oag.state.tx.us/opinions/opinions/50abbott/op/2011/htm/ga-0896.htm

Tinker v. Des Moines Independent School District, 393 U.S. 503 (1969).

Trolley, B., & Hanel, C. (2010). *Cyber kids, cyber bullying, cyber balance.* Thousand Oaks, CA: Corwin.

United States v. American Library Association, 539 U. S. 194 (2003).

United States v. Causby, 328 U.S. 256 (1946).

United States Copyright Office (2009). *Circular 21: Reproduction of copyrighted works by educators and librarians.* Washington, DC: Author

United States Department of Justice (2003). Accessibility of state and local government websites to people with disabilities. Washington, DC. Retrieved from http://www.ada.gov/websites2.htm

United States Department of Justice (2010). ADA standards for accessible design. Washington, DC. Retrieved from http://www.ada.gov/2010ADAstandards_index.htm

United States Supreme Court. (2010). *Federal rules of civil procedure.* Washington, DC: Author.

Vander Ark, T., & Wise, B. (2011). *Getting smart: How digital learning is changing the world.* New York, NY: Jossey-Bass.

Watson, J., Murin, A., Vashaw, L., Gemin, B., & Rapp, C. (2011). *Keeping pace with K-12 online learning: An annual review of policy and practice.* Durango, CO: Evergreen Education Group. Retrieved from http://kpk12.com/cms/wp-content/uploads/KeepingPace2011.pdf.

Williams, L. A., Atkinson, L. C., Cate, J. G., & O'Hair, M. J. (2008). Mutual support between learning community development and technology integration: Impact on school practices and student achievement. *Theory into Practice, 47,* 294–302.

CHAPTER 13

CONNECTED PRINCIPALS

In Pursuit of Social Capital
via Social Media

Candice Barkley and Jonathan D. Becker

INTRODUCTION

In connected teaching, individual educators...create their own online learning communities consisting of their students and their students' peers; fellow educators in their schools, libraries, and after-school programs; professional experts in various disciplines around the world; members of community organizations that serve students in the hours they are not in school; and parents who desire greater participation in their children's education....Episodic and ineffective professional development is replaced by professional learning that is collaborative, coherent, and continuous and that blends more effective in-person courses and workshops with the expanded opportunities, immediacy, and convenience enabled by online learning. (U.S. Department of Education, 2010, p. xii)

That passage comes from *The National Educational Technology Plan* in a section called "The Practice of Connected Teaching." This is a clear indication that

Principal 2.0: Technology and Educational Leadership, pages 211–232
Copyright © 2013 by Information Age Publishing
All rights of reproduction in any form reserved.

the U.S. Department of Education recognizes the affordances of the social web for professional learning. In fact, August 2012 was officially designated by the U.S. Department of Education as the first ever Connected Educators Month (CEM). CEM included a week of web conferences, the launch of an online book club, and announcements about new online communities for educators around the world. This was all hosted and supported by the U.S. Department of Education in collaboration with various partner organizations.

Connected learning through social media can occur between students, between students and educators, and between educators. As to the latter form of connected learning, for professional learning, a critical mass of educators is now engaged in multiple forms of social media-mediated informal professional learning, as illustrated through the following exemplary endeavors:

- #edchat—a Twitter-based, real-time chat that takes place twice every Tuesday. The topic of the chat is voted upon, and hundreds of educators worldwide participate in these chats. The #echat group on the Educator's PLN, an online community of educators, currently has 535 members, and all of the transcripts of the chats are archived and made available via a wiki.
- #edcamp— "Edcamps are based on Open Space Technology (OST) which states that 'whoever comes are the right people and whatever happens are the only things that could have'" (Edcamp Foundation website). These social-media initiated and fueled "unconferences" have been proliferating. These face-to-face meetings provide professional development for educators by educators, and social media is very much a catalyst. Since the first Edcamp was held in Philadelphia in May 2010, more than 90 Edcamps have been held by teachers in the United States, Chile, and Sweden as of the time of the writing of this chapter.
- Classroom 2.0/The Future of Education—Classroom 2.0 is an online community of nearly 69,000 educators. It serves as a conversation space as well as a central hub connecting educators to additional resources, including the *Future of Education* series. This interview series and the community around it are devoted to providing an opportunity for those who care about education to share their voices and ideas with others. It is a place for thoughtful discussion on a range of timely educational topics. These webinars, recorded and archived, occur multiple times per week and are hosted in a web conference platform open to any educator across the globe.

This intersection of social media, professional development, and informal learning is growing rapidly within education. School leaders, in addition to teachers, are very much involved. In the summer of 2010, two principals, George Couros from Canada and Patrick Larkin from Massachusetts (U.S.) decided to build an online community of practice dedicated to educational leadership issues. A multi-authored blog, Connected Principals, was born, and shortly after that a hashtag (#cpchat) was adopted for related content shared on Twitter. At the time, there were many principals with their own blogs and Twitter accounts, but this was likely the first time a group of principals was creating their own online learning community via a multi-authored blog and a dedicated Twitter hashtag.

This chapter includes a description of the Connected Principals community, as well as a section on how principals, or any educator for that matter, can become connected educators and take full advantage of all the affordances of the social web for professional learning. First, though, the next section is an exploration of the theory behind the purposes of social media-mediated professional learning in education: the pursuit of social capital.

SOCIAL CAPITAL, COMMUNITIES OF PRACTICE, AND THE SOCIAL WEB

Bordieu (1986) defines social capital as "the aggregate of the actual or potential resources which are linked to possession of a durable network of more or less institutionalized relationships of mutual acquaintance and recognition" (p. 248). In short, social capital is the benefits that come from cohesion and cooperation between individuals and groups. Onyx and Bullen (2000) concisely identified five main themes that are consistent throughout the literature on social capital. First, social capital depends upon networks of relationships among entities. The second is that social capital is based on reciprocity; that is, at some point, a participant will receive resources in return for those they have contributed. The third theme is that of trust. Trust, the authors state, "entails a willingness to take risks in a social context based on a sense of confidence that others will respond as expected" (Onyx & Bullen, 2000, p. 24). Fourth, social capital requires social norms; the shared values and common goals of the group that provide an informal social control. Finally, there is a theme of personal and collective efficacy. The members of the community have a willingness to participate within the group.

In the context of education, mentoring, networking, and mutual support associated with high levels of social capital all contribute to success (Coleman, 1988). Likewise, Cohen and Prusak (2001) state that social capital promotes knowledge sharing due to trust relationships, common norms, and shared goals. Others state that social capital facilitates the development of knowledge capital due to the exchange of information and sharing of knowledge (Nahapiet & Ghoshal, 1998).

For many school leaders, the development of knowledge capital through the exchange of information and ideas has come through participation in a community of practice (Boud & Middleton, 2003; Eraut, 2004; Gray, 2004; Johnson, 2001). Wenger (1998) wrote about "situated learning" and the idea of individuals learning collectively—that is, in the context of social relationships.

> Over time, this collective learning results in practices that reflect both the pursuit of our enterprises and the attendant social relations. These practices are thus the property of a kind of community created over time by the sustained pursuit of a shared enterprise. It makes sense, therefore, to call these kinds of communities *communities of practice*. (Wenger, 1998, p. 45)

These communities therefore have a joint enterprise, require mutual engagement that binds the community as a social group, and include a shared repertoire of communal resources (Wenger, 1998). Lesser and Prusak (1999) link social capital to communities of practice on three different dimensions. On the structural level, communities of practice foster the development of a network of individuals with relevant knowledge, allow for the evaluation of other members' knowledge, and connect individuals from the outside (Lesser & Prusak, 1999). The relational dimension is where the communities allow for interpersonal interactions that build trust, share relevant knowledge, and construct norms and values commonly held among the group (Lesser & Prusak, 1999). Finally, in the cognitive dimension, because of the commonality of the group, a shared vernacular and artifacts are created by the community (Lesser & Prusak, 1999).

Historically, educators have engaged in communities of practice most typically facilitated by professional organizations. They have been developed through professional conferences and various forms of communications that have become increasingly electronic such as newsletters and listservs. In recent years, communities of practice in education have taken advantages of the affordances of the social web. Thus, online communities of practice have become reasonably mainstream in the field of education.

Before the arrival and growth of social media as we know it now, McLure-Wasko and Faraj (2000) looked at electronic communities of practice (CoPs), noting that "[k]nowledge sharing is enabled through mechanisms that support posting and responding to questions, sharing stories of personal experience, and discussing and debating issues relevant to the community" (p. 161). They found that the participants in these electronic communities of practice considered knowledge to be a public good and felt an obligation to share. While technologies such as listservs, discussion groups, bulletin boards, and chat rooms aided such communities, the technology would soon make these electronic communities even stronger. The proliferation of social networking sites (SNS) and other online collaboration tools, coupled with communities of practice, has given rise to a new form of collective learning and knowledge sharing: virtual networks of practice (McLure-Wasko, Teigland, & Faraj, 2009).

Chiu, Hsu, and Wang (2006) defined virtual communities as "online social networks in which people with common interests, goals, or practices interact to share information and knowledge, and engage in social interactions" (p. 1873). Ardchivili (2008) found that participants in virtual communities of practice did so for profession-related benefits, increased self-esteem, community ties, and norms such as shared values and reciprocity. Gray (2004) found online CoPs to be ideal for individuals who are geographically dispersed or have few opportunities to meet face to face to share best practices. Finally, McLure-Wasko et al. (2009) defined electronic networks of practice as "a self-organizing, open, activity-system focused on practice that exists through computer-mediated communication" (p. 256). They found that electronic CoPs are sustained though generalized exchange, supported by a critical mass of members, and that the members develop strong ties with the community as a whole (McLure-Wasko et al., 2009).

In the world of education, the role of social networking sites (SNS) in informal learning for students has been examined at both the high school (Greenhow & Robelia, 2009) and college level (Ebner, Lienhardt, Rohs, & Meyer, 2009). However, there is little information on the use of SNS for the creation of electronic networks of practice for educational leaders. In the report *School Principals and Social Networking in Education*, a joint effort from edWeb.net, IESD, Inc., MMS Education, and MCH, Inc. (2010), the authors suggest that most principals surveyed indicated that social networking sites have value as a way to create professional learning communities. About half of the principals in the discussion group phase said they had used social networking sites to share ideas, questions, and/or solutions with other education professionals. These principals further stated that they used SNS to communicate with colleagues outside their school district. In these situations, SNS were seen as both a tool for sharing information, ideas, and experiences as well as providing access to information for themselves.

Although virtual communities of practice in the field of education are relatively new, there exist some analyses of a few successful groups such as Tapped In (Schlager & Fusco, 2003; Schlager, Fusco, & Schank, 2002), the Inquiry Learning Forum at Indiana University (Barab, MaKinster & Scheckler, 2004), and the Math Forum (Renninger & Schumar, 2004). Although these communities differ in design, in each case, the authors describe these projects along the lines of virtual CoPs. In particular, Tapped In was specifically designed to be a virtual community of practice for K–12 educators. The premise for Tapped In was that technology infrastructures could support teacher professional development that was transformative, sustainable, and scalable (Schlager et al., 2002). Although researchers have noted the limited impact on practice of Tapped In, it continues to provide a professional community for thousands of education professionals (Schlager, Farooq, Fusco, Schank, & Dwyer, 2009). However, the need for models of virtual CoPs for educators continues (Schlager et al. 2009). And, as the social media landscape changes and the horizons grow, the possibilities are nearly limitless.

The next section is a description of one such possibility: an example of a modern, virtual network of educational leaders from around the world. It is based on a thorough study, by the authors, of a group called Connected Principals over the course of a year, essentially from June 2010 to June 2011. The study involved content analysis of a simple random sample of blog posts during that year, social network analysis of data from Twitter, and interviews with key participants.

THE CASE OF CONNECTED PRINCIPALS

[T]he most important way for educators to confront and accept the challenge to educate effectively in this fast-changing era is to embrace both the responsibility and the opportunity to grow and learn, ourselves, each and every day, in collaboration with each other at schools which make serious commitments to this collaboration, and via the power of social networks online. (Martin, 2010, final paragraph)

The Connected Principals Blog

In the summer of 2010, Canadian principal George Couros (from Alberta, Canada) called fellow principal Patrick Larkin (from Burlington, MA, U.S.) and presented his idea about creating a blog where interested administrators could post their thoughts and ideas to promote conversations about leadership and education. Larkin agreed to come on board, and Couros set up the blog. At the end of June 2010, Couros added the first three posts to the Connected Principals blog. At the beginning of July, he added two more, including one inviting administrators to be a part of the group. With the exception of the post inviting administrators to the group, these first posts were re-posts from Couros' own blog. He wanted to ensure that when people visited the website there was content. Both Couros and Larkin then posted to Twitter what they were doing, and in a short period of time, six additional contributors began to post to the blog. In August 2010, the blog took off. In that month, there were 57 total posts; Couros posted his vision for the group, and Larkin announced the group's Twitter hashtag, #cpchat.

The group continued to grow, and as of December 2010, there were 45 contributors to the blog, and 718 users of the #cpchat hashtag. The first year of the Connected Principals blog consisted of 376 posts or an average of 31.33 posts per month (essentially one new post every day). The sample of posts ranged in length from 127 to 2,313 words with a mean of 720.88 words. Readers of the blog posts are allowed both to leave comments on the post and share the post through their own Twitter network. The number of comments for the sample of posts ranged from 0 to 26 with a mean of 4.54. The number of tweets for blog posts ranged from 0 to 143 with a mean of 22.18. In other words, on average, each post generated four or five comments and was shared via Twitter 22 times.

The Connected Principals site originally listed eight topic areas under which the contributors wrote their blog posts. The authors classified their blog posts according to these categories, with the ability to further classify a single post under multiple categories. Authors could also add a topic area for their posts if they did not feel one of the preexisting topic areas covered their posts. In addition to the eight topic areas listed in January of 2011, three additional topic areas were added by the authors. Some of those topic areas added by the authors later became part of the official list of topics on the Connected Principals website. Table 13.1 shows the frequency of these topic areas cited by the authors for the sample of blog posts. As seen in Table 13.1, Best Educational Practices and Leadership Essentials are the most frequently reported categories, with Technology Integration and Professional Development well behind and the other topics rarely reported.

TABLE 13.1   Connected Principal Blog Topic Information

Category	Number
Best Educational Practices	61
Leadership Essentials	30
Technology Integration	12
Professional Development	11
Distributed Leadership	8
Principal Quality Standard	5
School Branding	4
Parental Involvement	4
*Networked Leadership	3
*Students	2
*Grading and Assessment	1

* Topic areas not originally included as categories by *Connected Principals.*

The categories for blog posts were essentially predetermined for the authors, but the titles of the blog posts were determined by the authors, and therefore, may give more insight into what the areas of interest were for school leaders who wrote for Connected Principals. Figure 13.1 is a word cloud of the titles of the sampled blog posts. In word clouds, the words are sized by the number of mentions in the text. So, the larger the word, the more times it was used in the titles. In Figure 13.1, the most prominent words are learning, school, and students. Although titles are not necessarily descriptive of the content of a particular blog post, this word cloud does a reasonably good job of visualizing the content of the Connected Principals blog. Of particular importance is that much of the content centers around learning.

In summary, the content analysis of the blog yields two main insights. Primarily, the analysis shows what the Connected Principals wrote about and discussed, but to a smaller extent, it also shows both how the group interacted and the wider audience they reached. In terms of what was discussed by the group, the three main topic areas include teacher/classroom practices, leadership practices, and technology, and the comments show that the followers of the group were interested in the same topics. Additionally, the posts about the group itself give an insight into the value the members found in belonging to this group. As Lyn Hilt, an elementary school

Figure 13.1 Word cloud of blog post titles on *Connected Principals*.

principal and one of the earliest contributors to Connected Principals wrote, "One of the most positive aspects of interacting with other educators via social media, whether it be Twitter, Ning communities, or a meeting of the minds such as the Reform Symposium, is the array of talented individuals working in education today" (Hilt, 2010, first paragraph). This brief glimpse into the discussions on the blog post also hints at an even larger group included in what many of the authors describe as their professional learning network.

Connected Principals on Twitter

Not long after the establishment of the Connected Principals blog, co-founder Patrick Larkin established the #cpchat hashtag[1] on Twitter,[2] giving Twitter users the ability to continue discussions on blog posts or other topics of concern in the educational leadership field. In other words, the #cpchat hashtag extended the Connected Principals community into Twitter. This extended network created by those Twitter users who are a part of the Connected Principals community is an important aspect in understanding the group as a whole.

Figure 13.2 was generated using a service called hashtagify, which generates a graphic showing how a given hashtag is related to other hashtags on Twitter. The size of the circle represents the relative frequency of use of the hashtag, and the thickness of the line connecting two hashtags indicates the degree of overlap for two hashtags. So, of the hashtags that #cpchat is most associated with, #education and #leadership are the largest, but #edchat is the one with which it most frequently overlaps. In other words, of all of the other possible hashtags, if a tweet is tagged with a hashtag in addition to #cpchat, it is most likely to be #edchat, which is a real-time chat that takes place twice every Tuesday. The topic of the chat is voted upon, and hundreds of educators worldwide have been participating in these chats. It is noteworthy that #cpchat and #edchat overlap so much given the global reach and popularity of #edchat.

In order to better understand the #cpchat Twitter network, basic social network analysis was conducted. Data from Twitter were pulled on December 14, 2011, by using the import feature of NodeXL that allowed for data to be pulled specifically for users of the #cpchat hashtag. In the first 18 months or so of #cpchat, over 25,000 tweets were tagged with the hashtag by more than 700 unique contributors. Thus, Twitter clearly extended the Connected Principals community. With over 700 nodes (Twitter users) and over 25,000 edges (individual tweets), this is a very large network, creating some difficulty in generating a meaningful visualization. Nevertheless, a directed sociograph was created to visualize the #cpchat network. The graph

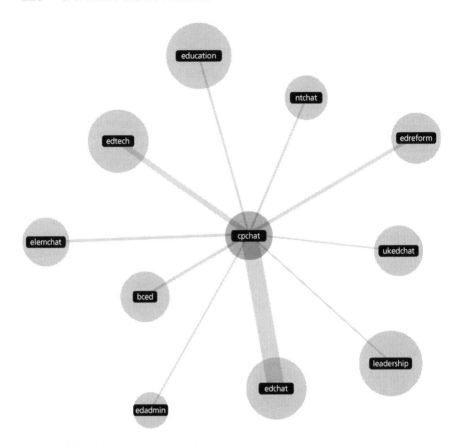

Figure 13.2 Relationship of #cpchat to other hasthags on Twitter.

is directed since relationships on Twitter are directional; some users "follow" other users and then may or may not be followed in return. Thus, in the sociograph that is Figure 13.3, the arrows point in the direction of who is followed in the relationship.

Finding key components of the network proved extremely complicated, but in Figure 13.3, the larger the circle, the more frequently the Twitter user chose to utilize the #cpchat hashtag. Additionally, the four different colors represent the four main clusters of relationships identified by the social network analysis.

Despite the dense appearance of the network sociograph, the network density was only .0488, meaning 4.88% of all possible edges existed within the network. In other words, of all the possible following relationships among #cpchat users, less than 5% actually exist. This low density metric is not uncommon for very large Twitter networks, and it points out how loosely connected the network is.

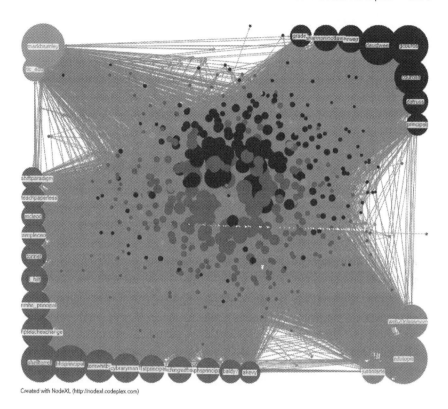

Created with NodeXL (http://nodexl.codeplex.com)

Figure 13.3   Sociograph of tweets labeled with #cpchat hashtag.

Although the overall graph metrics (e.g., density and distance) and clusters give some detail of the relationships within the network, it is also important to know about the key nodes within the network. This information is found through measures of centrality. For the Connected Principals' Twitter network, four measures of centrality were calculated, with the results of the top ten in each category given in Table 13.2. In-degree represents the number of arrows coming in to a node or, in Twitter terms, how many times a person/group has been followed. Out-degree then represents the number of arrows coming out of a node or the number of Twitter accounts that a particular node follows. Betweenness shows the key flow-through nodes, meaning that they are the main path through which information flows. Finally, closeness measures the shortest average distance from one node to another, indicating that the highest-ranking nodes in closeness can be connected to all other nodes in the fewest number of steps.

The average in-degree was 34.993, as was the average out-degree. In terms of the top ten shown in Table 13.2, the highest in-degree was 420 and

TABLE 13.2 *Connected Principals'* Twitter Network Measures of Centrality

Rank	In-Degree	Out-Degree	Betweenness	Closeness
1	web20classroom	markbrumley	edutopia	edutopia
2	edutopia	edutopia	markbrumley	web20classroom
3	nmhs_principal	davidwees	web20classroom	gcouros
4	tomwhitby	gcouros	gcouros	markbrumley
5	shellterrell	hpteachexchange	hpteachexchange	tomwhitby
6	gcouros	bhsprincipal	nmhs_principal	bhsprincipal
7	markbrumley	shellterrell	tomwhitby	nmhs_principal
8	cybraryman1	courosa	bhsprincipal	shellterrell
9	bhsprincipal	tonnet	teachpaperless	cybraryman1
10	courosa	datruss	cybraryman1	davidwees

the highest out-degree was 339, showing that the most central users were following and followed by hundreds of others. Although the nodes with the highest degree are not necessarily the same as those for betweenness, as seen in Table 13.2, several of the same nodes appear in all of the top ten lists. This is also true for the final centrality measure, closeness. In this case, within the top ten of all four centrality measures, there were only 15 different nodes represented. Of those 15 nodes, four were contributors to the Connected Principals blog, three were educational organizations, three were contributors to blogs on those educational organizations, and the remaining five were various educators/bloggers.

Connected Principals as Affinity Space

The data from the blog and from Twitter suggest that although the contributors to the blog are easily identified, that does not constitute all the "members," as many other people read and comment on those blogs. Additionally, on the Twitter network, 718 unique nodes show that there are many people involved in those discussions who are not contributors to the blog. From this perspective, it is difficult to say with any certainty who would claim that they are members of or belong to the Connected Principals community.

According to Gee (2004), the idea of community carries a connotation of close personal ties among members. He further states that the key problem with a CoP is that it attempts to label a group of people when it is not always possible to identify who is and is not a part of the group. Gee (2001) offered the idea of an "affinity space" where one can speak about the extent that a group of people interact even if they do not form a community:

What people in the group share, and must share to constitute an affinity group, is allegiance to, access to, and participation in specific practices that give each of its members the requisite experiences.... For members of an affinity group, their allegiance is primarily to a set of common endeavors or practices and secondarily to other people in terms of shared culture or traits. (p. 111)

Although these "affinity spaces" have much in common with CoPs, they have the key difference of so-called members of "affinity spaces" being able to move in and out of the space as it suits their needs. Connected Principals then meets all of the criteria for an "affinity space" as the "members" all have an allegiance to, access to, and choose to participate in the blog, the Twitter network, or both. The primary allegiance is to the needs of students in the world of education.

Finally, although the content analysis of the blog and the social network analysis of the Twitter data provide a nice snapshot of the group, collectively, they do not tell the full story of the group, nor do they give any indication of why this group has become so large and so popular. That can largely be explained by the words offered by key participants who were interviewed for the study of Connected Principals. As Eric Sheninger, a high school principal and key contributor to Connected Principals and the #cp-chat community stated:

I think the goals and purposes are to broaden our leadership horizons, push each other to get better, provide constructive feedback on ideas, to present new ideas that have worked, and to also add a layer of transparency to what we do as administrators. (E. Sheninger, personal communication, January 18, 2012)

This notion of pushing each other and sharing ideas is central to social capital. Also, as Patrick Larkin, one of the co-founders of Connected Principals, said:

What the whole thing is about for me is we share ideas not because we think that they're the best ones, but because we're excited about it, and we want to have a conversation. But then, you get people you're connected with and they take your ideas and take them a step further, making your ideas even better, so I think that's really the power of the thing. (P. Larkin, personal communication, January 18, 2012)

In addition to sharing ideas, the contributors provided one another with feedback and engaged in conversation. We can refer to Connected Principals as a community of practice, or as an affinity space. Regardless, it has become quite clear that social media affords tremendous opportunities for school leaders to improve their social capital. That is to say, educators engaging on the blog or utilizing the hashtag are involved in a group effort that is reciprocal and that is about increasing the collective efficacy of these school leaders around the world. This is the very essence of social capital.

HOW TO BECOME A "CONNECTED PRINCIPAL"

If the ideas in this chapter are new to you, it is probably also the case that you have not yet fully explored the affordances of social media for informal professional learning. Therefore, this final section is intended as a contemporary guide to becoming a connected educator. The section begins with a discussion and explanation of how Twitter can be used for professional networking purposes. The second part of the section describes other ways to use various forms of social media to be digitally present as a "connected principal."

Twitter

There are many ways to begin the journey to become a connected educator, but these days, Twitter is really the fastest way to connect with educators worldwide. Twitter, a micro-blogging service, has evolved from the simplistic "What are you doing?" platform to a space where, for instance, political revolutions have been facilitated. For example, Bhuiyan (2011) wrote about the effectiveness of social media in the political reform movement in Egypt. Specifically, social media helped mobilized "millions of citizens to participate in political action and emerged as authoring agents and organizational power structures" (Bhuiyan, 2011, p. 14). Twitter is a flexible tool that can be different things for different people. The following narrative describes some of the ways that Twitter is currently being utilized.

Human-Powered Search

When you're looking for restaurant recommendations, where do you go? You might check out newspaper/magazine reviews, or maybe Zagat. But most people prefer a good word-of-mouth recommendation—a positive review from a trusted source. Assuming the user has developed a reliable network of trusted friends and colleagues, Twitter can be a great place to ask for recommendations. Educators can ask for recommendations on curriculum resources, technology tools, or anything related to teaching and learning. Here, one of the chapter authors asks those he follows on Twitter for recommendations for an inexpensive laptop (see Figure 13.4). This becomes a compliment to researching via "traditional" consumer reports; it is search powered by humans within a purposefully constructed network.

Also, if you're looking for resources on a particular topic area, hashtags can be very useful. On Twitter, hashtags are keywords (with the # sign attached

Figure 13.4   Example of a human powered search using Twitter.

to it) that aid in the aggregation of ideas/topics. In addition to #cpchat, lots of school leaders use the #edadmin hashtag when tweeting about something related to educational leadership. Figure 13.5 shows an image of a tweet by Jessica Johnson, an elementary school principal. She posts this to Twitter to point out a resource for school leaders using iPads, and she appends the #cpchat hashtag so that anyone searching or following that hashtag will see the tweet irrespective of whether the user follows her on Twitter.

Conversation (Chat) Space

The power of the #cpchat hashtag for the Connected Principals community was documented earlier in this chapter. However, hashtags also serve as a means for aggregating many conversations on Twitter. Most conversations on Twitter are spontaneous and do not have a specific hashtag (or any hashtag), but some educators use Twitter to participate in synchronous conversations around

Figure 13.5   Example of resource sharing on a particular topic area using #hashtags.

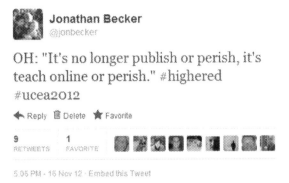

Figure 13.6 Example of communication using a professional conference #hashtag.

specific topics. One of the most popular Twitter "chats" is #edchat which occurs every Tuesday at noon EST and again at 7 p.m. on Tuesdays. This chapter ends with a link to a set of resources for connected educators, which includes a link to a Google calendar with a listing of education-related Twitter chats.

Additionally, numerous professional conferences adopt official hashtags so that attendees can use Twitter as a backchannel and so that those not in attendance can participate virtually by following the tweets tagged with the official hashtag. Here, again, is one of the authors of this chapter using Twitter at a recent educational leadership conference (Figure 13.6). He uses the official conference hashtag (#ucea2012) so that the tweet is archived and easily searchable and so that followers have some context for the tweet. Thus, used in this way, Twitter and other forms of social media have enabled educators to make important professional connections. A number of educators have received job offers because of connections made on Twitter.

Faculty Lounge/Water Cooler

And, yes, Twitter can be that place where people share what they're having for breakfast....

Figure 13.7 Example of informal communication using Twitter.

But, you know what? That's OK—even good. Twitter is a form of *social* media; and it's beautiful in that way. Sharing "personal" or "social" information builds social capital and makes Twitter the powerful networking platform that it is. If you think relationships matter, professionally or personally, Twitter is ALL about relationships.

Ways of Being Digitally Present beyond Twitter

Twitter is certainly a great way to network and connect with other educators across the globe. Building a strong and supportive network on Twitter will yield valuable social capital rewards, and you will discover new ways to connect from those you connect with on Twitter. That is, should you use Twitter as your gateway to becoming a connected educator, you are certain to learn of other ways to connect professionally online. Professional networking via social media works a lot like face-to-face networking; the greatest value comes from simply being present and making yourself known. Here are a couple of additional ways to connect.

Blogging
Twitter is microblogging, 140 characters at a time. There are advantages and disadvantages to that format. There are also good reasons to adopt a platform for longer forms of writing and reflection, and that is where a full-fledged blog is a better approach. Blogs afford the opportunity to write in a range of ways and in modes that are potentially more engaging than through more traditional media. The technological literacy needed to start a blog has decreased dramatically, and the barrier to entry to blogging is incredibly low. These days, if you can send an email, you can be a blogger. As a result, hundreds of school leaders around the world are sharing their ideas and engaging in discussions around those ideas with commenters ranging from local community members to educators around the world.

Join Existing Online Communities of Practice
Another great way to "meet" and connect with educators around the world is to join one of the many existing online communities of practice.

- Classroom 2.0 was one of the original social networking sites for educators, especially those inclined towards technology. As of the writing of this chapter, the community was approaching 70,000 members, 9,000 forum discussions, and 1,000 groups. Classroom 2.0 is a great place to meet other educators, discuss educational policy and practice, and to find out about other learning opportunities, virtual or face-to-face.

- *The Future of Education* interview series is about providing an opportunity for those who care about education to share their voices and ideas with others. This interview series provides a forum for synchronous, thoughtful discussion on a variety of topics. Steve Hargadon, an educational technology pioneer and social networking expert, interviews the most important thinkers and visionaries in education, and the chat spaces during the interviews become reasonably rich discussion areas around what is being shared by the individual(s) being interviewed. If you cannot attend the discussions real-time, the webinars, which occur multiple times per week and are hosted in a web conference platform open to any educator across the globe, are recorded and archived.
- There are other existing and vibrant online communities of practice for you to consider joining. The U.S. Department of Education's new community directory (http://connectededucators.org/communities/?sort=views) is a growing compilation of links to many of those active virtual communities.

CONCLUSION

Ultimately, the key to connected learning is developing the habits of mind as well as the digital habits to be a viable node on the virtual learning networks to which you attach yourself. You can gain valuable insights by being a lurker (i.e., one who virtually "looks in" without actually participating) and by checking in with your network on occasion. However, this is about developing social capital through social media. It is very much a social endeavor—a many-to-many give and take. The more you give, the more you get back. And the more you get back, the better you become as a school leader. That is the essence of social capital. As George Couros, one of the founding members of Connected Principals, said himself:

> I think when you use traditional things like newsletters or even a traditional 1.0 website, there is only talking, there's no listening, and I think in this medium you're showing your willingness to be open, and connect and listen to the thoughts of others to become a better administrator. (Couros, G., personal communication, February 1, 2012)

The link and the QR code (a barcode-like graphic that can be scanned by a QR code reader on a laptop or mobile device that will open a webpage) on the final page of this chapter takes you to an ever-updating bundle of resources related to social media-mediated informal professional learning in education. Take some time to peruse those resources and, if you have not

Figure 13.8   QR code to scan for additional educator resources.

already done so, join the vast and growing network of educators committed to learning in new and exciting ways.

CONNECTED EDUCATOR RESOURCES

The best way to learn about the affordances of Twitter, though, is to start a Twitter account, jump in, tinker around, and figure out how it can work for you. Also, educators have created and curated lots of resources about the use of Twitter for professional purposes.

To access a bundle of resources on connected learning and social media-mediated informal professional learning in education, go to the following URL by typing it into your browser. Or, to access it directly on a mobile device with a camera, use a QR code reader to scan the QR code which takes you to the same site (see Figure 13.8). http://bit.ly/connectedprincipals

NOTES

1. *Hashtags* denoted by the # symbol, according to the Twitter website, are used to mark keywords or topics in a Tweet. It was created organically by Twitter users as a way to categorize messages. When a Tweet is posted with a specific hashtag, it signifies to other users that the Tweet pertains to a particular interest area.
2. *Twitter* is the oldest and best known micro-blogging service (Galagan, 2009). On this service, users send their messages called "tweets." Users may "follow" other users, meaning that the follower will receive the followed user's updates.

FOR FURTHER READING

Abdal-Haqq, I. (1995). *Making time for teacher professional development* (Digest 95-4). Washington, DC: ERIC Clearinghouse on Teaching and Teacher Education.

Burbank, M. D., & Kauchak, D. (2003). An alternative model for professional development: Investigations into effective collaboration. *Teaching and Teacher Education, 19,* 499–514.

Garber, D. H. (1992). Networking on the job: School administrators making contact. *NASSP Bulletin, 76*, 121–124.

Garet, M. S., Porter, A. C., Desimone, L., Birman, B. F., &Yoon, K. S. (2001). What makes professional development effective? Results from a national sample of teachers. *American Educational Research Journal, 38*(4), 915–945.

Gee, J. P. (2005). Semiotic social spaces and affinity spaces: From the age of mythology to today's schools. In D. Barton & K. Tusting (Eds.), *Beyond communities of practice: Language, power, and social context.* (pp. 214–243). Cambridge, UK: University of Cambridge Press.

Grissom, J. A., & Harrington, J. R. (2010). Investing in administrator efficacy: An examination of professional development as a tool for enhancing principal effectiveness. *American Journal of Education, 116*(4), 583–612.

Grogan, M., & Andrews, R. (2002). Defining preparation and professional development for the future. *Educational Administration Quarterly, 38*(2), 233–256.

Hallinger, P., & Heck, R. H. (1998). Exploring the principal's contribution to school effectiveness: 1980–1995. *School Effectiveness and School Improvement, 9*(2), 157–191.

Ingersoll, R., & Smith, T. M. (2004). Do teacher induction and mentoring matter? *NASSP Bulletin, 88*, 28–40.

Jacobs, J. (1965). *The death and life of great American cities.* New York, NY: Penguin Books.

Little, J. W. (1993). Teachers' professional development in a climate of educational reform. *Educational Evaluation and Policy Analysis, 15*(2), 129–151.

Livingstone, D. W. (2001). *Adults' informal learning: Definitions, findings, gaps and future research* (Working Paper No. 21). Toronto, ON: Centre for the Study of Education and Work.

Marsick, V. J., & Volpe, M. (1999). The nature and need for informal learning. *Advances in Developing Human Resources, 1*, 1–9.

National Staff Development Council. (2000). *Learning to lead, leading to learn.* Oxford, OH: Author.

Penuel, W. R., Fishman, B. J., Yamaguchi, R., & Gallagher, L. P. (2007). What makes professional development effective? Strategies that foster curriculum implementation. *American Educational Research Journal, 44*(4), 921–958.

Peterson, K. (2002). The professional development of principals: Innovations and opportunities. *Educational Administration Quarterly, 38*(2), 213–232.

Putnam, R. T., & Borko, H. (2000). What do new views of knowledge and thinking have to say about research on teacher education? *Educational Researcher, 29*(1), 4–15.

Sailors, M., & Price, L. R. (2010). Professional development that supports the teaching of cognitive reading strategy instruction. *The Elementary School Journal, 110*, 301–322.

Stockard, J., & Lehman, M. B. (2004). Influences on the satisfaction and retention of 1st-year teachers: The importance of effective school management. *Educational Administration Quarterly, 40*(5), 742–771.

Waters, T., Marzano, R. J., & McNully, B. (2003). *Balanced Leadership: What 30 years of research tells us about the effect of leadership on student achievement.* Aurora, CO: Mid-Continent Research for Education and Learning.

REFERENCES

Ardchivili, A. (2008). Learning and knowledge sharing in virtual communities of practice: Motivators, barriers, and enablers. *Advances in Developing Human Resources, 10*(4), 541–554.

Barab, S. A., MaKinster, J. G., & Scheckler, R. (2004). Characterizing an online professional development community. In S. A. Barab, R. Kling, & J. H. Gray (Eds.), *Designing for virtual communities in the service of learning* (pp. 53–90). Cambridge, UK: University of Cambridge Press.

Bourdieu, P. (1986). Forms of social capital. In J. C. Richards (Ed.), *Handbook of theory and research for sociology education* (pp. 241–258). New York, NY: Greenwood Press.

Boud, D., & Middleton, H. (2003). Learning from others at work: Communities of practice and informal learning. *Journal of Workplace Learning, 15*(5), 194–202.

Bhuiyan, S. I. (2011). Social media and its effectiveness in the political reform movement in Egypt. *Middle East Media Educator, 1,* 14–20.

Chiu, C., Hsu, M., & Wang, E. T. (2006). Understanding knowledge sharing in virtual communities: An integration of social capital and social cognitive theories. *Decision Support Systems, 42,* 1872–1888.

Cohen, D., & Prusak, L. (2001). *In good company: How social capital makes organizations work.* Boston, MA: Harvard Business Press.

Coleman, J. S. (1988). Social capital in the creation of human capital. *The American Journal of Sociology, 94,* S95–S120.

edcamp Foundation. (2012). Occupy professional development: Take control of your professional learning with the edcamp format. Retrieved September 12, 2012 from http://edcamp.org/?s=%22edcamps+are+based+on+open+space+technology%22&x=0&y=0

edWeb.net, IESD, Inc., MCH, Inc., & MMS Education. (2010). School principals and social networking in education: Practices, policies, and realities in 2010. Retrieved from http://www.mmseducation.com/SiteData/docs/PrincipalsReport/6a66e4004f61eb5c328378a80cf6f734/PrincipalsReport.pdf

Ebner, M., Lienhardt, C., Rohs, M., & Meyer, I. (2009). Microblogs in higher education: A chance to facilitate informal and process-oriented learning? *Computers & Education, 55,* 92–100.

Eraut, M. (2004). Informal learning in the workplace. *Studies in Continuing Education, 26*(2), 247–273.

Galagan, P. (2009). Twitter as a learning tool. Really. Retrieved September 12, 2012 from http://www.astd.org/Publications/Newsletters/Learning-Circuits/Learning-Circuits-Archives/2009/06/Twitter-as-a-Learning-Tool-Really

Gee, J. P. (2001). Identity as an analytic lens for research in education. *Review of Research in Education, 25,* 99–125.

Gee, J. P. (2004). *Situated language and learning: A critique of traditional schooling.* New York, NY: Routledge.

Gray, B. (2004). Informal learning in an online community of practice. *Journal of Distance Education, 19*(1), 20–35.

Greenhow, C., & Robelia, B. (2009). Informal learning and identity formation in online social networks. *Learning, Media, and Technology, 34*(2), 119–140.

Hilt, L. (2010, August 10). It's people, not programs. [Weblog post]. Retrieved from http://www.connectedprincipals.com/archives/339

Johnson, C. M. (2001). A survey of current research on online communities of practice. *Internet and Higher Education, 4,* 45–60.

Lesser, E., & Prusak, L. (1999). Communities of practice, social capital and organizational knowledge. In E. L. Lesser, M. A. Fontaine, & J. A. Slusher (Eds.), *Knowledge and communities* (pp. 123–131). Boston, MA: Butterworth Heinemann.

Martin, J. (2010, November 16). Appreciating NETP: Advancing 21st c. learning. [Weblog post]. Retrieved from http://www.connectedprincipals.com/archives/1648

McLure-Wasko, M., & Faraj, S. (2000). "It is what one does": Why people participate and help others in electronic communities of practice. *Journal of Strategic Information Systems, 9,* 155–173.

McLure-Wasko, M., Tiegland, R., & Faraj, S. (2009). The provision of online public goods: Examining social structure in an electronic network of practice. *Decision Support Systems, 47,* 254–265.

Nahapiet, J., & Ghoshal, S. (1998). Social capital, intellectual capital, and the organizational advantage. *Academy of Management Review, 23*(2), 242–266.

Onyx, J., & Bullen, P. (2000). Measuring social capital in five communities. *The Journal of Applied Behavioral Science, 36*(1), 23–42.

Renninger, K. A., & Shumar, W. (2004). The centrality of culture and community to participant learning at and with the math forum. In S. A. Barab, R. Kling, & J. H. Gray (Eds.), *Designing for virtual communities in the service of learning* (pp. 53–90). Cambridge, UK: University of Cambridge Press.

Schlager, M. S., Farooq, U., Fusco, J., Schank, P., & Dwyer, N. (2009). Analyzing online teacher networks: Cyber-networks require cyber-research tools. *Journal of Education, 60*(1), 86–100.

Schlager, M. S., & Fusco, J. (2003). Teacher professional development, technology, and communities of practice: Are we putting the cart before the horse? *The Information Society, 19,* 203–220.

Schlager, M. S., Fusco, J., & Schank, P. (2002). Evolution of an on-line education community of practice. In K. A. Renninger and W. Shumar (Eds.), *Building virtual communities: Learning and change in cyberspace* (pp. 129–158). NY: Cambridge University Press.

U.S. Department of Education. (2010). *Transforming American education—Learning powered by technology: National Education Technology Plan 2010.* Washington, DC: Office of Educational Technology, U.S. Department of Education.

Wenger, E. (1998). *Communities of practice: Learning, meaning, and identity.* Cambridge, MA: Cambridge University Press.

CHAPTER 14

SCHOOL LEADERS' PERCEPTIONS OF THE TECHNOLOGY STANDARDS

Matthew Militello and Alpay Ersozlu

INTRODUCTION

It's just a hell of a time to be alive, is all—just this goddamn messy business
of people having to get used to new ideas. And people just don't, that's all.
I wish this were a hundred years from now, with everybody used to the change.

—Vonnegut, *Player Piano* (1952, p. 37)

Today, there is contentious debate on the role and functionality of technology in schools. While pundits believe that technological innovations will reconceptualize teaching and learning, critics purport the computer is nothing more than an enchanting, sophisticated replication of our current system (modern-day "Emperor's New Clothes"). As a result, technophiles continue to pump technology into schools at record rates, using the sheer abundance of technology as proxy measures of success. In turn, we see warnings of technology as the new blunt instrument led by policy charlatans that will attempt to change extant behavior with "toolishness" (McKenzie, 2002), faddism, and rampant featurism (Cuban, 2001). Or, in

Principal 2.0: Technology and Educational Leadership, pages 233–247
Copyright © 2013 by Information Age Publishing
All rights of reproduction in any form reserved.

Shakespearian tongue, does technology have the "full sound and fury signifying nothing"? (cf., *Macbeth*, Act 5, Scene 5, Lines 27–8).

The tension between the availability of technology and the effectiveness of its use has been further complicated with the added pressures of standards and accountability. In 2002, No Child Left Behind (NCLB) not only called for increased accountability and testing measures related to student achievement, but the legislation also stated that by 2006 "technology will be fully integrated into the curricula and instruction of schools" (NCLB, 2002a). Moreover, Title II of NCLB earmarked 25% of the money spent on technology to professional development (in comparison, in 1996 only 9% of the money went to professional development) (NCLB, 2002b). NCLB transformed the philosophical question of *why* implement technology into analytical and practical questions of *how* do principals lead *with* technology to support teaching with technology in order to improve student learning.

The purpose of this chapter is to understand the perceptions of school leaders in regard to technology. More specifically, we focus on how school leaders perceive the current school leader technology standards. We begin with highlighting what we know about school leadership and technology. Next, we summarize the standards for technology to which school leaders must adhere to. We then offer results from a research study aimed at understanding the perceptions school principals have about the technology standards they are suppose to meet. We conclude with what we have learned and how it might provide insights for current and future school leaders.

WHAT WE KNOW

Let's begin with some basic facts:

1. *Technology is ubiquitous*—technological innovations are progressing at a rapid pace as is the accessibility (i.e., size and cost) to these innovations. As a result, technologies play a large role in both teaching and learning in schools.
2. *Technology mediates student learning*—recent innovations with technology have influenced what we know about learning (i.e., learning theory) and how teachers are teaching (i.e., new pedagogical tools).
3. *Technology impacts content*—the world indeed is much "flatter," to steal a phrase from Thomas Friedman (2007). Technology is a powerful, liberating force that democratizes information. Innovations allow for unprecedented access to people around the world, to geography, history, and culture—to information.
4. *Leaders matter in schools*—school leaders have the most influence on how teachers teach (Leithwood & Jantzi, 2008). As a result, there is a

close degree of separation among how leaders lead, teachers teach, and student learn.

5. *Standards matter*—the old adage, "what gets measured gets done," is truer now more than ever. In this era of accountability based on student standardized test scores, educators pay specific attention to initiatives that have a proven impact on learning. As a result, research-based technology standards have more prominence.

Administrative leadership may be the single most important factor affecting schools' successful integration of technology (Schrum, Galizio, & Ledesma, 2011). There have been clear and constant calls for school leaders to develop a vision and plans for technology that match their administrative goals (cf., Means, 2010; Papa, 2011). Creighton (2003) stated, "The crucial task at hand now is to decide how to implement this technology effectively into instruction" (p. 2). However, infrastructure changes are not enough; administrative support and leadership are equally if not more crucial to success. Administrators must model, budget, develop a vision, and create meaningful professional development with curricular aspects. As a result, it is the school leader who is uniquely positioned to transform technology into pedagogical practices and, thus, to positively impact student learning (Dexter, 2011).

Uniquely positioned and ready and able are different enterprises. We know there is dissonance between what *should be* and what *is* relative to technology leadership in schools. There are three mediating components for implementation with fidelity: knowledge, dispositions, and resources. First, it is imperative that the school leader has a developmental knowledge of technology's relationship to pedagogy and learning. That is, what do leaders know about school technology in general, and what specific links to proven teaching strategies can they share? Secondly, what is the *will* of the leader? Dispositions, beliefs, and motivations are synonymous with successful implementation of innovation. Finally, school leaders must attend to resources and support structures that pave the way for implementation. Resources and support are distinct from one another. Resources can be categorized as physical or monetary-based infrastructures that are needed (e.g., computers, iPads, etc.). Support includes macro issues such as a clearly articulated, ongoing professional development initiative, and micro activities such as crucial, honest one-to-one conversations about instructional practices.

In this section we demonstrated that school leaders are uniquely positioned to support effective implementation of technological innovations to improve student learning. Principals must first have the knowledge and skills necessary to implement new technologies, and they must have the will to infuse technology within the work of the school. At the same time NCLB provided mandates related to technology and professional development, national standards were developed that serve as a valuable resource to guide teachers' and administrators' efforts to integrate technology in schools. In the next section we summarize these standards.

THE NATIONAL STANDARDS FOR ADMINISTRATORS (NETS-A)

The International Society for Teachers in Education (ISTE, 2002, 2009) created NETS-A to "represent a national consensus of the things PK–12 school administrators need to know and do to support technology integration effectively in schools" (Brooks-Young, 2009, p. 2). The original set of standards was created by TSSA: Technology Standards for School Administrators in 2001. TSSA was comprised of various experts and organizational partners. These standards were later adopted by the International Society for Technology in Education (ISTE, 2002) and came to be known as the National Educational Technology Standards for Administrators (NETS-A). The standards have changed over time as technologies in general and specifically educational technologies have made advancements.

The NETS-A are made up of five standards (ISTE, 2009):

1. Visionary Leadership: Educational administrators inspire and lead development and implementation of a shared vision for comprehensive integration of technology to promote excellence and support transformation throughout the organization.
2. Digital-age Learning Culture: Educational administrators create, promote, and sustain a dynamic, digital-age learning culture that provides a rigorous, relevant, and engaging education for all students.
3. Excellence in Professional Practice: Educational administrators promote an environment of professional learning and innovation that empowers educators to enhance student learning through the infusion of contemporary technologies and digital resources.
4. Systemic Improvement: Educational administrators provide digital-age leadership and management to continuously improve the organization through the effective use of information and technology resources.
5. Digital Citizenship: Educational administrators model and facilitate understanding of social, ethical, and legal issues and responsibilities related to an evolving digital culture.

These standards are supported by a number of key school administrator organizations including: National Association of Secondary School Principals (NASSP), National Association of Elementary School Principals, American

Association of School Administrators, National School Board Association, and North Central Regional Educational Laboratory to name a few.

In the next section, we will explore the results of a research study that analyzed school administrators' perceptions of the school technology standards in their current leadership practice.

ADMINISTRATORS' PERCEPTIONS OF NETS-A

The researchers in this study used Q methodology to identify, describe, and examine distinct perceptions of technology leadership among 27 current school administrators in North Carolina Public Schools. The group of administrators included representation from all levels of schooling. Q methodology is a research method that was conceptualized and developed by the British physicist-psychologist William Stephenson in 1935. Q builds on both qualitative and quantitative instruments for data collection and analysis (Brown, 1993; Militello & Janson, 2007; Stainton Rogers, 1995). The methodology is designed to understand the unique, idiosyncratic subjectivity of individuals. Therefore, it was well suited to this investigation of administrators' perceptions related to the technology standards. Brown (1997) stated that "subjectivity is the purpose of Q methodology to enable the person to represent his or her vantage point for purposes of holding it constant for inspection and comparison" (p. 2). Basically, Q allows the researcher to quantify subjectivity (Watts & Stenner, 2012)—a most difficult task, to be sure. But if we want to understand how principals understand the technology the standards purport they enact, then we need a methodology that is able to (1) ascertain individual perceptions, and (2) quantify perceptions among a number of participants.

Each administrator who participated in this study was asked to rank, or sort, a set of items, referred to as a "Q sample." For this study, we chose to create a 21-item Q sample based upon the NETS-A standards document. We used the descriptions and elements of the five NETS-A standards to create a set of 21 statements. We eliminated duplicate statements and combined statements that expressed similar ideas while retaining statements that held unique expressions. Table 14.1 is the Q sample for this study.

These 21 technology statements were posted on a web application called Q-Assessor (see http://q-assessor.com/). The administrator participants were invited via email to link to the on-line web application. The portal allowed participants to sort the 21 statements in a drag and drop fashion (similar to playing Solitaire online). The administrators had a range of choices to drop the statements, from –3 ("Least like my perspective of technology leadership") to +3 ("Most like my perspective of technology leadership").

TABLE 14.1   Q Sample

No.	Q Sample Statement
1	Model and promote the frequent and effective use of technology for learning.
2	Stay abreast of educational research and emerging trends regarding effective use of technology and encourage evaluation of new technologies for their potential to improve student learning.
3	Inspire and facilitate among all stakeholders a shared vision of purposeful change that maximizes use of digital-age resources to meet and exceed learning goals, support effective instructional practice, and maximize performance of district and school leaders.
4	Recruit and retain highly competent personnel who use technology creatively and proficiently to advance academic and operational goals
5	Promote, model, and establish policies for safe, legal, and ethical use of digital information and technology.
6	Promote and model effective communication and collaboration among stakeholders using digital-age tools.
7	Allocate time, resources, and access to ensure ongoing professional growth in technology fluency and integration.
8	Provide learner-centered environments equipped with technology and learning resources to meet the individual, diverse needs of all learners.
9	Engage in an ongoing process to develop, implement, and communicate technology infused strategic plans aligned with a shared vision.
10	Ensure effective practice in the study of technology and its infusion across the curriculum.
11	Establish and maintain a robust infrastructure for technology including integrated, interoperable technology systems to support management, operations, teaching, and learning.
12	Model and facilitate the development of a shared cultural understanding and involvement in global issues through the use of contemporary communication and collaboration tools.
13	Collaborate to establish metrics, collect and analyze data, interpret results, and share findings to improve staff performance and student learning.
14	Promote and model responsible social interactions related to the use of technology and information.
15	Ensure instructional innovation focused on continuous improvement of digital-age.
16	Ensure equitable access to appropriate digital tools and resources to meet the needs of all learners.
17	Facilitate and participate in learning communities that stimulate, nurture, and support administrators, faculty, and staff in the study and use of technology.
18	Promote and participate in local, national, and global learning communities that stimulate innovation, creativity, and digital-age collaboration.
19	Lead purposeful change to maximize the achievement of learning goals through the appropriate use of technology and media-rich resources.
20	Advocate on local, state and national levels for policies, programs, and funding to support implementation of a technology-infused vision and strategic plan.
21	Establish and leverage strategic partnerships to support systemic improvement.

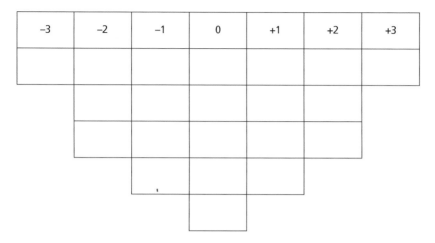

−3	−2	−1	0	+1	+2	+3

Figure 14.1 Q Sort distribution.

Figure 14.1 illustrates forced distribution into which the administrators had to sort the statements.

After performing the sorting procedure, each administrator responded to a series of prompts, including:

- Why did you place Statement #X into the +3 column?
- Why did you place Statement #X into the −3 column?
- What statement(s) did you have most difficulty placing? Why?
- Do you believe there were statement(s) that were missing? If so, what would the statement have said and where would you have placed it? Why?

After each of the administrator participants completed the online sorting procedure and the series of prompts, the 21 Q sorts were analyzed. Q methodology uses a by-person correlation and factor analytic procedure (McKeown & Thomas, 1988). Rather than analyzing the statements themselves, the Q process analyzes how individual participants sorted their statements in comparison to others. Following factor analysis, the factors are rotated to simple structure (using a Varimax rotation). In the end, four factors emerged from the analysis. The four-factor rotation accounted for 48% of the total variance. Next we describe each factor.

WHAT WE FOUND

Based upon the data analysis in this research study, four factors emerged. Table 14.2 summarizes where each of the 27 administrator participants fell

TABLE 14.2   Participants' Q-sort According to Factor Array

Participant	Factor A	Factor B	Factor C	Factor D
1	.12	−.31	−.24	.51*
2	−.22	.10	.12	−.08
3	.07	.80*	−.00	.26
4	.27	−.05	−.15	.59*
5	.21	−.71*	.08	−.06
6	.04	−.07	−.15	.19
7	.09	.06	.77*	−.06
8	.74*	−.18	−.22	.19
9	.68*	.01	.29	−.04
10	−.01	−.01	.28	.85*
11	.58*	.20	.10	.17
12	.79*	−.05	−.00	.02
13	.32	.39	.31	−.03
14	.02	.43*	.19	−.23
15	.08	.23	−.12	.81*
16	.36	.09	.35	.18
17	.59*	.14	.20	.04
18	.01	.18	.80*	−.04
19	.82*	.06	−.14	.02
20	.18	.00	.16	−.16
21	.19	.39	.54*	−.12
22	.01	.01	−.10	.24
23	.29	.27	.64*	−.00
24	.59*	.03	.02	.38
25	.09	.79*	.19	.16
26	.66*	.18	−.17	.04
27	.46*	.36	.36	−.11

*Signify significance, p<.05

on each of the factors. In quantitative analysis, researchers seek to determine significance in order to decide whether the findings happened by chance or whether the data reflect a pattern. Participants with a score or .43 or above on one of the factors was deemed significant (in Q methodology this is determined by the standard error multiplied by the level of significance). This level of significance ensures that the outcomes are not as a result of chance, at least 95% of the time for this study.

Of the 27 participants, 21 (78%) fell on one of the four factors, which we labeled as: (1) learning-based technology leaders, (2) organizational technology leaders, (3) change-agent technology leaders, and (4) facilitative technology leaders. Six participants did not have a level of significance on these four factors. That is, these six did not identify with any of the four factors.

Factor A: Learning-based Technology Leaders

Nine of the administrators were significantly associated with the factor we refer to as learning-based technology leadership. The nine participants on this factor all obtained master's degrees and were current principals (4) or assistant principals (5). Four of them have worked in education for more than 16 years while the others have been educators for at least six years. These administrators conceptualized technology leadership anchored in principals of learning.

More specifically, this perspective emphasized that technology leaders support effective use of technology for instructional practices, and they encourage evaluation of new technologies to improve student learning. Statements that were on the positive side of the distribution, meaning that administrators responded +1 through +3 (Most like my perspective of technology leadership), included:

- Model and promote the frequent and effective use of technology for learning (Statement 1)
- Inspire and facilitate among all stakeholders a shared vision of purposeful change that maximizes use of digital-age resources to meet and exceed learning goals, support effective instructional practice, and maximize performance of district and school leaders (Statement 3)
- Stay abreast of educational research and emerging trends regarding effective use of technology and encourage evaluation of new technologies for their potential to improve student learning (Statement 2)
- Lead purposeful change to maximize the achievement of learning goals through the appropriate use of technology and media-rich resources (Statement 19).

Interestingly, these statements fall throughout the NETS-A standard domains. Statement 1 falls under Digital-age Learning Culture, statement 3 in Visionary Leadership, statement 2 in Excellence in Professional Practice and 19 under Systemic Improvement. However, each has an element of learning that they attribute to educational technology. One principal who had affinity with this factor stated, "The change or improvement in any area of education must be centered around the student, and I feel that if all students are allowed access through the tools and resources then needs can be met. This begins with teacher learning. Learning is the key at the end, the middle and the beginning." As a result, we named these leaders "Learning-based Technology Leaders."

Factor B: Organizational Technology Leaders

Four administrators, three principals and one assistant principal, were significantly associated with the second factor. All four have more than 11 years of experience in education, and one had a doctoral degree.

These administrators conceptualized technology leadership through their role in the organization. That is, these leaders facilitate technology leadership through their ability to organize resources, both technical and human. The statements on the positive side of the distribution included:

- Provide learner-centered environments equipped with technology and learning resources to meet the individual, diverse needs of all learners (Statement 8)
- Recruit and retain highly competent personnel who use technology creatively and proficiently to advance academic and operational goals (Statement 4)
- Ensure equitable access to appropriate digital tools and resources to meet the needs of all learners (Statement 16)
- Collaborate to establish metrics, collect and analyze data, interpret results, and share findings to improve staff performance and student learning (Statement 13).

These principals looked at leadership for technology in a systemic manner. These leaders believed that resources and support for technology must be developed and implemented equally and systemically. They ensure the infrastructure is in place for technology to have an impact. One principal stated, "I believe that it is extremely important that all students and staff have access to student-centered technology. This is the way of the world and students are eager to use technology. They will find a way to use it and educators need to capitalize on this." Another said that providing the support and resources for teachers to use technology with students was "my job."

Factor C: Change-agent Technology Leaders

Four administrators were significantly associated with this factor related to promoting a culture of technology in schools via a departure from current practices. The participants included experienced educators (all more than 11 years' experience). Three were principals and one an assistant principal. One of the principals also had a doctoral degree.

These administrators conceptualized collective technology leadership through the development of a *new* technology culture. More specifically, this perspective stressed the necessity of promoting effective use of technology innovations to achieve planning goals and learning goals.

These administrators supported the development of a school culture that embraced technology and experimented with new ways that technology could be integrated into the work of the school. The positive side of the distribution included:

- Ensure instructional innovation focused on continuous improvement of digital age (Statement 15)
- Ensure effective practice in the study of technology and its infusion across the curriculum (Statement 10)
- Advocate on local, state, and national levels for policies, programs, and funding to support implementation of a technology-infused vision and strategic plan (Statement 20)
- Lead purposeful change to maximize the achievement of learning goals through the appropriate use of technology and media-rich resources (Statement 19).

These leaders are focused on improvement, vision, and purposeful change. One leader who was significant on this factor stated, "In order to promote 21st century skills and effective technology integrating, we need teachers who are willing to think outside the box, explore new interesting ways to teach, and hire those who can inspire children to reach beyond current limits." Another leader said, "This is the digital age. It is critical for our students to learn to be responsible users of technology. In order to teach students how to use technology effectively, I must ensure the teachers I hire are competent in this area. I must help them understand that how they teach may need to look very different."

Factor D: Facilitative Technology Leaders

Four administrators were significantly associated with this factor, which we refer to as facilitative technology leaders. The administrators included three principals and one assistant principal. They all had more than 16 years of experience, and they all had master's degrees.

These administrators conceptualized technology leadership by means of their coordination or facilitation. That is, these leaders wanted to integrate technology through their ability to provide direction, secure resources, and model for others. Statements in the positive side of the distribution included:

- Recruit and retain highly competent personnel who use technology creatively and proficiently to advance academic and operational goals (Statement 4)
- Promote, model, and establish policies for safe, legal, and ethical use of digital information and technology (Statement 5)
- Collaborate to establish metrics, collect and analyze data, interpret results, and share findings to improve staff performance and student learning (Statement 13)
- Model and promote the frequent and effective use of technology for learning (Statement 1).

One leader on this factor stated, "Recruiting the right staff is critical to implement any and all use of technology in the classrooms." Another stated, "Principals should use technology regularly and demonstrate its value for teaching, learning, communication, information gathering, decision making, etc. The principal must hire people who understand, are willing to learn, and will use tech."

DISCUSSION

School leaders are expected to play a key role in the usage of technology. This study focused on this press through technology standards for school leaders. Our goal was to ascertain how current school leaders perceived these standards in their practice.

Four factors emerged in this study to understand the perceptions of school leaders regarding technology leadership. This research indicated that principals have diverse perspectives. There is no one best model array—no *one* best archetype of a technology leader. There can and should be many routes to being an effective technology leader in schools. Nonetheless, there are indications for the literature and lessons from studies such as this that illuminate promising practices.

The current school leaders in this study were Organizational Technology Leaders (Factor 2), who pave the way for the Learning-based Technology Leaders (Factor 1) who teach and model. They were Change-agent Technology Leaders (Factor 3) looking to change the status quo. Finally, they were Facilitative Technology Leaders (Factor 4) who combined many of the traits of the previous factors. While these factors do not provide the *one* archetypical technology leader, they provide valuable insight into the specific dimensions of technology leadership. They highlight the multidimensionality needed in our school leaders today.

Regardless of which factor leaders represent, there are two important features that are telling about leaders of technology. First, leaders must understand, reflect, and hone their own knowledge, dispositions, and skills in the arena of technology. Refusal to promote or integrate technology may be a function of ignorance or inexperience in one or all dimensions of their knowledge, skills, and dispositions. Assessing where one is on this triumvirate is a beginning. It allows leaders to understand what they need through reflection and inquiry before proceeding directly to action.

Second, school leaders must address the very personal and very powerful elements associated with change. Lortie (1975) stated, "Teachers have built-in resistance to change because they believe that their work environment has never permitted them to show what they really can do" (p. 235). It is the school leader who plays an important role in the psychological and emotive dance of change. Leaders need to help teachers *develop capacity* and *see how* the change will impact student learning. The integration of any innovation hinges on how a leader can help teachers own the innovation.

CONCLUSION

Research has clearly indicated that advanced technologies can enhance teachers' pedagogy and students' learning. The catalyst for this enhancement can be the technology itself. However, there must be *access* to advanced technologies, resources, and support. As the economy of technology hardware and software becomes more prevalent and relevant, there will be undoubtedly more access and use. However, the catalyst can also be *the school leader* herself. It is the leader who is a gatekeeper for resources and support. The leader has some power of the purse string: budgetary discretion. She also has the ability to recruit and hire effective teachers. She is the chief evaluator of teachers, a powerful mechanism for change. Finally, she is well positioned to model educational technology for her teachers, students, and parents. For all these reasons, school leaders must be the chief technology leaders in the school.

Are we asking too much of our school leaders: management, instruction, communication, and now technology? Administrators have visionary, structural, and positional power. That is, they can establish a clear, articulate vision of the use of technology in schools, and they can procure funds, establish support structures, and evaluate its use in concert with the vision. The broad scope and nuances of educational technologies "will require uniquely skilled administrators who understand technology and stay current with all its vagaries. These administrators will need to be capable of managing computer personnel, advising the staff on rapidly changing products, providing vision in a changing technological landscape, and managing a large budget" (Weiss, 1996, pp. 410–411). As a result, if new understandings of student learning and teaching pedagogy are required for meaningful use of educational technologies, attention must be paid to the street-level managers of implementation, the school leaders. Leaders will have to be transformational, not transactional, if pedagogy is to be reconceptualized (see Moore-Johnson, 1996). Transformational leadership will be required for educators to own the innovation and for the "purpose of bringing about a 'major change in form, nature, and function of some phenomenon'" (Spillane, Halverson, & Diamond, 2001, p. 24).

Leaders must stop buffering and marginalizing reforms; instead, "the problem is finding structures that reflect and reinforce competing theories of good teaching and learning" (Sykes & Elmore, 1988, p. 84). Advancements in technology may be the catalyst for major reform. However, the reform will be as powerful and effective as the school technology leadership. Reform efforts begin with changing the traditional leadership practices based on managing the school, to instructionally based transformational leadership that is distributed across the school, allowing all educators in the school ecology to co-evolve. The innovation of instructional technology in conjunction with such transformational leadership may have tremendous impact on how teachers teach, and thus, how students learn.

If we want different outcomes for student learning using educational technologies, then we must also have different inputs: the technology itself and the pedagogical delivery of the technology. Here we submit it is the function of the school leader to be the inquiry and action leader of a technology fortified school filled with technology-savvy teachers and learners. The concept of the school principal as chief technology leader may be worrisome, but the alternative is worse.

REFERENCES

Brooks-Young, S. (2009). *Making technology standards work for you: A guide for school administrators.* Washington, DC: ISTE Publications.

Brown, S. R. (1993). A primer on Q methodology. *Operant Subjectivity, 16*(3/4), 91–138.

Brown, S. R. (1997). *The history and principles of Q methodology in psychology and the social sciences.* Retrieved from http://facstaff.uww.edu/cottlec/Qarchive/Bps.htm

Creighton, T. (2003). *The principal as technology leader.* Thousand Oaks, CA: Corwin Press.

Cuban, L. (2001). *Oversold and underused: Computers in the classroom.* Cambridge, MA: Harvard University Press.

Dexter, S. (2011). School technology leadership: Artifacts in systems of practice. *Journal of School Leadership, 21*(2), 166–189.

Friedman, T. (2007). *The world is flat 3.0: A brief history of the twenty-first century.* New York, NY: Farrar, Straus and Giroux.

International Society for Technology in Education (ISTE). (2002). *National educational technology standards for administrators*. Retrieved from http://www.iste.org/docs/pdfs/nets-for-administrators-2002_en.pdf?sfvrsn=2

International Society for Technology in Education (ISTE). (2009). *National educational technology standards for administrators*. Retrieved from http://www.iste.org/docs/pdfs/nets-a-standards.pdf?sfvrsn=2

Leithwood, K., & Jantzi, D. (2008). Linking leadership to student learning: The contributions of leader efficacy. *Educational Administration Quarterly, 44*(4), 496–528.

Lortie, D. (1975). *Schoolteacher*. Chicago, IL: University of Chicago Press.

McKenzie, J. (2002). Leading by example: The high touch high tech principal. *From Now On* Retrieved March 12, 2010, from http://www.fno.org/sum02/principal.html

McKeown, B., & Thomas, D. (1988). *Q methodology*. London, UK: Sage Publications.

Means, B. (2010). Technology and education change: Focus on student learning. *Journal of Research on Technology in Education, 42*(3), 285–307.

Militello, M., & Janson, C. (2007). Socially-focused, situationally-driven practice: A study of distributed leadership practices among school principals and counselors. *Journal of School Leadership, 17*(4), 409–441.

Moore-Johnson, S. (1996). *Leading to change: the challenge of the new superintendency*. San Francisco, CA: Jossey-Bass.

No Child Left Behind (NCLB) Act of 2001, Pub. L. No. 107-110, § 115, Stat. 1425 (2002a).

No Child Left Behind. (2002b). *The facts about No Child Left Behind: 21st century technology*. Retrieved from www.NoChildLeftBehind.gov

Papa, R. (2011). *Technology leadership for school improvement*. Thousand Oaks, CA: Sage.

Schrum, L., Galizio, L., & Ledesma, P. (2011). Educational leadership and technology integration: An investigation into preparation, experiences, and roles. *Journal of School Leadership, 21*(2), 241–261.

Spillane, J., Halverson, R., & Diamond, J. B. (2001). Investigating school leadership practice: A distributed perspective. *Educational Researcher, 30*(3), 23–28.

Stainton Rogers, R. (1995). *Q methodology*. London, UK: Sage.

Sykes, G., & Elmore, R. (1988). Making schools manageable: Policy and administration for tomorrow's schools. In J. Hannaway & R. Crowson (Eds.), *The politics of reforming school administration: The 1988 yearbook of the Politics of Education Association* (pp. 77–94). New York, NY: Falmer Press.

Vonnegut, K. (1952). *Player Piano*. New York, NY: Dell Publishing.

Watts, S., & Stenner, P. (2012). *Doing Q methodological research: Theory, method and interpretation*. Thousand Oaks, CA: Sage.

Weiss, A. (1996). System 2000: If you build it, can you manage it? *Phi Delta Kappan, 77*(6), 408–415.

CHAPTER 15

SUPPORTING EFFECTIVE TECHNOLOGY INTEGRATION AND IMPLEMENTATION

Scott McLeod and Jayson W. Richardson

INTRODUCTION

Schools have made significant progress regarding their implementation and integration of digital technologies compared to where they were three decades ago. That progress often has been quite slow, however. Although Apple 1 computers were donated to schools as early as 1975 (*Computers in the classroom,* n.d.), it was not until the mid-1980s that computers started to become something other than a novelty in teachers' classrooms. Technology use by educators and students continued to be relatively rare through the mid-1990s until the federal Technology Literacy Challenge Fund helped schools to work toward the goal of making computers available to every student (Riley, 1996). Fostered by additional funding, investment in infrastructure, multiple national educational technology plans (United States Department of Education, 1996, 2000, 2004, 2010), and concurrent growth of the Internet and home computing use, digital technologies proliferated more quickly in U.S. schools in the beginning decades of the 21st century.

Principal 2.0: Technology and Educational Leadership, pages 249–272
Copyright © 2013 by Information Age Publishing
All rights of reproduction in any form reserved.

Technological changes in school learning environments over the past 15 years have been substantial, particularly related to computer and Internet access and usage. For instance, in 1994 only 3% of public school classrooms, computer labs, and library media centers had Internet access (National Center for Education Statistics [NCES], 1997). Fourteen years later, 97% of public school classrooms had an Internet connection (NCES, 2010a). Student-to-computer ratios also decreased significantly over this time. In 1996, the national student-to-computer ratio in public schools was 11:1 (United States Department of Education, 1996) but by 2009 that ratio had dropped to just 1.7 students per computer (NCES, 2010b). Today many schools are implementing so-called 1:1 programs in which every student is provided a laptop, netbook, tablet computer, or some other handheld device. Schools that allow students to bring their own technology from home are even seeing student-to-computer ratios tip the other direction, since it is not uncommon for students to possess multiple computing devices. As students incorporate laptops, tablets, smartphones, and other digital devices into their daily learning experiences in the years to come, it will be the norm for student-to-computer ratios in schools to be 1:2, 1:3, or even lower.

Progress in other areas of school technology has been significant as well. For example, in 2002 only 9% of U.S. public schools reported having students who were taking online courses (NCES, 2005). Those students accounted for a mere 328,000 course enrollments. Given that some students took more than one online course, approximately 0.5% of the national student population was taking an online class a decade ago. By 2009 there were an estimated 1.8 million online enrollments of traditional students and another 200,000 children taking multiple courses as students in full-time online schools (International Association for K–12 Online Learning [iNACOL], 2012). At least 5% of the national student population is taking at least one online course today, which constitutes a tenfold increase in just a few years (United States Department of Education, 2012). Similarly, while in 1999 less than 10% of teachers reported using the Internet to access research and best practices for teaching (United States Department of Education, 2000), a decade later 94% of teachers reported using the Internet "sometimes or often" for classroom, instruction, or administrative tasks (NCES, 2010b).

As computers and the Internet have become more prevalent in U.S. schools, many analysts' concerns have shifted from *whether* educators and students have access to digital technologies to *how* they use the technology as learning tools. Some scholars have focused on teachers' lack of usage (e.g., Collins & Halverson, 2009; Cuban, 2001; Moe & Chubb, 2009), while others note that teachers may use technology in their instruction but may not use it very effectively (see, e.g., Jacobs, 2010; Lemke, Coughlin, Garcia,

Reifsneider, & Baas, 2009; Richardson & Mancabelli, 2011). This chapter emphasizes leadership models and practices that enhance the adoption and effective use of learning technologies in schools.

STANDARDS, MODELS, AND FRAMEWORKS

In an attempt to increase and improve educators' use of digital learning tools, some researchers and organizations have created theoretical models or standards documents to guide teachers' and administrators' practice. The dominant conceptual model used by most instructional technology experts today is Mishra and Koehler's Technological Pedagogical Content Knowledge Framework [TPACK] (2006), which focuses on the intersections between teachers' content knowledge, their pedagogical knowledge, and their knowledge of digital technologies. In addition to the TPACK framework, technology curricula for P–12 students, professional development initiatives for teachers, and pre-service teacher preparation programs also are typically being guided by the International Society for Technology in Education (ISTE) National Educational Technology Standards for students (NETS-S) and teachers (NETS-T) (ISTE, 2007, 2008). ISTE was founded in 1979 and is the world's largest organization focused on educational technology issues. In addition to its standards for students, teachers, and administrators, there also are sets of standards from ISTE for administrators (NETS-A), instructional technology coaches (NETS-C), and computer science educators (NETS-CSE) (ISTE, 2009b, 2011a, 2011b), but these have gained much less traction in the field. Few pre-service administrator preparation programs, for example, are making use of the NETS-A (McLeod, 2011).

In addition to its standards regarding what students, teachers, and administrators need to know and be able to do when it comes to digital technologies, ISTE has published a list of *Essential Conditions* (2009a) that are necessary "to effectively leverage technology for learning" (p. 1). These conditions include vision, leadership, technical support, curriculum frameworks, and supporting policies. It is ISTE's belief that school leaders who acquire and effectively implement the competencies outlined in the NETS-A will enable the environmental conditions necessary for students and teachers to thrive in their technological practices in support of learning. ISTE's *Essential Conditions* list has been utilized by researchers (e.g., Borthwick, Hansen, Gray, & Ziemann, 2008; Bucci, Cherup, Cunningham, & Petrosino, 2003; Judge & O'Bannon, 2007) and provides a useful framework for examining administrators' behaviors and belief systems as they work to support technology usage by teachers and students (Thomas & Knezek, 2008).

ESSENTIAL CONDITIONS

There are 14 essential conditions described by ISTE as necessary for effective technology integration and implementation in schools. Principals and superintendents arguably are primarily responsible for the climate, culture, and other environmental characteristics that define students' and teachers' work. Accordingly, if the necessary conditions for successful technology usage are lacking in schools, administrators are the first place to look for the solution. In the sections that follow, we outline in concrete terms a number of leadership actions that promote and facilitate powerful usage of technology for learning.

Shared Vision

Facilitating organizational vision is an imperative component of any leader's roles and responsibilities. When it comes to technology, any vision for powerful integration and implementation must by necessity begin with a rich understanding of the complex and interdependent characteristics of the new technology-infused environments in which schools are encompassed. Our world is now digital rather than merely analog. Our interactions occur electronically and online rather than just face to face. We increasingly have mobile access—anytime and anywhere—through our Internet-connected devices to the entire world's information, crossing both geographic and linguistic borders. Like our individual selves, most of that information is networked and interconnected. It is also largely open and free and thus much more convenient and accessible (Willinsky, 2006).

Because the barriers to publishing are so low, billions of people now can be content creators instead of just being information consumers (Shirky, 2008). Ideas and resources blossom and create an often-overwhelming ecosphere of information, forcing us to devise new knowledge aggregation and curation tools. We are developing techniques such as "crowdsourcing" and "crowdfunding" that allow us to create content and tools that were literally impossible to make in the past.

Because of online and electronic learning environments, our dependency on place-bound information repositories and/or live humans as instructors is decreasing. For hundreds of millions of people whose learning needs were previously unmet, this is a tremendous blessing, particularly as informal, technology-mediated learning opportunities become robust enough to sometimes substitute for formal, face-to-face learning institutions such as schools and universities (Christensen, Horn, & Johnson, 2008). Our learning resources now come to us in the form of interactive multimedia, including not just static and hyperlinked text but also audio, video, images, charts, diagrams, maps, games, and simulations. Our barriers to access have decreased significantly and thus our learning is more empowered because it can be more autonomous, self-directed, and personalized.

All of these developments, both individually and as part of the larger, commingled whole, have profound implications for how we think about learning, teaching, and schooling. Most schools continue to utilize traditional analog pedagogical techniques rather than being primarily digital. They are predominantly locally oriented rather than globally oriented. Many of the devices that bring the world's information to us are banned in schools, and educators infrequently understand or use with students the technologies that are transforming everything else around us.

Principals must be purposeful and intentional about developing school internal cultures that are relevant to students' external cultures. If they are to see desired movement in necessary directions, principals must be able to communicate these societal and technological shifts in emotionally and intellectually resonant ways to their internal and external communities. If staff, parents, and other community members lack a felt need to change, principals must enact sustained initiatives of communication and education until long-term change mindsets are firmly in place that digital technologies are here to stay, that they are important, and that they will continuously and disruptively foster numerous changes in schooling practice. These mindsets then must be continually nurtured and supported in order to stave off complacency or a return to traditional modes of operating (Kotter, 2008).

Numerous avenues are available to principals to do this visioning work. In the past, school leaders wishing to find support for a change initiative would "pound the pavement," connecting with staff and community members face to face and trying to recruit allies to the cause. That face time still is critically important for technology-related change efforts, but it is also often inefficient since it depends on interactions that are primarily one-to-one or one-to-few. Principals have new tools available to them that can increase their reach and impact. Daily sharing on a blog, weekly podcasts, monthly videos (instead of paper newsletters) to the community and ongoing interactions on the school website and Facebook pages all are possible mechanisms for spreading the word, drumming up support, and maintaining a sense of urgency.

Empowered Leaders

Facilitating distributed leadership structures is another critical task for principals in their roles as technology leaders. In the past, school leadership was viewed primarily as the domain of a single person in charge (Gronn,

2008). That person made decisions and then employees carried out the orders. We now know that school organizational structures that distribute leadership functions across more people result in better outcomes, whether those be employee involvement and engagement (Hulpia, Devos, & Van Keer, 2011; Murphy, Smylie, Mayrowetz, & Louis, 2009) or student achievement (Heck & Hallinger, 2009).

Distributed leadership is vital for a school's operations generally. It is also important for its technology functions specifically (Levin & Schrum, 2012). Every principal should have a technology advisory team that consists of teachers, parents, students, and interested community members. That team should have meaningful input into the school's technology-related goals and decision-making processes, including purchasing, instructional integration, professional development, and staffing for both technology support and technology integration. The technology advisory team also should be charged with collecting both qualitative and quantitative data from all stakeholders (including students), evaluating the success of the school's technology initiatives, and reporting frequently and publicly.

Another aspect of empowered, distributed leadership is the creation of structures that facilitate team members' learning. Schools that create ways to "bring the outside in" for staff and technology advisory teams will have access to a greater diversity of ideas and resources than those whose ideas are devised locally in-house. In their seminal book, *The Power of Pull*, Hagel, Brown, and Davison (2010) describe the incredible power of members at the outside edges of organizations bumping up against, intersecting with, and learning from individuals at other organizations' edges (see also Cross & Parker, 2004; Benkler, 2006). Online—and often informal—learning structures that span institutional barriers can be powerful ways to facilitate distributed learning and leadership. A variety of technology tools are available for this purpose, including blogs, Twitter, Facebook, wikis, webinars, and social bookmarking.

Implementation Planning

Any effective technology implementation will be well-planned. However, the speed at which digital technologies change these days brings unique challenges. For example, the days of three- or five-year technology plans are probably numbered. Any school technology plan that is not able to adapt yearly or even quicker is one that may be outdated the moment it is written. Technology planning should be organized around essential student learning outcomes and staff learning goals, not particular devices. For example, a goal statement in a technology plan might read, "To enable greater access to online learning resources by primary grade students" rather than, "To purchase 250 iPads for use in the elementary school." Technology plan goal statements that are learning-oriented rather than tool-oriented are more flexible and can better accommodate rapid changes in available devices and systems.

A truism for all technology implementations is that schools likely never can have enough bandwidth. Principals should plan on probably upgrading the capacity of their school network yearly as student and staff computers become ubiquitous. Technology users in the organization also will access more multimedia as mobile computing devices become more prevalent, thus putting additional strains on network capacity. Principals should work closely with their school and district technology support staff regarding technology deployment and network load management. This includes advocacy for greater bandwidth and other supports for rich technology integration by students and staff. While perhaps preservative of the integrity of the existing school network, locking or disabling access to particular sites or certain functions of the network often goes against the educational mission of school organizations. Robust conversations must be held in which principals, teachers, and students have meaningful input into the purchasing of specific learning technologies and services, the management of the school network, access to the Internet, and local policies that affect access and usage. The National Center for Technology Planning (www.nctp.com) can be a helpful resource to principals and local technology advisory teams as they and their communities do the difficult work of technology planning.

Consistent and Adequate Funding

Another component of effective technology planning and implementation is ensuring a steady and adequate stream of funding. Technology-oriented grants, donations, short-term business partnerships, or other one-time monies are useful for jumpstarting new programs, funding pilots, and enhancing current practice but should not be relied upon for long-term, systemic deployments. Currently, schools utilize a variety of strategies to fund their ongoing technology initiatives. Many reallocate general funds. Others rely upon facility, equipment, and/or technology levies. While the latter are often dependent on voter approval, these referenda still may be more stable revenue streams than grants, donations, or temporary set-asides. Some states have allocated portions of statewide tax revenues to help schools with technology-related purchasing and deployment. Principals and their technology advisory teams should stay abreast of any and all possible avenues for technology funding and should have a long-term goal of sustaining instructional and organizational technology initiatives through reliable funding streams rather than short-term, temporary mechanisms.

One promising trend for technology funding is that an increasing number of states now allow schools to repurpose textbook monies for digital learning devices and materials. Rather than being forced to buy paper textbooks, schools can use those funds to create or purchase electronic textbooks, laptop or tablet computers, digital learning systems, access to online services, and other learning technologies. As they gain flexibility regarding funding and usage requirements, many schools are getting creative with their technology initiatives and are implementing more innovative programs such as wireless-enabled school buses (Dillon, 2010), learning projects that utilize mobile technologies such as smartphones and tablets (Toppo, 2011), 3-dimensional printers that can create tangible objects from liquefied materials (Dimension Printing, 2012), and "maker labs" in which youth have access to workspaces containing a wide variety of digital and physical tools (Youth Radio, 2012). Similar creativity is necessary to fund and sustain these inventive programs. Schools should make every attempt possible to stay abreast of emerging technologies and their potential instructional uses.

Equitable Access

Equitable opportunities with learning technologies have been a concern from the beginning of their deployment in schools. Most of the attention has focused on typically underserved students' access to computers and the Internet (e.g., Becker, 2006; Warschauer, Knobel, & Stone, 2004). Many educational policy and funding initiatives have been aimed at closing this so-called "digital divide." Although access gaps are smaller today than a decade or two ago (Warschauer & Matuchniak, 2010), principals still must pay attention to the issue, particularly as the emergence of new technologies often creates new disparities (Reich, Murnane, & Willett, 2012).

In addition to technology access divides, it also is common in schools to see technology usage divides. As Neuman (1991) noted:

> Economically disadvantaged students, who often use the computer for remediation and basic skills, learn to do what the computer tells them, while more affluent students, who use it to learn programming and tool applications, learn to tell the computer what to do. (p. 1)

This "secondary digital divide" is of grave concern. Students living in poverty, students of color, students from diverse linguistic backgrounds, students with special needs, and others may be particularly dependent on schools to close technology access and usage gaps since their existing economic, social, and/or cultural capital may not be sufficient to do so.

Principals must attend to both primary and secondary digital divide concerns. Otherwise, students who are already disadvantaged will fall further behind as our world becomes even more technology-suffused than it is already. Principals must be proactive, taking actions such as investigating potential gaps in their schools and using federal Title I and other monies to remedy access and usage disparities. Instead of giving new technology equipment and opportunities to high-achieving or already-advantaged students, schools can intentionally give academically struggling or disadvantaged students first exposure to those learning tools.

Many schools have tried to address disparate technology access and usage at home, not just at school. For instance, some schools provide students with portable computers, subsidize mobile phone Internet subscriptions, implement wireless Internet hotspot checkout programs, or create parent education and training opportunities in a deliberate attempt to close technology and learning equity gaps. Similarly, some schools have worked with local community groups or telecommunications companies to provide discounted or free home Internet access to low-income families (McLeod, 2009). A new national nonprofit organization, Connect2Compete (www. connect2compete.org), has received billions of dollars in commitments from the federal government, Internet service providers, and other corporations and foundations to provide reduced-cost home Internet access and digital programming to lower-income students and their families.

Skilled Personnel

The existence of digital learning technologies in schools does not mean that educators know how to use them. Wide variability in educators' technology knowledge and skills exists both within and across school organizations. While some educators seem to be quickly fluent with any technology that crosses their horizons, others still are struggling to master basic technologies such as email, file management systems, Internet browsers, and office productivity software.

Overall, teachers report that they are more fluent with digital technologies than they used to be. For example, over half of all public school teachers report that they use word processing, spreadsheet, desktop publishing, and presentation software "sometimes or often" (NCES, 2010b). Smaller but still substantial percentages report that they use database, image editing, and simulation and visualization programs. Nonetheless, a broad continuum of faculty technology fluency persists in most schools, particularly when it comes to newer tools such as blogs, wikis, social networking, and other social media (NCES, 2010b).

One way that principals can work to ensure that they have teachers and other personnel who are skilled with digital technologies is to incorporate technology expectations into hiring and annual review criteria. For instance, many schools create detailed job descriptions and interview protocols for hiring new faculty but fail to include meaningful technology integration as an essential component of their job announcements and interview processes. Students and technology-savvy teachers should be integrally involved with the selection and on-campus interviews of potential hires. Interview protocols should include detailed questions designed to determine how and how often teacher candidates will incorporate technology into student learning experiences.

Another way for principals to influence the supply of technology-fluent teachers is to work closely with teacher education programs. As schools create technology-rich learning environments and focus more on higher-order thinking skills, many administrators are finding that pre-service programs have not adapted yet to provide new graduates with skills that are relevant for their classrooms. For example, when asked how well their teacher education program prepared them to make effective use of technology for instruction, only 33% of public school teachers replied "to a moderate or major extent" for their graduate program, and only 25% of public school teachers reported the same for their undergraduate teacher education program (NCES, 2010b). Principals should initiate constructive, nonthreatening dialogues with university faculty and administrators about the technology skill sets that they need new teachers to have. Realigned postsecondary curricula, joint research initiatives, observation programs, mentoring systems, internships, partnerships, political advocacy platforms, and assessments of technological and human capacity are just some of the potential outcomes of such conversations.

Ongoing teacher observation and evaluation processes should stress that technology integration is a core component of educators' work rather than an optional or marginal add-on. In order for that to occur, principals must be able to identify and differentiate between effective technology usage by students and teachers to support learning, and simply using technology for technology's sake. Principals also can facilitate school-wide discussions, the creation of videotaped exemplars, and other mechanisms to foster explicit recognition and analysis of relevant, authentic technology integration. Additionally, school leaders should facilitate appropriate assistance and intervention opportunities for teachers who are struggling to meaningfully integrate digital technologies into their classrooms. These might include technology "boot camps" that create peer-to-peer training opportunities and focus on specific skills, ongoing mentoring, and other professional learning mechanisms.

Ongoing Professional Learning

Whether teachers are trying to remediate gaps in their knowledge and skills or extend and enhance those that they already have, all teachers deserve rich professional learning opportunities related to technology. Unfortunately, the majority of public school teachers report that they receive eight hours or less of technology-related training per year; one in seven reports no technology training whatsoever (NCES, 2010b). In an era when digital technologies, workforce demands, and other societal factors are changing quite rapidly, low exposure to technology-oriented professional development opportunities does nothing to ameliorate schools' typically sluggish rates of change.

Principals need to find ways to continually nurture and upgrade their teachers' technology knowledge, skills, and inclinations. If funds are limited for more traditional mechanisms such as sending faculty to state or national educational technology conferences, plenty of other opportunities abound. For instance, principals could work with other local leaders to facilitate regional or in-house technology workshops. Every school has teachers who are technologically fluent. Typically those teachers are more than happy to share their skills and talents with their peers. Whether it is through after-school training, release time during the school day, participant-driven "unconferences," or other structures, principals should work with district technology staff, professional development personnel, and other leaders to find ways for technology-savvy faculty to teach and facilitate other teachers within their buildings.

In addition to utilization of internal technology integration expertise, principals often bring in outside experts to train teachers how to use specific technology tools. These may be provided by vendors or may be independent national-level trainers or consultants. Regardless of the provider, technology training experiences always should comply with best practices regarding adult learning. Similar to non-technology-related training, technology professional development should occur within learning communities, be differentiated by learning needs, facilitate active engagement by participants, be recurrent and build upon past learning rather than only occurring once, be aligned with desired curriculum standards, and be rooted in learning and teaching needs rather than the technical aspects of a particular tool (Learning Forward, 2011).

One of the very best ways to facilitate teachers' technology learning is to have dedicated technology integration personnel. Similar to instructional coaches, technology integration personnel usually have advanced training related to teaching with technology and have different skill sets than those technical support personnel charged with hardware, software, or network maintenance and troubleshooting. Whether technology integration personnel are staffed within a particular building or shared with other buildings across a larger system, teachers better integrate technology into their classrooms when they have regular access and exposure to such individuals (e.g., Hew & Brush, 2006; Zhao, Pugh, Sheldon, & Byers, 2002). When it comes to technology, most school organizations invest in technical support but lack a concurrent commitment regarding teacher integration. Whether due to a lack of funding, knowledge, or vision, this underinvestment perpetuates teachers' infrequent and/or shallow use of learning technologies within their instructional practice (Collins & Halverson, 2009; Cuban, 2001). Principals must recognize that technology purchases require parallel investments in educator capacity-building in order to maximize usage.

If dedicated technology integration personnel are unavailable, other possibilities still exist for schools. Hughes and Ooms (2004), for example, facilitated teacher inquiry groups in which teacher teams of similar content and grade area worked to find technology-supported solutions. These groups experienced great success as they engaged in action research projects designed to support their technology integration experiences. Other alternatives might be to create student-led technology support teams or to assign a student technology mentor to every teacher. Organizations such as Generation YES (www.genyes.org) work with schools around the world to implement student-driven technology support structures.

In addition to providing formal technology learning avenues for teachers, principals also should strive to connect their faculty with informal opportunities. Many educators find great value in online, networked learning spaces, sometimes called personal (or professional) learning networks (PLNs). Using tools such as webinars, blogs, RSS readers, Twitter, and social networks, teachers are connecting with each other within PLNs in ways that were impossible prior to the advent of the Internet. Communities of practice are emerging that are global rather than just local. As illustrated by the extraordinary enthusiasm of many of the educators participating in these loose, diffuse networks, helping teachers connect with other role-alike peers around the world can have a transformative impact on their instructional practices. Research shows that administrators who are trained in and model the use of digital technologies often see increased usage by teaching faculty (Dawson & Rakes, 2003). Principals should be active participants themselves when it comes to our new technological landscape.

Technical Support

Although school systems invest in technical support personnel much more often than they do technology integration personnel, public schools still typically are understaffed compared to for-profit and other institutions. This state of affairs leads to personnel-to-computer support ratios that dwarf those found in private organizations. It is not uncommon for public school technology personnel to support 600 to 1,500 computers apiece (Stansbury, 2008). This compares quite unfavorably to their counterparts in industry or private schools who may only manage between 40 and 200 computers each (Apel, 2009; McLeod, 2003). Some schools have outsourced their technology support and/or integration functions to private vendors, regional educational service agencies, or other entities. Schools are constantly at risk of technical support personnel succumbing to burnout or leaving for greener pastures elsewhere. Given the difficulty of hiring and keeping replacements, principals should do everything possible to nurture, support, assist, and retain technical support staff members. The Consortium for School Networking (www.cosn.org) has a wealth of free tools available to principals and technical support staff related to leadership, planning, and staffing.

Despite their best intentions, technical support personnel often are accused of being gatekeepers or blockers when asked by teachers or administrators to enable technology-related learning opportunities. Citing the demands of safety, security, network integrity, bandwidth, and other factors, technical personnel may be perceived as denying students and educators the chance to engage in powerful learning through use of the Internet and other digital technologies. Sometimes these responses are due to sheer time and work overload. Other times such responses are a result of genuine disagreement over the utility or wisdom of allowing certain learning opportunities to occur. Principals should engage in constructive dialogues with technical support personnel, recognizing their needs and concerns but affirming at all times that the technology function of the organization is there to serve the educational function, not the other way around. Strong, visible leadership support can alleviate technical support staff members' concerns that they will be blamed if a negative incident occurs and can help technical support staff better support the learning mission of the school.

Curriculum Framework

Technology usage in schools always should be in service of instructional and curricular goals. Unfortunately, many learning technologies are purchased without careful consideration of how they will facilitate and enhance organizational learning objectives. Technology purchasing and deployment should be informed by the needs of students and teachers, not just administrators. Principals and superintendents should ensure that both instructional and administrative management technologies are chosen with due concern for the requirements of end users.

An issue that frequently arises related to technology purchasing is administrators' susceptibility to vendor pitches. Tales of principals or superintendents buying hardware and software for their schools without consulting classroom educators or technology support personnel are legion. Whether this occurs because of administrators' own lack of technology fluency, an unwillingness to involve teachers and other staff, or other reasons, any technology that is purchased without involvement of the people who will be using it runs a high risk of being used infrequently at best. Before making any sizable technology purchase, principals should ensure that teachers, students, administrative assistants, and other end-users are meaningfully included in the decision-making process.

Attempts to align particular computer tools with various instructional or curricular frameworks are fairly common. These lists purport to identify specific technologies that are appropriate for teaching certain topics, skills, or levels of thinking. Sometimes tools such as the Geometer's Sketchpad (www.dynamicgeometry.com) or the iCivics web site (www.icivics.org) are indeed only relevant for certain courses. Principals should be aware, however, that most non-subject-specific learning technologies can be used for a variety of instructional purposes. There are few general technology tools that only are suitable for lower- or higher-order thinking tasks, for example. Where a technology falls along an instructional or curricular continuum nearly always depends on how that technology is used by the teacher.

Management software also can be used to facilitate curricular and instructional goals. Plano, Texas Independent School District, for example, maintains for its teachers an online database of effective lessons and activities connected to curricular standards (http://k-12.pisd.edu/curriculum. html). Curriculum alignment software, electronic grade books, formative assessment tools, student information systems, learning analytics, data warehouses, adaptive learning systems, parent portals, and standards-based grading software are just a few of the many technologies available to principals to enhance the instructional and management functions of their schools.

Student-Centered Learning

Although most learning technologies are general enough to be used quite flexibly, by design some technologies are more teacher-centric rather than student-centric. For instance, tools such as interactive whiteboards, student response systems, digital projectors, and document cameras are technologies designed to facilitate the presentation of material by one teacher to many students. Even when a student rather than a teacher is using the technology, the vast majority of children are passively watching the facilitator rather than actively using the technology themselves. Similarly, tools such as DVD players, preselected online videos, prefiltered web sites for research, and content management systems usually are implemented in ways that are more teacher-directed than student-directed. Teacher-centric technologies mirror traditional educational practices related to information transmission and—unlike laptop or tablet computers, digital cameras or camcorders, scientific probeware, and other technologies that typically are used primarily by students—are generally replicative rather than transformative. Principals should strive to create opportunities for students to have greater autonomy and ownership over how and when they use technology tools. It is important for teachers to use technology in their instruction in ways that are meaningful, relevant, and powerful. It is arguably more important, however, to empower students to do the same. Schools that mostly invest in teacher-centric rather than student-centric technology tools will struggle to adequately prepare graduates who are ready for a hyperconnected, hypercompetitive, technology-infused global information society.

Many schools are trying to give every student a mobile computing device. These programs usually give students a laptop, netbook, or tablet computer. A few smartphone pilot programs also are in place around the world. Regardless of the device provided, educators in such programs are finding that technology can facilitate incredible opportunities to enable student agency and voice. As students' autonomy and ownership of their learning experiences increases in conjunction with their access to powerful technology tools, their ability to do more authentic, real-world work is greatly improved. Schools that enable student-centered instructional and curricular processes along with regular access to robust computing devices typically find that student academic engagement is extremely high and that traditionally desired learning outcomes often are enhanced (Sauers & McLeod, 2012). New school models such as those in the High Tech High (www.high techhigh.org), New Tech (www.newtechnetwork.org), and other networks can give principals glimpses of what all schools may one day be like. In these schools, students have greater agency over their own learning, are focused on deeper thinking, and have access to technological tools as needed.

Assessment and Evaluation

Any technology implementation should include measures for evaluating its success. Those measures should focus primarily on classroom integration and learning goals and should be created and monitored with student and teacher input. The overall goal of any technology deployment should not be merely to make technology available to students and teachers but also to make sure it is used and used well. Both implementation fidelity and implementation impact are important. Among other things, evaluation measures should address essential integration metrics such as frequency of use ("How often do students and teachers use technology for learning and teaching purposes?"), type of use ("What do students and teachers do when they use technology?"), and depth of cognitive work enabled by such use ("Are learning technologies being used for deeper learning or merely low-level thinking work?").

Summative outcome measures and progress monitoring benchmarks can be identified for all technology deployments. Both qualitative and quantitative data on a variety of different metrics should be gathered, with particular attention given to student technology usage, learning outcomes, and perceptions. Data collection should be the responsibility of all staff and should be coordinated and analyzed by the principal and the school's technology advisory team. Regular public reports should be made to school board members, parents, and the general community. The emphasis of all data collection, analysis, and reporting should be on learning, growth, and improvement, not on allocating shame or blame. The Consortium for School Networking (www.cosn.org) has free toolkits available for principals who are concerned with return-on-investment and other productivity analyses.

Engaged Communities

Social media and other technologies can be excellent vehicles for fostering community engagement. For instance, Cox (2012) found that many school leaders are leveraging social media in powerful ways with both external and internal stakeholders. Principals increasingly use tools like Facebook, YouTube, blogs, and Twitter to connect with students, staff, parents, and community members. These tools generally have an immediacy, visibility, and authenticity that more traditional communication channels may lack. New communication technologies thus are frequently more impactful than weekly flyers, email listservs, stagnant web sites, and local cable television channels (Stock, 2009). Corporations and nonprofits can serve as models for principals who wish to enhance their school's technology-facilitated communication strategies.

In addition to new information-sharing and interaction spaces, principals also have access to new information-gathering tools. Crowdsourcing community members' input through the use of wikis, blog comment areas, online surveys, virtual chat areas, or Twitter is among the possible mechanisms for collecting feedback on proposed policies or activities. The more involvement that relevant stakeholders have in the development of ideas and actions, the more buy-in there will be regarding implementation of needed changes. Social media and data collection technologies can be excellent tools for facilitating community members' engagement. Additionally, virtual book clubs with faculty or parents can be fantastic opportunities to facilitate needed discussions on important topics.

Support Policies

Numerous internal policies are necessary to facilitate effective technology integration and implementation. Any school policy related to student learning or teachers' pedagogy should include references to digital technologies. Any policy relating to educators' correspondence with students, parents, and the world at large should reference electronic communication channels. Any policy relating to student or teacher privacy concerns should reference school-provided computing devices and networks as well as off-campus uses of social media and other technologies. And so on. Principals, superintendents, and school board members should review every school and district policy to assess its potential connection to today's technology-suffused information landscapes and learning environments.

Most internal policy reviews should focus on three primary concerns. The first concern is one of relevance: Does the policy make sense given how the world works today? Internal policies that operate under old assumptions, ignore modern realities, or try to preserve outmoded ways of thinking and being will need substantial revision. The second primary concern for school leaders when they review internal policy relates to support and empowerment: Does the policy get in the way of enabling powerful learning opportunities for students? Some internal policies may be based on misunderstandings of how modern technologies operate or on misconceptions about youth, media, and technology. These, too, will need significant modification. The third primary concern relates to messaging: Does the policy send the message we want? School leaders always should remember that policies send messages about what their organization values (Martinez, 2008). Many current school technology policies are rooted in unsubstantiated fears. Principals should recognize that they probably do not want to send their communities the message that the technologies that are transforming everything around us should first and foremost be feared. Principals who are engaged in this difficult policy revision work should be prepared for contentious discussions as committee members likely will vociferously disagree with each other about desired outcomes, the means to achieve them, and the role that digital technologies should or should not play in the process.

Principals can serve extremely important educational roles when it comes to policy evaluation and implementation. When board members, parents, staff, or the community express concerns about certain technology-related aspects of schooling, principals can educate and inform them about the needs of today and tomorrow, not just romanticized notions of yesteryear. Whether we like it or not, the Internet and digital technologies continue to permeate nearly every aspect of our lives. Their influence on how we live, work, think, learn, and play will continue to increase. Either we learn to accommodate these tools as educational organizations or we expose our irrelevance to our children's futures. Stakeholders who attempt to effectively block out these tools from children's learning experiences are denying students opportunities to be appropriately prepared for their lives when they leave school. Overzealous blocking and filtering, for example, has very real and significant impacts on information access, student learning, pedagogy, ability to address required curricular standards, and teachers' willingness to integrate technology into their instruction. Similarly, "walled garden" online environments not only prevent the occurrence of serendipitous learning connections with the outside world but also create artificial communication spaces that are a mere shadow of how the Internet really works. Principals should do everything they can to create internal policy environments that are supportive of students' and teachers' current and future needs.

Supportive External Context

In addition to the work that school leaders must do within their educational organizations, they also must educate and advocate in their local and larger external community. Administrators need to bring parents and community members on board. They also must successfully educate local school board members and state and federal policymakers. Many changes in local, state, and federal policies must be made in order to productively transition schools and communities into this digital, global world that we all now inhabit.

Right now most school leaders are not actively involved in state or federal policy discussions. They rely instead on their organizations and membership associations to serve as the representative voice of both themselves and their communities. In the years to come, principals will need to play a much more active role in policymaking conversations if we are to see the schooling changes necessary for our new information, economic, and learning landscapes. Although external policymaking is an area in which principals have much less direct control, its importance cannot be overstated. As we live through seismic shifts in nearly everything we do, our laws and policies are struggling to keep up. Right now we have people making decisions and enacting policy about technologies and environments that they don't really understand. Principals' individual education and advocacy efforts never have been more imperative.

One technique that principals can use to help convince skeptics about the power of learning technologies is to frequently and visibly highlight the amazing work that their students are doing with digital tools. Student displays at school events, demonstrations to school boards, presentations to legislators, and ongoing sharing through various electronic communication channels such as school blogs, Facebook pages, and Twitter feeds can be powerfully persuasive. It is difficult for people to understand the learning power of digital technologies—and easy to dismiss their instructional utility—if they are not familiar enough with the tools to understand their positive affordances. Principals and their staff and students must regularly remind others of how learning technologies facilitate powerful learning work and why such technology-infused work is important.

CONCLUSION: PREPARATION, TRAINING, AND SUPPORT CONCERNS

A number of the competencies necessary for principals to effectuate ISTE's essential conditions for effective technology integration and implementation are delineated in both ISTE's own NETS-A standards (ISTE, 2009a) and the *Educational Leadership Policy Standards* (Council of Chief State School Officers, 2008) that guide most states' licensure requirements for principals and superintendents. As we have demonstrated through our inclusion of concrete action ideas in this chapter, principals will have to be deeply knowledgeable and highly skilled in a number of different areas in order to accomplish these complex, technology-oriented leadership goals. Unfortunately, right now principals have few places to turn to enhance their own knowledge and skills when it comes to technology leadership. The educational leadership preparation programs at most universities, for example, lack both the faculty expertise and the coursework to prepare technology-savvy administrators (McLeod, Bathon, & Richardson, 2011). Most national and state educational leadership associations, state departments of education, and school districts are not investing heavily in the development of technology-fluent principals and superintendents. While there are annual educational technology conferences in most states, they generally focus on teachers, technology coordinators, and media specialists. Rarely is there a dedicated strand or a separate conference for administrators. The research literature on effective technology leadership is quite sparse (McLeod & Richardson, 2011; Richardson, Bathon, Flora, & Lewis, in press), as is corporate or foundation funding for school technology leadership training programs.

Our underinvestment in principals as school technology leaders is troubling. Scholarly research has shown quite consistently that school leadership is "second only to teaching among school-related factors in its impact on student learning" (Leithwood, Louis, Anderson, & Wahlstrom, 2004, p. 3). We know that principals' leadership of both learning and organizational transformation is necessary for significant, long-lasting changes in classroom cultures and student outcomes (e.g., Duke, 1987; Hallinger, 1992). If as a society we want effective technology integration and implementation to occur in our schools, we must begin by recognizing that ultimately it is principals, superintendents, and school board members, not teachers, who control all of the resources necessary for systemic change, including vision, money, time, professional development, personnel allocation, and internal policy. Most principals currently struggle when it comes to the extremely complex and challenging work of creating and maintaining technology-rich learning environments (Levin & Schrum, 2012). Some of the examples in this chapter—and other schools that already have begun traveling the path of deep, rich, technology-infused learning—can serve as models for school leaders regarding the possibilities for powerful learning that await our youth.

APPENDIX

ISTE National Educational Technology Standards for Administrators
http://www.iste.org/standards/nets-for-administrators

ISTE National Educational Technology Standards for Coaches
http://www.iste.org/standards/nets-for-coaches

ISTE National Educational Technology Standards for Computer Science Educators
http://www.iste.org/standards/nets-for-computer-science-educators

ISTE National Educational Technology Standards for Students
http://www.iste.org/standards/nets-for-students

ISTE National Educational Technology Standards for Teachers
http://www.iste.org/standards/nets-for-teachers

REFERENCES

Apel, W. (2009). *International school technology survey, 2009. Part 1: Technology staffing.* Amsterdam, Netherlands: Author.

Becker, J. D. (2006). Digital equity in education: A multilevel examination of differences in and relationships between computer access, computer use, and state-level technology policies. *Education Policy Analysis Archives, 15*(3), 1–38.

Benkler, Y. (2006). *The wealth of networks: How social production transforms markets and freedoms.* New Haven, CT: Yale University Press.

Borthwick, A., Hansen, R., Gray, L., & Ziemann, I. (2008). Exploring essential conditions: A commentary on Bull et al. (2008). *Contemporary Issues in Technology and Teacher Education, 8*(3). Retrieved from http://www.citejournal.org/vol8/iss3/editorial/article2.cfm

Bucci, T. T., Cherup, S., Cunningham, A., & Petrosino, A. J. (2003). ISTE standards in teacher education: A collection of practical examples. *The Teacher Educator, 39*(2), 95–114.

Christensen, C. M., Horn, M. B., & Johnson, C. W. (2008). *Disrupting class: How disruptive innovation will change the way the world learns.* New York, NY: McGraw-Hill.

Collins, A., & Halverson, R. (2009). *Rethinking education in the age of technology: The digital revolution and schooling in America.* New York, NY: Teachers College Press.

Computers in the classroom. (n.d.). In *Wikipedia.* Retrieved from http://en.wikipedia.org/wiki/Computers_in_the_classroom

Council of Chief State School Officers (CCSSO). (2008). *Educational leadership policy standards: ISLLC 2008.* Washington, DC: Author.

Cox, D. D. (2012). *School communications 2.0: A social media strategy for K–12 principals and superintendents.* Unpublished doctoral dissertation, Iowa State University, Ames, IA.

Cross, R., & Parker, A. (2004). *The hidden power of social networks: Understanding how work really gets done in organizations.* Boston, MA: Harvard Business School Press.

Cuban, L. (2001). *Oversold and underused: Computers in the classroom.* Cambridge, MA: Harvard University Press.

Dawson, C., & Rakes, G. C. (2003). The influence of principals' technology training on the integration of technology into schools. *Journal of Research on Technology in Education, 36*(1), 29–49.

Dillon, S. (2010, February 12). Wi-Fi turns rowdy bus into rolling study hall. *The New York Times,* p. A22.

Dimension Printing. (2012). *Southview Middle School gets a grip on design with Dimension 3D printing.* Retrieved from http://www.dimensionprinting.com/successstories/successstoryview.aspx?view=57&title=Southview+Middle+School+Gets+a+Grip+on+Design+with+Dimension+3D+Printing

Duke, D. L. (1987). *School leadership and instructional improvement.* New York, NY: Random House.

Gronn, P. (2008). The future of distributed leadership. *Journal of Educational Administration, 46*(2), 141–158.

Hagel, J., Brown, J. S., & Davison, L. (2010). *The power of pull: How small moves, smartly made, can set big things in motion.* New York, NY: Basic Books.

Hallinger, P. (1992). The evolving role of American principals: From managerial to instructional to transformational leaders. *Journal of Educational Administration, 30*(3), 35–48.

Heck, R. H., & Hallinger, P. (2009). Assessing the contribution of distributed leadership to school improvement and growth in math achievement. *American Educational Research Journal, 46*(3), 659–689.

Hew, K. F., & Brush, T. (2006). Integrating technology into K–12 teaching and learning: Current knowledge gaps and recommendations for future research. *Educational Technology Research and Development, 55*(3), 223–252.

Hughes, J. E., & Ooms, A. (2004). Content-focused technology inquiry groups: Preparing urban teachers to integrate technology to transform student learning. *Journal of Research on Technology in Education, 36*(4), 397–411.

Hulpia, H., Devos, G., & Van Keer, H. (2011). The relation between school leadership from a distributed perspective and teachers' organizational commitment: Examining the source of the leadership function. *Educational Administration Quarterly, 47*(5), 728–771.

International Association for K-12 Online Learning (iNACOL). (2012). *Fast facts about online learning*. Vienna, VA: Author.

International Society for Technology in Education (ISTE). (2007). *National educational technology standards for students*. Eugene, OR: Author.

International Society for Technology in Education (ISTE). (2008). *National educational technology standards for teachers*. Eugene, OR: Author.

International Society for Technology in Education (ISTE). (2009a). *Essential conditions*. Eugene, OR: Author.

International Society for Technology in Education (ISTE). (2009b). *National educational technology standards for administrators*. Eugene, OR: Author.

International Society for Technology in Education (ISTE). (2011a). *National educational technology standards for coaches*. Eugene, OR: Author.

International Society for Technology in Education (ISTE). (2011b). *National educational technology standards for computer science educators*. Eugene, OR: Author.

Jacobs, H. H. (2010). *Curriculum 21: Essential education for a changing world*. Alexandria, VA: ASCD.

Judge, S., & O'Bannon, B. (2007). Integrating technology into field-based experiences: A model that fosters change. *Computers in Human Behavior, 23*(1), 286–302.

Kotter, J. P. (2008). *A sense of urgency*. Boston, MA: Harvard Business Press.

Learning Forward. (2011). *Standards for professional learning*. Dallas, TX: Author.

Leithwood, K., Louis, K. S., Anderson, S., & Wahlstrom, K. (2004). *How leadership influences student learning*. New York, NY: Wallace Foundation.

Lemke, C., Coughlin, E., Garcia, L., Reifsneider, D., & Baas, J. (2009, March). *Leadership for Web 2.0 in education: Promise and reality*. Culver City, CA: Metiri Group.

Levin, B. B., & Schrum, L. (2012). *Leading technology-rich schools: Award-winning models for success*. New York, NY: Teachers College Press.

Martinez, S. (2008). *What message does your AUP send home?* Retrieved from http://blog.genyes.org/index.php/2008/05/08/what-message-does-your-aup-send-home

McLeod, S. (2003). *National district technology coordinators study. Technical report 1: Personal and professional characteristics*. Naperville, IL: North Central Regional Educational Laboratory, United States Department of Education.

McLeod, S. (2009). Toward real digital learning. *Threshold, 7*(2), 29–32.

McLeod, S. (2011). Are we irrelevant to the digital, global world in which we now live? *UCEA Review, 52*(2), 1–5.

McLeod, S., Bathon, J. M., & Richardson, J. W. (2011). Studies of technology tool usage are not enough. *Journal of Research in Leadership Education, 6*(5), 288–297.

McLeod, S., & Richardson, J. W. (2011). The dearth of technology-related articles in educational leadership scholarship. *Journal of School Leadership, 21*(2), 216–240.

Mishra, P., & Koehler, M. J. (2006). Technological pedagogical content knowledge: A framework for integrating technology in teacher knowledge. *Teachers College Record, 108*(6), 1017–1054.

Moe, T. M., & Chubb, J. E. (2009). *Liberating learning: Technology, politics, and the future of American education.* San Francisco, CA: Jossey-Bass.

Murphy, J., Smylie, M., Mayrowetz, D., & Louis, K. S. (2009). The role of the principal in fostering the development of distributed leadership. *School Leadership & Management, 29*(2), 181–214.

National Center for Education Statistics. (1997). *Advanced telecommunications in U.S. Public elementary and secondary schools, Fall 1996.* Washington, DC: United States Department of Education.

National Center for Education Statistics. (2005). *Distance education courses for public elementary and secondary school students: 2002–03.* Washington, DC: United States Department of Education.

National Center for Education Statistics. (2010a). *Educational technology in U.S. public schools: Fall 2008.* Washington, DC: United States Department of Education.

National Center for Education Statistics. (2010b). *Teachers' use of educational technology in U.S. public schools: Fall 2009.* Washington, DC: United States Department of Education.

Neuman, D. (1991). *Technology and equity* (ERIC Digest). Syracuse, NY: ERIC Clearinghouse on Information Resources. ED339400. Retrieved from http://www.ericdigests.org/1992-5/equity.htm

Reich, J., Murnane, R., & Willett, J. (2012). The state of wiki usage in U.S. K–12 schools: Leveraging Web 2.0 data warehouses to assess quality and equity in online learning environments. *Educational Researcher, 41*(1), 7–15.

Richardson, J. W., Bathon, J., Flora, K., & Lewis, W. D. (in press). NETS-A scholarship: A review of published literature. *Journal of Research on Technology in Education.*

Richardson, W., & Mancabelli, R. (2011). *Personal learning networks: Using the power of connections to transform education.* Bloomington, IN: Solution Tree.

Riley, R. W. (1996). *Application for state grants under the Technology Literacy Challenge Fund.* Washington, DC: United States Department of Education.

Sauers, N. J., & McLeod, S. (2012, May). *What does the research say about school one-to-one computing initiatives?* [research brief]. Lexington, KY: UCEA Center for the Advanced Study of Technology Leadership in Education.

Shirky, C. (2008). *Here comes everybody: The power of organizing without organizations.* New York, NY: Penguin Press.

Stansbury, M. (2008, January 9). *Schools need help with tech support.* Retrieved from http://www.eschoolnews.com/2008/01/09/schools-need-help-with-tech-support

Stock, M. J. (2009). *The school administrator's guide to blogging: A new way to connect with the community.* Lanham, MD: Rowman & Littlefield.

Thomas, L. G., & Knezek, D. G. (2008). Information, communications, and educational technology standards for students, teachers, and school leaders. In J. Voogt & G. Knezek (Eds.), *International handbook of information technology in primary and secondary education, 20*(4), 333-348.

Toppo, G. (2011, July 25). Social media find place in classroom. Available from *USA Today* at http://www.usatoday.com/news/education/2011-07-24-schools-social-media_n.htm

United States Department of Education. (1996). *Getting America's students ready for the 21st century: Meeting the technology literacy challenge.* Washington, DC: Author.

United States Department of Education. (2000). *e-Learning: Putting a world-class education at the fingertips of all children.* Washington, DC: Author.

United States Department of Education. (2004). *Toward a new golden age in American education: How the Internet, the law, and today's students are revolutionizing expectations.* Washington, DC: Author.

United States Department of Education. (2010). *Transforming American education: Learning powered by technology.* Washington, DC: Author.

United States Department of Education. (2012). *The condition of education 2012.* Washington, DC: Author.

Warschauer, M., Knobel, M., & Stone, L. (2004). Technology and equity in schooling: Deconstructing the digital divide. *Educational Policy, 18*(4), 562–588.

Warschauer, M., & Matuchniak, T. (2010). New technology and digital worlds: Analyzing evidence of equity in access, use, and outcomes. *Review of Research in Education, 34*, 179–225.

Willinsky, J. (2006). *The access principle: The case for open access to research and scholarship.* Cambridge, MA: MIT Press.

Youth Radio. (2012, April 5). *Maker lab teaches rockets, circuits, and soldering.* Available at http://www.youthradio.org/news/in-tech-education-void-maker-lab-teaches-rockets-circuits-and-soldering

Zhao, Y., Pugh, K., Sheldon, S., & Byers, J. L. (2002). Conditions for classroom technology innovations. *Teachers College Record, 104*(3), 482–515.

ABOUT THE CONTRIBUTORS

April Adams has held the position of principal at Liberty High School for four years. Prior to this role, she was a high school assistant principal with experiences ranging from managing the alternative high school and sophomore discipline to coaching new teachers and ensuring instructional and curriculum alignment within the comprehensive high school. April entered education as a special education teacher, and her passion to make an even larger impact on the learning of children was the driving force to enter administration. As a lead principal, she is passionate about teacher development and the positive effects this has on student achievement. The digital integration movement has taken hold in her building and, in collaboration with a high quality team of faculty, staff, and administrators, learning at Liberty High School is becoming more aligned to the needs and thinking process of the iGeneration of students.

Candice Barkley is a mathematics teacher at New Kent High School in New Kent, Virginia. She has taught mathematics for the past 16 years at the junior high, high school, community college, and university levels. The chapter in this book is based on the research Candice did for her dissertation that was successfully completed, culminating her doctoral program in educational leadership at Virginia Commonwealth University. Candice's education and research interests include school leaders use of technology, improvement of advanced placement programs, and mathematics instruction and coaching.

Principal 2.0: Technology and Educational Leadership, pages 273–281
Copyright © 2013 by Information Age Publishing
273

Justin Bathon is an assistant professor in the Department of Educational Leadership Studies at the University of Kentucky and a Director of the UCEA Center for the Advanced Study of Technology Leadership in Education (CAS-TLE). Justin focuses on the underlying code of education and the changes necessitated by the digital, global age. This work looks at the intersections of education, law, and technology and translates research into specific actions for local learning communities. Justin has legal and educational experience at the local, state, national, and international levels including as a high school teacher in southern Illinois. He holds a JD from Southern Illinois University and a PhD in education policy from Indiana University.

Jonathan D. Becker is an assistant professor in the Department of Educational Leadership of the School of Education at Virginia Commonwealth University, Richmond, VA. Jonathan's teaching and scholarly endeavors occur at the intersection of educational technology, policy, law, and leadership. Currently, Jonathan serves as the evaluator of a multimillion dollar, multiyear grant program funded by the U.S. Department of Education to develop simulations and to support leadership preparation, and he is a co-investigator of an NSF-funded grant targeted at research and development of science curriculum modules for students in underserved areas.

Kevin P. Brady is an associate professor of educational leadership in the Department of Leadership, Policy and Adult and Higher Education at North Carolina State University. His research focuses primarily on educational law issues, including student and teacher free speech and expression, student discipline, and special education law as well as educational technology issues involving today's school leaders. Dr. Brady's scholarship appears in a wide array of leading educational law, policy, and technology-based journals, including the *Brigham Young University, Children's Legal Rights Journal, Distance Education, Education and Urban Society, Journal of Education Finance, Journal of Interactive Online Learning, Journal of Online Learning and Teaching, Journal of School Leadership, Review of Research in Education,* and *West's Education Law Reporter.* Dr. Brady currently has over 30 publications, including a recent book, *Debating Issues in American Education: Technology in Schools* (2012, SAGE Publications).

Mark Cantu is an educator from San Marcos, Texas. He earned a bachelor's degree in interdisciplinary studies with an emphasis in middle school English language arts and reading, and a master's degree in educational administration from the University of Texas Pan-American. He taught middle school English language arts and English as a second language for several years at Edcouch–Elsa ISD. Currently, this is his third year as principal at Waelder Independent School District, a small, rural public school that serves about 300 students from Pre-K–12th grade. Mark is also enrolled at

Texas State University where he is pursuing his PhD in school improvement. His interests include community development and leadership, creating spaces to promote social justice and equity, youth engagement, and culturally appropriate pedagogy.

Dan Cox is the principal at Hoover Middle School in Waterloo, Iowa and has served as an adjunct instructor in educational administration at Iowa State University. Previously he served as an assistant principal at an urban Iowa high school and as chief administrator of a Lutheran secondary school. Prior to becoming an administrator, he taught high school Spanish in two rural Iowa school districts. His research interests include the use of social media by school administrators, school marketing and branding, and effective communication practices.

Alpay Ersozlu is an assistant professor in the Educational Administration, Supervision, Planning and Economics Department at Gaziosmanpasa University, Turkey and has been working as a post doctoral research scholar with the Department of Science, Technology, Engineering, and Mathematics Education at North Carolina State University. Prior to his academic career, Ersozlu served as a teacher for 11 years at the vocational and technical high school in Bilecik, Tokat City. His research is focused on educational leadership, organizational behavior, human relations and social capital. In addition to publications, Ersozlu, is co-author of *Egitim Orgutlerinde Sosyal Sermaye ve Yonetimi (Social Capital and its Management in Educational Organizations)* (2010, Ideal Kultur Press).

Lee Francis IV is a doctoral student at Texas State University – San Marcos in the Department of Education. He received his MA in educational leadership from the University of New Mexico and serves as the national director for the non-profit Native American writers' organization, Wordcraft Circle. His scholarship revolves around the intersections of politics, education, technology, and community development, and he has worked in and around K–16 settings for most of his career, starting as a teacher with the Pueblo of Laguna. He has numerous publications in poetry and is an award-winning performance poet.

Alexander Friend's motto would be "ad astra per aspera" even if he was not from Kansas. He enjoys sounds, flavors, and colors arranged into various shapes and magnitudes—such as gardens, music, clouds, bugs, and books—in proximity to candy. He composes music and plays saxophone, keyboard, and cowbell in Kansas City groups. He will open the first 24/7 breakfast restaurant in space.

Jennifer Friend is an associate professor in the Educational Leadership, Policy and Foundations program at the University of Missouri-Kansas City. Her prior experience includes work as a middle grades language arts teacher, associate principal, and principal. She has recently published research in *Educational Studies, Journal of Research on Leadership Education,* and *Middle School Journal.* She served as the president of the Missouri Professors of Educational Administration and as Secretary for the Learning and Teaching in Educational Leadership (LTEL)-SIG. Her research agenda focuses on equity issues related to urban educational leadership, educational leadership preparation, middle-level education, and documentary film as research.

Francisco Guajardo is an associate professor of educational leadership at the University of Texas Pan American. He is co-founder of the Llano Grande Center for Research and Development at Edcouch–Elsa High School, a community-based youth leadership organization, and is founding director of the Center for Bilingual Studies at UT Pan American. His research interests include community leadership, the use of storytelling for school and community leadership, and Latino epistemologies.

Miguel A. Guajardo is an associate professor in the Education and Community Leadership Program at Texas State University–San Marcos and co-founder and co-chairman of the board of directors of the Llano Grande Center for Research and Development. He was a fellow with the Kellogg International Leadership Program and the Salzburg Seminar. Dr. Guajardo's work has been informed by the local ecology and the values of fairness, good work, and democracy. He has traveled to five continents and engaged in conversations with indigenous leaders, teachers, and citizens on issues of education, development, community building, citizenship, and identity. He earned a PhD in educational leadership with an emphasis on the politics and policy of education from the University of Texas at Austin.

Chris Janson is an associate professor in the Department of Leadership, School Counseling, and Sport Management at the University of North Florida. Janson has public school experience as a junior high school teacher and high school counselor. His research interests include interprofessional relationships in schools, collective leadership, the career and academic goals of students in urban schools, and community-based learning. He has published in journals such as *Professional School Counselor, Journal of School Leadership,* and *Journal of Special Education Leadership.* He earned his PhD in counselor education from Kent State University.

Shawndra T. Johnson is a doctoral student in educational leadership, policy, and law at Alabama State University. Additionally, she is an instructor in instructional technology and serves as the ASU eLearning coordinator. Previously, she served as an instructional technology specialist for the Alabama State Department of Education, director of professional learning for an IT firm, and a school technology teacher. She has presented at numerous state and national conferences. Currently her research interests include curriculum and technology integration, technology professional development, and distance learning.

Jacqueline Jones is currently an assistant principal for Duval County Public Schools in Jacksonville, FL. She is a doctoral candidate at the University of North Florida and participates in the state of Florida's Turnaround Leadership program. Jacqueline has a love for serving schools and youth of low social economical communities. It is her passion to motivate great teaching and authentic learning every day. Eventually, Jones hopes to become a middle or high school principal, a UNF faculty member, and expand her influence as a school district administrator.

Scott McLeod is an associate professor of educational leadership at the University of Kentucky. Dr. McLeod also is the founding director of the UCEA Center for the Advanced Study of Technology Leadership in Education (CASTLE), the nation's only academic center dedicated to the technology needs of school administrators, and was a co-creator of the wildly popular video series, *Did You Know? (Shift Happens)*. He has received numerous national awards for his technology leadership work, including recognitions from the cable industry, Phi Delta Kappa, the National School Boards Association, and the Center for Digital Education. In spring 2011 he was a Visiting Canterbury Fellow at the University of Canterbury in New Zealand. Dr. McLeod blogs regularly about technology leadership issues at *Dangerously Irrelevant* and *Education Recoded* and occasionally at *The Huffington Post*. He also just completed his first book, *What School Leaders Need to Know About Digital Technologies and Social Media* (2012, Jossey Bass).

Dominic Militello is a tenth-grade student at Athens Drive High School in Wake County public schools in Raleigh, North Carolina. He is the oldest of four boys and takes amazing care of all his brothers, especially his two-year-old brother Oscar. Dominic is a car aficionado and is addicted to the TV show Top Gear, British version only. He is also a swimmer for his high school.

Luke Militello is a seventh grader at Reedy Creek Middle School in Wake County public schools in Raleigh, North Carolina. He is the second oldest of the four boys. Luke loves hockey. He plays and is captain of a travel team: the Carolina Lighting. Luke also plays the saxophone and runs track for his middle school.

Gabriel Militello is a fourth grader at A. B. Combs Elementary School in Wake County public schools in Raleigh, North Carolina. He is the third out of four boys. Gabe plays basketball and lacrosse, but his real passion is football. He is a huge fan of the University of Michigan, North Carolina State University, and the New England Patriots.

John Militello is head of creative on Google's creative content development team. In addition to his day job, John is an adjunct professor at the School of Visual Arts in New York City. Before joining Google, John led his own design firm and was a founding member of a leading boutique creative agency in NYC where he served as a VP and creative director partnering with such clients as Volvo Cars of North America and Mercedes-Benz. John earned a bachelor of fine arts from the College for Creative Studies in Detroit, where he received the Leo Brunett Scholarship.

Matthew Militello is an associate professor in the leadership, policy, and adult and higher education department and a research fellow at the Friday Institute for Educational Innovation at North Carolina State University. Prior to his academic career, Militello was a middle and high public school teacher, assistant principal, and principal in Michigan. His research focuses on developing principals' knowledge and skills in the areas of school law, school data, and collective leadership. Militello has more than 50 publications including two books: *Leading with Inquiry and Action: How Principals Improve Teaching and Learning* (2009, Corwin Press) and *Principals Teaching the Law: 10 Legal Lessons Your Teachers Must Know* (2010, Corwin Press).

Ronald Militello began his career as a 6th and 7th grade teacher at Divine Child in Dearborn, Michigan. In 1965 he became a high school teacher in Lincoln Park, Michigan where he wrote and directed an exemplary and innovative program funded by a federal Title III grant. He went on to become a high school assistant principal and principal at Menominee Area Public Schools for 21 years. He finished his career as a superintendent for eight years before his retirement in 1999. Militello received his bachelor and master degrees from Wayne State University.

Levertice Moses is currently a student at Florida State College in Jacksonville, Florida. He is earning a degree in nursing and plans to enroll in medical school when he completes his bachelor's degree. Moses also plans to continue playing organized football, a sport that he loves.

John B. Nash is an associate professor in the department of educational leadership studies at the University of Kentucky. Dr. Nash is also a director of the UCEA Center for the Advanced Study of Technology Leadership in Education (CASTLE) and founding director of the Laboratory on Design

Thinking in Education (dLab) at the University of Kentucky. Nash is a specialist in the design and prototyping of innovations in educational organizations with research interests on how technology, innovation, and policy interact and influence schools and educators in different contexts. He is the co-founder of the OpenEye Innovation Management, an international consultancy focused on shortening time-to-impact in the social sector. Nash was the director of evaluation at the Stanford Center for Innovations in Learning, and prior to that he was director of research and assessment at the Stanford Learning Lab.

John A. Oliver is an assistant professor of educational leadership at Texas State University–San Marcos. His research includes the intersection of adult–youth partnerships for community change and effective partnerships among higher education, schools, and communities. John was a public school educator and assistant principal for over eight years. John worked on the national evaluation team for a W. K. Kellogg-funded grant that focused on intersections of community leadership development among institutions, communities, and families. He also works with the W. K. Kellogg-funded grant Community Learning Exchange (www.community learningexhange.org), a network of resilient local communities, vibrant organizations, and active change agents who share their local wisdom and collective leadership approaches with each other so they can be more effective in addressing critical social issues.

Sejal B. Parikh is an assistant professor of counselor education at the North Carolina State University. She has experience as a professional school counselor working in elementary, high school, urban, and suburban school settings. She received her PhD in counseling from the University of North Carolina at Charlotte where she was the recipient of the Dean's Distinguished Dissertation Award for Social Sciences. Her primary research focus includes social justice and advocacy in school counseling, multicultural counseling, and school counselor training development.

Terrinikka Ransome is currently a student at Florida State College in Jacksonville, Florida. There she is pursuing a double major in nursing and business. She dreams of owning her own healthcare company. Ransome is active, outgoing, and always looking for opportunities to express her love for people.

Jayson W. Richardson is an assistant professor of educational leadership at the University of Kentucky and a Director of the UCEA Center for the Advanced Study of Technology Leadership in Education (CASTLE). His research focuses on understanding the technology leadership in various contexts. His work also explores how technology and leadership can propel school reform in less developed countries. He is the founding chair of the Information and Communication Technology for Development (ICT4D) SIG in the Comparative and International Education Society (CIES). Dr. Richardson has over 30 publications and 70 presentations. He has recently published work in *Educational Administration Quarterly, Journal of Research in Leadership in Education, Journal of Educational Administration, Journal of School Leadership*, and *Comparative Education Review*.

Michael J. Schmedlen is the director of worldwide commercial and public sector marketing at Lenovo. Prior to his career at Lenovo, he worked at IBM for nine years, serving educational institutions across North and South America. He founded and served as the chair of the Education Research Initiative (ERI) and served as a director or advisor to a diverse range of education advocacy groups such as the World Economic Forum Global Education Initiative, the Partnership for 21st Century Skills, the Jiayu School, and the North Carolina Public School Forum. Mike was named a 2013 Eisenhower Fellow to Ireland and the United Nations Educational, Scientific and Cultural Organization (UNESCO). Mr. Schmedlen holds a BA in classics from Colgate University and an MBA from the Fuqua School of Business at Duke University.

Tricia J. Stewart is an associate professor in educational leadership, policy, and law at Alabama State University. Her prior experience includes teaching alternative high school equivalency to ages 16 to 86, teaching middle level social studies and language arts, and serving as project manager/researcher for a large grant-funded bicoastal research project. She has published research in *The Journal of School Leadership, Education Research International*, and *School Business Affairs*. Her research agenda focuses on social class and inequality in education, educational policy studies, and program evaluation in high needs school districts—urban and rural.

David Ta-Pryor is an instructional designer at the University of Missouri–Kansas City where he works with instructors on education technology, online course design, learning outcomes, and assessments. He is also a doctoral student in the School of Information Science and Learning Technologies at the University of Missouri–Columbia. His research interest looks at affective learning, motivation, and the use of new media and technology in higher education. In particular, he is interested in examining how certain platforms contribute to how users communicate and how communication elicits presence.

Jonathan T. Ta-Pryor is a doctoral student in educational leadership and policy analysis at the University of Missouri–Columbia. Additionally, he is the LGBTQIA coordinator at the University of Missouri–Kansas City, where he facilitates educational programs and serves as a resource for the LG-BTQIA student population. He has presented at several national conferences in the field of higher education and student affairs. Currently his research interests focus on the LGBTQIA college student experience and student leadership and involvement in higher education.

Mónica Valadez is a former bilingual educator. Currently she coordinates the Proyecto Maestría program in the office of bilingual/bicultural education at the University of Texas–Austin and is a part of the teaching faculty in the educational leadership program at Texas State University–San Marcos. Mónica continues to actively work within PK–12 educational settings, providing insight and facilitating learning opportunities to promote and develop both campus and teacher leaders working with diverse populations. Mónica recently completed her PhD from Texas State University–San Marcos.